Mastering Scala
Functional and Object-Oriented Programming

Contents

4

Introduction

Scala is a powerful programming language that uniquely combines functional and object-oriented paradigms. Originating as a successor to languages like Java, Scala offers a succinct syntax and efficient run-time performance on the Java Virtual Machine (JVM). This book, "Mastering Scala: Functional and Object-Oriented Programming," aims to provide a comprehensive introduction to the language and its core features, serving as a robust foundation for both beginners and experienced programmers.

The motivation behind this book is to offer a structured and accessible guide to mastering Scala. The language's design emphasizes simplicity and scalability, motivating its adoption in both academic settings and commercial industries. By focusing on key concepts and providing detailed explanations, this book ensures that readers gain a deep understanding of Scala, enabling them to write clean, efficient, and maintainable code.

Scala's history and evolution are rooted in the need for a modern programming language that addresses the limitations of older languages while introducing new paradigms. It was designed by Martin Odersky and first released in 2003, with continuous improvements that have cemented its place as a versatile and powerful language. Its primary goal was to provide a more expressive syntax without sacrificing performance, allowing developers to write concise code that performs efficiently.

One of the defining features of Scala is its seamless integration of functional programming (FP) and object-oriented programming (OOP). This hybrid model allows developers to choose the most appropriate paradigm for specific problems, thus facilitating more flexible and efficient code design. From immutable data structures to higher-order functions and rich type inference, Scala's feature set is designed to improve developer productivity and code robustness.

The Scala ecosystem is rich and continually growing. Key tools such as sbt (Scala Build Tool) streamline project management, dependency resolution, and build automation. The language's compatibility with both Java and a myriad of external libraries provides developers with extensive resources for tackling various programming challenges. Leveraging the strengths of the JVM, Scala can interoperate with existing Java code, making it a favorable choice for projects in diverse environments.

As we progress through this book, we will start with the basics of setting up the Scala development environment, running simple programs, and understanding the core syntax. Subsequent chapters delve into more advanced topics, such as collections, data structures, functional programming principles, object-oriented design, concurrency, error handling, and data processing. By the end of this book, readers should be proficient in developing complex applications in Scala, utilizing both functional and object-oriented paradigms to their advantage.

Scala's growing popularity can be attributed to its ability to solve real-world problems efficiently and elegantly. It encourages best practices, promotes readable code, and provides powerful constructs that simplify many programming tasks. Whether you are looking to enhance your skills, begin a new project, or explore the latest trends in software development, mastering Scala offers immense rewards.

We invite you to immerse yourself in the nuanced and robust world of Scala, where you will find a confluence of elegant syntax, efficient performance, and a rich set of features. This book is structured to guide your learning systematically and progressively, ensuring that you build a solid foundation and advance confidently to more complex topics.

Thank you for choosing "Mastering Scala: Functional and Object-Oriented Programming." We hope that this journey will be intellectually enriching and practically valuable in your programming endeavors.

Chapter 1

Introduction to Scala

Scala Is a versatile programming language that blends functional and object-oriented paradigms. Born out of the need to improve upon older languages like Java, it offers concise syntax and efficient performance on the JVM. This chapter covers Scala's history, key features, ecosystem, and basic setup, providing a foundational understanding for beginners. Through detailed explanations and practical examples, readers will gain the knowledge needed to write their first Scala program and explore its rich toolset.

1.1   What is Scala?

Scala, short for *Scalable Language*, is a robust and versatile programming language that aims to address the limitations of older languages like Java while providing advanced features for modern application development. It is designed to seamlessly integrate functional and object-oriented programming paradigms, offering powerful capabilities for developers to create expressive, concise, and high-performance code.

Scala runs on the Java Virtual Machine (JVM), allowing it to interoperate with Java seamlessly. This means that Scala can leverage the vast ecosystem of Java libraries and frameworks, making it a practical choice for enterprises already invested in Java technology.

One of Scala's core principles is to provide a concise syntax without sacrificing clarity. This is achieved through features such as type inference, expressive type system, and powerful abstraction mechanisms. These attributes not only reduce boilerplate code but also enhance the readability and maintainability of programs.

To illustrate the conciseness and power of Scala, let's consider a simple example. Here is a Scala function to compute the factorial of a number:

```scala
def factorial(n: Int): Int = {
  if (n <= 1) 1
  else n * factorial(n - 1)
}
```

This function demonstrates the elegance of Scala's syntax, combining simplicity with readability. The function factorial takes an integer n and recursively calculates the factorial of n. The notation is precise and straightforward.

In addition to simplicity, Scala is designed to be a scalable language. This means it can be used for small scripts as well as large, complex systems. The scalability of Scala is chiefly due to its combination of functional programming constructs and a strong static type system. Functional programming, with its emphasis on immutability and first-class functions, helps in writing modular and testable code. The static type system provides compile-time type checking, reducing runtime errors and improving the robustness of applications.

For example, in functional programming, higher-order functions play a significant role. These functions take other functions as parameters or return them as results. Here is an example of a higher-order function in Scala:

```scala
def applyFunctionTwice(f: Int => Int, x: Int): Int = {
  f(f(x))
}

val increment = (x: Int) => x + 1

val result = applyFunctionTwice(increment, 5)
println(result) // Output: 7
```

In this example, applyFunctionTwice is a higher-order function that takes a function f and an integer x. It applies the function f to x twice. The increment function increments a given integer by one. When we pass increment and the integer 5 to applyFunctionTwice, the result is 7. This example demonstrates how functional programming in Scala can lead to concise and expressive code.

Scala's rich type system provides another layer of scalability. By supporting advanced type features such as generic types, singleton types, and path-dependent types, Scala enables the creation of highly abstract and reusable code components. Here is an example demonstrating the use of generics in Scala:

```
class Box[T](value: T) {
  def get: T = value
}

val intBox = new Box[Int](123)
val stringBox = new Box[String]("Hello, Scala!")

println(intBox.get) // Output: 123
println(stringBox.get) // Output: Hello, Scala!
```

In this code, Box is a generic class that can hold a value of any type T. The get method returns the value. When creating instances of Box with specific types, such as Int and String, Scala ensures type safety, preventing type mismatch errors at compile time.

Scala also supports pattern matching, an advanced feature that allows easy deconstruction and analysis of data. Pattern matching simplifies the code required for data manipulation, enhancing readability. Consider the following example:

```
def describe(x: Any): String = x match {
  case 0 => "zero"
  case true => "true"
  case "hello" => "greeting"
  case _ => "something else"
}

println(describe(0)) // Output: zero
println(describe(true)) // Output: true
println(describe("hello")) // Output: greeting
println(describe(42)) // Output: something else
```

In this example, the describe function uses pattern matching to return a description for various input values. The match keyword and case statements enable a clear and concise way to handle multiple conditions.

By combining these advanced features with compatibility with existing Java infrastructure, Scala offers a powerful environment for both academic and commercial software development. The language design decisions aim to optimize developer productivity, code safety, and the ability to build complex, scalable systems efficiently. Through this section, we have explored the core principles and features of Scala, highlighting its strengths in adopting a modern approach to programming on the JVM.

1.2   History and Evolution of Scala

Scala, a portmanteau of "scalable" and "language," was designed to address the limitations of existing programming languages while offering the flexibility of both object-oriented and functional programming paradigms. Scala's development commenced in 2001 at the École Polytechnique Fédérale de Lausanne (EPFL) under the guidance of Professor Martin Odersky, motivated by the drive to improve upon Java's verbosity and rigidity.

The first public release of Scala, Scala 1.0, was made available in 2003. Notably, it ran on the Java Virtual Machine (JVM), emphasizing interoperability with Java. The blending of functional and object-oriented programming allowed developers to leverage Java's robust ecosystem while writing more concise and expressive code. Early versions of Scala introduced several core features, including a sophisticated type system to ensure type safety and support for advanced functional programming constructs like higher-order functions and pattern matching.

Scala 1.x Series

During the 1.x series, Scala began attracting attention largely due to its innovative features. Several academics and early adopters contributed to its evolution by testing and porting critical libraries and frameworks. Although adoption was gradual, a dedicated community began to form around Scala, enabling iterative enhancements to be made rapidly.

Scala 2.0: A Significant Milestone

A landmark in Scala's history was the release of Scala 2.0 in March 2006. This version constituted a substantial overhaul of the language, with the introduction of numerous features that enhanced both performance and usability. Some of the hallmarks of Scala 2.0 included:

- Mixin composition through traits, which offered a more flexible alternative to multiple inheritance.

- Pattern matching, which provided a robust mechanism for deconstructing data structures and improved readability.

- Advanced type inference, reducing the verbosity seen in Java by inferring most types automatically.

- The introduction of the for-comprehensions, enabling a more intuitive way to work with collections and monadic constructs.

14

Growth and Adoption

Post-2.0, Scala witnessed increased adoption across both academia and industry. Influential contributions such as the development of the Akka library for concurrent and distributed systems and the Play Framework for web development significantly boosted its appeal. Additionally, companies like Twitter and LinkedIn began adopting Scala for backend services, citing benefits such as reduced boilerplate code and improved application performance.

Scala 2.8: Enhancements and Stability

Released in 2010, Scala 2.8 introduced major improvements designed to stabilize and mature the language further. Key enhancements included:

- The collections library overhaul, facilitating more efficient and consistent manipulation of data structures.

- Improved compiler optimizations, leading to faster runtime performance and lower memory footprint.

- The introduction of named and default parameters, enabling more flexible and readable function definitions.

- A more consistent and predictable approach to generic programming.

Scala 2.11 and 2.12 Series: Industry-wide Adoption

The Scala 2.11 and 2.12 series, released in 2014 and 2016 respectively, marked a period of optimization and refinement. The focus for these series included:

- Enhanced Java 8 compatibility, allowing the smooth integration of Java 8 features such as lambdas and streams.

- Performance improvements regarding both compilation time and runtime efficiency.

- Modularization of the standard library, optimizing the dependency management process and reducing unnecessary baggage.

These versions also saw widespread adoption, with Scala gaining significant traction in big data ecosystems, notably by becoming the language of choice for Apache Spark – a unified analytics engine for large-scale data processing.

Transition to Scala 3

Scala 3, initially known as Dotty, represents the latest evolution and reimagining of the language. Officially released in May 2021, Scala 3 focuses on simplifying the language, improving compiler performance, and introducing advanced new features while ensuring backward compatibility with Scala 2. Major features introduced in Scala 3 include:

- Opaque Types and Union Types, extending the type system to offer more precise type definitions and flexibility.

- A new, concise syntax for control abstractions, improving readability.

- Support for Contextual Abstractions, providing a mechanism for implicit definitions that simplify dependency injection and context-passing.

- Compiler improvements, incorporating a more scalable and maintainable codebase.

As Scala continues to evolve, its commitment to ensuring robust and scalable programming models endures, driven by both community input and academic research. The language remains a mainstay in both functional and object-oriented programming communities, consistently contributing to more efficient and expressive software development.

```scala
// Sample Scala code to demonstrate pattern matching from Scala 2.0
sealed trait Shape
case class Circle(radius: Double) extends Shape
case class Rectangle(length: Double, width: Double) extends Shape

def calculateArea(shape: Shape): Double = shape match {
  case Circle(radius) => Math.PI * Math.pow(radius, 2)
  case Rectangle(length, width) => length * width
}

// Usage
val circleArea = calculateArea(Circle(5))
val rectangleArea = calculateArea(Rectangle(4, 7))

println(s"Circle Area: $circleArea")
println(s"Rectangle Area: $rectangleArea")
```

```
Circle Area: 78.53981633974483
Rectangle Area: 28.0
```

1.3 Features of Scala

Scala is designed to be highly expressive, concise, and efficient, incorporating both functional and object-oriented programming paradigms. Its features enable developers to write robust, high-performance applications with fewer lines of code. Below are some of the key features that make Scala a powerful and flexible language:

1. Statically Typed

Scala is statically typed, meaning that type checking is performed at compile-time rather than at runtime. This allows for early detection of errors, providing a layer of safety and robustness to the code. Scala's type inference allows it to deduce types automatically, minimizing the required explicit type declarations.

```
val x = 5 // Type inferred as Int
val y: Double = 5.0 // Explicit type declaration
```

2. Type Inference

Scala's ability to infer types from context reduces boilerplate code and enhances readability without sacrificing type safety.

```
def add(a: Int, b: Int) = a + b // No need to explicitly specify the return type
```

3. Immutable Collections

Scala encourages the use of immutable collections. Immutable data structures do not change after they are created, which makes them inherently thread-safe and easier to reason about.

```
val list = List(1, 2, 3) // Immutable list
// list = list :+ 4 // This would cause an error
```

4. Pattern Matching

Pattern matching in Scala is a powerful feature that simplifies the manipulation of data structures. It is similar to the switch statement in other languages, but far more expressive.

```
val number: Int = 2
val result = number match {
  case 1 => "One"
  case 2 => "Two"
  case 3 => "Three"
  case _ => "Other"
}
```

5. First-Class Functions

Scala treats functions as first-class citizens. Functions can be passed as parameters, returned from other functions, and assigned to variables.

```
val addOne = (x: Int) => x + 1 // Function assigned to a variable
val result = addOne(5) // result: 6
```

6. Higher-Order Functions

Higher-order functions are functions that can take other functions as parameters or return functions. This capability allows for a high degree of abstraction and code reuse.

```
def applyFunction(f: Int => Int, x: Int) = f(x)
val doubled = applyFunction((x) => x * 2, 3) // doubled: 6
```

7. Traits

Traits in Scala are used to share interfaces and fields between classes. They are similar to Java interfaces but can contain concrete methods and state.

```
trait Greeting {
   def greet(name: String): String = s"Hello, \$name!"
}

class Person(val name: String) extends Greeting

val john = new Person("John")
println(john.greet(john.name)) // Output: Hello, John!
```

8. Concurrency

Scala offers several powerful tools for handling concurrency, including the Actors model (via the Akka toolkit), parallel collections, and Futures and Promises.

```
import scala.concurrent.Future
import scala.concurrent.ExecutionContext.Implicits.global

val futureResult = Future {
  // Long-running computation
  Thread.sleep(1000)
  42
}

futureResult.foreach(result => println(s"Got the result: \$result"))
```

9. Interoperability with Java

Scala runs on the Java Virtual Machine (JVM) and is fully interoperable with Java. This allows Scala developers to leverage existing Java libraries and frameworks seamlessly.

```
import java.util.Date

val now = new Date
println(now)
```

10. Rich Standard Library

Scala's standard library is rich, encompassing a wide array of functionality that caters to both functional and object-oriented programming needs. It includes powerful collections, concurrent programming abstractions, and utilities for I/O operations.

Scala's features promote concise, elegant, and efficient code, aligning with modern software development demands. Its blend of functional and object-oriented paradigms, coupled with strong typing and powerful standard libraries, significantly enhances productivity and code quality.

1.4 Scala Ecosystem

The Scala ecosystem encompasses a comprehensive range of tools, libraries, and frameworks designed to enhance the development experience, streamline workflows, and leverage the language's capabilities. Developers can leverage a rich toolset to build applications for diverse domains including web, data processing, and distributed systems. This section provides a detailed overview of the crucial components within the Scala ecosystem, ensuring clarity and ease of understanding for both novice and advanced programmers.

Scala Standard Library

Scala's standard library is extensive, providing a robust foundation for development. Key components include collections, concurrent programming, and input/output functionalities. The collections framework provides immutable and mutable data structures, offering a broad spectrum of containers such as lists, sets, maps, and sequences. These collections support higher-order functions, enhancing expressiveness and enabling functional programming paradigms.

For example, the use of List in a Scala program is as follows:

```
val fruits = List("apple", "banana", "cherry")
val upperFruits = fruits.map(_.toUpperCase)
println(upperFruits)
```

19

The output displays:

List(APPLE, BANANA, CHERRY)

Build Tools: sbt (Simple Build Tool)

sbt is the de facto build tool used in Scala projects. It facilitates project management through dependency resolution, compilation, testing, and packaging. sbt uses a straightforward and declarative syntax for build definitions. Consider a basic build.sbt file:

```
name := "MyScalaProject"

version := "0.1"

scalaVersion := "2.13.3"

libraryDependencies += "org.scalatest" %% "scalatest" % "3.1.2" % Test
```

This build file specifies the project name, version, Scala version, and a dependency on the ScalaTest library.

Testing Frameworks

Robust testing is imperative in software development. Scala features several testing frameworks such as ScalaTest, Specs2, and JUnit, allowing developers to write unit tests, integration tests, and behavior-driven development (BDD) tests. ScalaTest supports a variety of styles, including FunSuite and FlatSpec. Below is an example of a FunSuite test:

```
import org.scalatest.funsuite.AnyFunSuite

class HelloWorldTest extends AnyFunSuite {
  test("sayHello should return Hello, World!") {
    assert(HelloWorld.sayHello() === "Hello, World!")
  }
}
```

Web Frameworks: Play and Akka HTTP

Scala excels in web development with frameworks such as Play and Akka HTTP. Play is a high-productivity framework that features reactive principles and a stateless architecture. It is particularly suitable for building scalable applications. A simple Play controller might look like this:

```
import javax.inject._
import play.api.mvc._

@Singleton
class HomeController @Inject()(val controllerComponents: ControllerComponents)
      extends BaseController {
  def index() = Action { implicit request: Request[AnyContent] =>
    Ok("Hello, World!")
```

```
  }
}
```

On the other hand, Akka HTTP provides a toolkit for building HTTP servers and clients. Akka HTTP is built on Akka, a toolkit for building highly concurrent, distributed, and resilient message-driven applications. An example of an Akka HTTP server route might be:

```
import akka.actor.ActorSystem
import akka.http.scaladsl.Http
import akka.http.scaladsl.server.Directives._

object WebServer extends App {
  implicit val system = ActorSystem("my-system")
  implicit val executionContext = system.dispatcher

  val route = path("hello") {
    get {
      complete("Hello, World!")
    }
  }

  Http().newServerAt("localhost", 8080).bind(route)
}
```

Data Processing: Apache Spark

Apache Spark, an open-source distributed computing system, integrates seamlessly with Scala, empowering developers to process large datasets efficiently. Spark's core abstraction, RDD (Resilient Distributed Dataset), and high-level APIs in DataFrame and Dataset offer robust tools for scalable data processing. A sample Spark application that counts words from a text file is as follows:

```
import org.apache.spark.sql.SparkSession

object WordCount {
  def main(args: Array[String]): Unit = {
    val spark = SparkSession.builder.appName("WordCount").getOrCreate()
    val input = spark.read.textFile("input.txt")
    val counts = input.flatMap(line => line.split(" "))
                  .groupBy("value")
                  .count()
    counts.show()
    spark.stop()
  }
}
```

IDE Support

Integrated Development Environments (IDEs) provide vital support in Scala development. Popular IDEs for Scala include IntelliJ IDEA and Eclipse with the Scala IDE plugin. These IDEs offer features such as intelligent code completion, debugging, and refactoring tools tailored for

Scala, enhancing developer productivity. For instance, IntelliJ IDEA can be configured to support sbt projects seamlessly.

Libraries and Frameworks

The Scala ecosystem's strength lies in its libraries and frameworks for various domains such as:

- Cats and Scalaz for functional programming abstractions.

- Akka for building concurrent and distributed systems.

- Slick for functional relational mapping (FRM).

- Finagle for asynchronous RPC systems.

- Doobie for functional JDBC layer.

- Circe for JSON processing.

Build Automation: Jenkins and GitHub Actions

For continuous integration and continuous deployment (CI/CD), tools such as Jenkins and GitHub Actions are widely used in Scala projects. They automate building, testing, and deploying Scala applications, ensuring consistency and reliability in software delivery pipelines. A sample GitHub Actions workflow configuration for a Scala project is as follows:

```
name: Scala CI

on: [push, pull_request]

jobs:
  build:
    runs-on: ubuntu-latest
    steps:
    - uses: actions/checkout@v2
    - name: Setup JDK
      uses: actions/setup-java@v1
      with:
        java-version: '11'
    - name: Cache sbt
      uses: actions/cache@v2
      with:
        path: |
          ~/.ivy2/cache
          ~/.sbt
        key: ${{ runner.os }}-sbt-${{ hashFiles('**/build.sbt') }}
        restore-keys: ${{ runner.os }}-sbt-
    - name: sbt test
      run: sbt test
```

The Scala ecosystem's depth and breadth provide a robust platform for developers to explore and harness the language's full potential, ensuring efficient and effective software development. Incorporating the right tools and libraries as per project requirements can significantly enhance productivity and code quality, demonstrating Scala's versatility and strength in various application domains.

1.5 Setting Up the Scala Development Environment

To get started with Scala, it is crucial to set up a robust and efficient development environment. This section provides meticulous instructions to install Scala on your machine, configure necessary tools, and verify the installation to ensure a seamless development experience.

Step 1: Install Java Development Kit (JDK)

Scala runs on the Java Virtual Machine (JVM); thus, you must have the Java Development Kit (JDK) installed. We recommend installing JDK 8 or later.

- For Windows:

  1. Download JDK from the official Oracle website.
  2. Run the installer and follow the on-screen instructions.
  3. Set the $JAVA\_HOME$ environment variable to point to your JDK installation directory.
  4. Add the bin directory of the JDK to your system $PATH$.

- For macOS:

  1. Use the Homebrew package manager by running the following command in the terminal:
     ```
     brew install openjdk
     ```
  2. Set the $JAVA\_HOME$ environment variable in your $/.bash\_profile$ or $/.zshrc$ file:
     ```
     export JAVA_HOME=$(/usr/libexec/java_home)
     ```

- For Linux:

23

1. Use the package manager specific to your distribution. For example, on Ubuntu, use:

```
sudo apt-get update
sudo apt-get install openjdk-8-jdk
```

2. Verify the installation by running:

```
java -version
```

Step 2: Install Scala

- For Windows:

    1. Download the Scala binaries from the official Scala website.

    2. Run the installer and follow the on-screen instructions.

    3. Add the bin directory of the Scala installation to your system PATH.

- For macOS:

    1. Use the Homebrew package manager:

    ```
    brew install scala
    ```

- For Linux:

    1. Download the Scala binaries from the official Scala website.

    2. Extract the downloaded archive and move it to a directory of your choice:

    ```
    tar xzf scala-2.13.6.tgz
    sudo mv scala-2.13.6 /usr/local/share/scala
    ```

    3. Update your PATH environment variable:

    ```
    export PATH=$PATH:/usr/local/share/scala/bin
    ```

    4. Verify the installation:

    ```
    scala -version
    ```

Step 3: Install sbt (Scala Build Tool)

Scala Build Tool (sbt) is essential for managing Scala projects and their dependencies.

- For Windows:

    1. Download the sbt installer from the official sbt website.

    2. Run the installer and follow the on-screen instructions.

- For macOS:

    1. Use Homebrew to install sbt:

    ```
    brew install sbt
    ```

- For Linux:

    1. Add the sbt repository to your package manager. For example, on Ubuntu:

    ```
    echo "deb https://repo.scala-sbt.org/scalasbt/debian all main" | sudo tee
        /etc/apt/sources.list.d/sbt.list
    curl -sL "https://keyserver.ubuntu.com/pks/lookup?op=get&search=0
        x99E82A75642AC823" | sudo apt-key add
    sudo apt-get update
    sudo apt-get install sbt
    ```

Step 4: Verify the Installation

Once Scala and sbt are installed, verify the installation by checking the versions and creating a simple sbt project.

- Check Scala version:

```
scala -version
```

- Check sbt version:

```
sbt sbtVersion
```

- Create a simple sbt project to ensure everything is configured correctly. First, create a directory for your project and navigate into it:

```
mkdir HelloScala
cd HelloScala
```

- Initialize a new sbt project:

```
sbt new scala/scala-seed.g8
```

- Follow the prompts to set up the project. Once the project is set up, navigate into the project directory and run sbt:

```
cd helloscala
sbt
```

- In the sbt console, compile the project:

```
compile
```

```
[info] Compiling 1 Scala source to /path/to/helloscala/target/scala-2.13/classes ...
[success] Total time: 2 s, completed <Date>
```

- Run the project:

```
run
```

```
[info] running Hello
Hello, Scala!
[success] Total time: 1 s, completed <Date>
```

With these steps completed, your Scala development environment is now properly set up. You are ready to start developing Scala applications effectively.

1.6   First Scala Program

To begin writing our first Scala program, we must first ensure that the necessary Scala development environment has been correctly set up, as discussed in the earlier section. This includes having the Scala compiler and the necessary tools like the Scala Build Tool (sbt) installed.

In Scala, a simple program can be written inside a singleton object. Singleton objects in Scala are created using the object keyword. They are essentially classes with only one instance, and they're used to define methods and fields which are globally accessible. Here, we will create a basic Scala application that prints "Hello, World!".

Consider the following code snippet:

```
object HelloWorld {
  def main(args: Array[String]): Unit = {
    println("Hello, World!")
  }
}
```

In this program:

- object HelloWorld declares a singleton object named HelloWorld.

- The main method serves as the entry point to the program. It takes an array of strings as an argument (args: Array[String]) and returns Unit, which is analogous to void in languages like Java.

- println("Hello, World!") is a simple function call that prints "Hello, World!" to the standard output.

To compile and run this program using the Scala compiler, follow these steps:

1. Save the above code in a file named HelloWorld.scala. 2. Open a terminal or command prompt and navigate to the directory containing HelloWorld.scala. 3. Compile the program using the Scala compiler by exccuting the command:

```
scalac HelloWorld.scala
```

This command generates several files, including HelloWorld.class, in the current directory.

4. Run the compiled program using the Scala command:

```
scala HelloWorld
```

The program output should be:

```
Hello, World!
```

Now, we will explore a slightly more complex example that demonstrates the use of variables, functions, and simple control structures in Scala. Let's write a program that computes the factorial of a given number.

```
object FactorialCalculator {
  def main(args: Array[String]): Unit = {
    val number = 5
    println(s"Factorial of $number is ${factorial(number)}")
  }

  def factorial(n: Int): Int = {
    if (n <= 1) 1
    else n * factorial(n - 1)
  }
}
```

In this program:

- val number = 5 declares an immutable variable number and assigns it the value 5.

27

- println(s"Factorial of $number is $factorial(number)") uses string interpolation to print the result of the factorial function.

- The factorial method is a recursive function:

  - If n <= 1, it returns 1.

  - Otherwise, it multiplies n by the result of factorial(n - 1).

Follow the same steps for compilation and execution as previously outlined. Save the code in a file named FactorialCalculator.scala, compile it with scalac FactorialCalculator.scala, and run it using scala FactorialCalculator. The expected output is:

Factorial of 5 is 120

Compiling and running programs in an Integrated Development Environment (IDE) like IntelliJ IDEA can simplify this process significantly. Setting up your project correctly within the IDE allows you to compile and run applications seamlessly, leveraging features like syntax highlighting, code suggestions, and error checking.

Experimenting with slightly more complex programs soon becomes intuitive. Writing idiomatic Scala code often involves leveraging core features like immutability, higher-order functions, pattern matching, and a rich collection of data structures. As one codes more Scala programs, the distinctions and efficiencies provided by its syntax and functional paradigms become increasingly clear. This encourages more concise and expressive code, often manifesting in fewer lines than equivalent Java implementations.

1.7   Scala REPL

The Scala REPL (Read-Eval-Print Loop) serves as an interactive shell for writing and evaluating Scala code. It provides immediate feedback, making it an invaluable tool for experimenting with Scala and quickly testing code snippets. By interactively writing code and seeing results instantly, developers can refine their understanding of Scala's syntax and semantics.

To invoke the REPL, navigate to the terminal and type:

```
scala
```

This command initiates the environment wherein you can begin to input Scala commands. Upon successful execution of the above command, the prompt will update to:

```
Welcome to Scala 2.13.5 (OpenJDK 64-Bit Server VM, Java 1.8.0_242).
Type in expressions for evaluation. Or try :help.

scala>
```

The REPL accepts single-line and multi-line inputs. For instance, a simple arithmetic operation can be performed:

```
scala> 1 + 1
```

The REPL will instantly evaluate this expression and return:

```
res0: Int = 2
```

In this output, res0 is the default name given to the result of the evaluated expression. Future results will increment this identifier (e.g., res1, res2, etc.).

Variables can be declared just like within a typical Scala program:

```
scala> val x = 5
```

```
x: Int = 5
```

You can refer to these variables in subsequent operations. For example:

```
scala> val y = x * 2
```

```
y: Int = 10
```

The REPL can also handle more complex constructs, including function definitions:

```
scala> def add(a: Int, b: Int): Int = a + b
```

Once the function is defined, it can be called:

```
scala> add(3, 4)
```

```
res2: Int = 7
```

To quit the REPL, use the command:

```
:quit
```

The command :quit or simply :q will exit the current REPL session.

Additionally, the Scala REPL supports a variety of commands beyond just standard Scala code. These can enhance and facilitate the interactive programming experience. Accessing the help for these commands can be done via:

```
:help
```

This displays a list of available commands, such as:

```
:help                       Display this help message
:quit            Exit the interpreter
:type      \t      expr         Print type of expression without evaluating it
:doc       \t      sym      \t          Display documentation for symbol
:load      \t      file            \t      Load and execute a Scala source file
:reset              \t            Reset the interpreter and delete all defined variable names
```

A particularly useful command is :load, which allows you to execute predefined scripts stored in files:

```
:load filename.scala
```

This makes it easier to work with larger chunks of code without manually inputting each line.

Another beneficial feature is the ability to get the type of any expression without evaluating it, using :type:

```
:type 1 + 1
```

```
Int
```

This aids in understanding the types Scala infers, enhancing the learning experience by emphasizing the strong type system of Scala.

:reset is useful if you wish to clear the current session and start anew without quitting the REPL. This command will clean the namespace of previous variable and function definitions:

```
:reset
```

The REPL also allows you to check documentation for Scala symbols using :doc. For example:

```
:doc List
```

This command leverages integrated documentation systems to provide useful information about Scala classes, methods, and objects.

In essence, the Scala REPL is a robust environment for experimenting, learning, and quick prototyping. It allows developers to explore Scala's syntax and features dynamically, making it an essential tool for both beginners and experienced Scala programmers.

1.8   Introduction to sbt (Scala Build Tool)

The Scala Build Tool (sbt) is a powerful and flexible build tool that is specifically designed for Scala and Java projects. It provides an efficient way to manage dependencies, compile Scala code, run tests, and package projects. sbt is a build tool akin to Apache Maven and Gradle, but it offers a more streamlined set of functionalities tailored for Scala developers.

sbt uses a build definition written in Scala-based syntax, which allows a higher level of customization and programmatic control over the build process. The build definition is typically divided across several files and directories:

- build.sbt: The primary build file where you define project settings.

- project/: Contains auxiliary build definitions and configuration files.

- src/: The main source directory, typically split into main, test, and other subdirectories.

- lib/: Includes any unmanaged dependencies.

```
name := "MyScalaProject"

version := "0.1"

scalaVersion := "2.13.4"

libraryDependencies += "org.scalatest" %% "scalatest" % "3.2.3" % Test
```

The build.sbt file illustrated in Listing **??** defines a basic project configuration. Here, name specifies the project's name, version denotes the project's version, and scalaVersion sets the version of Scala to be used. The libraryDependencies setting is used to declare dependencies, where scalatest is added for testing purposes.

sbt supports incremental compilation, meaning it only recompiles the necessary parts of the codebase, which can save significant amounts of time for larger projects. This is achieved through tracking dependencies and automatically determining the minimal set of files that need recompilation.

```
sbt
```

31

Running sbt, as shown in Listing **??**, starts an interactive shell where various commands can be executed. Some of the most commonly used sbt commands include:

- compile: Compiles the source code.

- test: Runs the tests.

- run: Runs the main class of the project.

- package: Packages the code into a JAR file.

- clean: Cleans up generated files.

```
> compile
[info] Compiling 1 Scala source to /path/to/project/target/scala-2.13/classes ...
[success] Total time: 2 s, completed Jan 1, 2023 12:00:00 PM
```

The output above results from executing the compile command, showcasing sbt's logging feature which provides detailed information on the progress and success of the compilation process.

sbt also allows for defining custom tasks and settings. A task is an action that sbt can perform, such as compiling or packaging code. This flexibility is one of sbt's strengths, enabling users to define specific behaviors for their build process.

```
lazy val hello = taskKey[Unit]("Prints 'Hello, World!'")

hello := {
  println("Hello, World!")
}
```

In Listing **??**, a custom task is defined using taskKey, which is a key type for tasks. The task hello is then assigned a simple println statement.

```
> hello
[info] Hello, World!
```

Executing the hello task would produce the output shown above, demonstrating how easy it is to extend sbt's capabilities with user-defined tasks.

Dependency management is a critical feature of sbt, enabling projects to easily manage and resolve library dependencies. sbt integrates with repositories such as Maven Central to automatically download and include libraries specified in the libraryDependencies setting.

A more sophisticated usage involves defining multiple modules or subprojects within a single build. These modules can depend on each other, offering a structured way to manage complex projects.

```
lazy val root = (project in file("."))
  .aggregate(core, utils)

lazy val core = (project in file("core"))

lazy val utils = (project in file("utils"))
```

Listing **??** shows how to define a multi-project build where root aggregates two subprojects, core and utils. Each subproject is defined in a separate directory and can have its own build.sbt file.

Moreover, sbt facilitates the integration with continuous integration (CI) tools, offering plugins for Jenkins, Travis CI, and others. This capability is essential for maintaining code quality and automating the build process.

In practice, leveraging sbt's powerful features facilitates efficient and scalable development workflows. By managing dependencies, supporting incremental compilation, and providing customizable tasks, sbt helps developers maintain high productivity in Scala projects.

1.9 Comparing Scala with Java and Other Languages

Scala is often juxtaposed with Java due to their shared platform, the Java Virtual Machine (JVM). This comparison, while useful, extends to other languages as well, such as Python and Haskell, each offering unique paradigms and features. This section elucidates the fundamental differences and similarities of Scala with these languages, highlighting the benefits and trade-offs inherent in each.

Scala vs. Java

Java, a stalwart in the programming community, is renowned for its robustness, widespread use, and extensive libraries. Scala, designed to address some of Java's limitations, provides several key enhancements:

- Conciseness: Scala's syntax is notably more concise than Java's. This reduction in verbosity is achieved by eliminating boilerplate code. Examples include type inference, which allows the omission of explicit type declarations, and case classes, which provide a succinct way to define immutable data objects.

```
// Java
public class Person {
    private String name;
    private int age;

    public Person(String name, int age) {
        this.name = name;
        this.age = age;
    }

    // getters and setters
}
// Scala
case class Person(name: String, age: Int)
```

- **Functional Programming**: Scala integrates functional programming features, enabling functions as first-class citizens. Higher-order functions and immutability are core to Scala, contrasting with Java's primarily object-oriented nature (though Java 8 and beyond introduce some functional concepts like lambdas).

```
// Java
List<Integer> numbers = Arrays.asList(1, 2, 3, 4, 5);
numbers.stream().map(n -> n * 2).collect(Collectors.toList());

// Scala
val numbers = List(1, 2, 3, 4, 5)
numbers.map(_ * 2)
```

- **Advanced Type System**: Scala's type system is more expressive than Java's, supporting features like traits (a more flexible form of interfaces), generics with variance annotations, and pattern matching.

```
// Java
interface Animal {
    void sound();
}

class Dog implements Animal {
    public void sound() {
        System.out.println("Woof");
    }
}
// Scala
trait Animal {
    def sound(): Unit
}

class Dog extends Animal {
    def sound() = println("Woof")
}
```

Scala vs. Python

Python is celebrated for its simplicity and readability, traits that have catapulted it to prominence across various domains, from web development to data science. Scala, while more complex, offers benefits in certain contexts:

- Performance: Scala, running on the JVM, often performs better in high-computation scenarios compared to Python, which is an interpreted language. This makes Scala suitable for performance-critical applications.

- Static vs. Dynamic Typing: Scala's statically-typed nature contrasts with Python's dynamic typing. Static typing can catch errors at compile-time, leading to more robust and maintainable code. Python's dynamic typing, on the other hand, offers more flexibility and ease of use.

- Concurrency: Scala's Akka library provides robust concurrency and parallelism tools, making it easier to build scalable and responsive applications. Python's Global Interpreter Lock (GIL) often limits concurrent execution, though libraries like asyncio and threading offer some solutions.

Scala vs. Haskell

Haskell is a purely functional programming language with strong static typing, making it semantically similar to Scala but differing in several aspects:

- Purity: Haskell emphasizes pure functions, where side effects are managed through monads, ensuring referential transparency. While Scala promotes functional paradigms, it is not purely functional and allows mutable state and side effects.

- Lazy Evaluation: Haskell uses lazy evaluation by default, meaning expressions are not evaluated until their results are needed. Scala uses strict evaluation but offers lazy evaluation through the lazy keyword and Stream class.

```
// Haskell
let infiniteList = [1..]
take 5 infiniteList

// Scala
val infiniteList = Stream.from(1)
infiniteList.take(5).toList
```

- Interoperability: Scala's seamless integration with Java is advantageous compared to Haskell, as it allows leveraging existing Java libraries and frameworks. This interoperability makes Scala more pragmatic for many enterprise applications.

- Syntax: Haskell's syntax is often more mathematical and abstract, which can be both a strength (for expressing complex algorithms concisely) and a barrier (due to its steep learning curve). Scala's syntax, though complex, is more accessible to those familiar with C-like languages.

Scala, by bridging functional and object-oriented paradigms, serves as a versatile tool in modern programming. It retains the familiar structure and performance benefits of the JVM while introducing advanced functional programming concepts that streamline code development and enhance readability. Through its conciseness, powerful type system, and functional capabilities, Scala addresses many of the shortcomings found in other languages, making it an apt choice for a wide range of applications.

1.10   Why Learn Scala?

Scala is a powerful and versatile programming language that adheres closely to both functional and object-oriented programming paradigms. This dual nature is one of the primary reasons developers and organizations are increasingly adopting Scala for a variety of projects. This section offers a detailed exploration of the specific advantages of learning and using Scala.

- **Concise Syntax:** One of the key advantages of Scala is its concise and expressive syntax. Scala's syntax is designed to reduce boilerplate code, which simplifies the codebase and enhances readability. For instance, consider a simple example of defining a class in Scala:

```
class Person(val name: String, val age: Int)
```

The above code snippet succinctly defines a class Person with two properties, name and age. In contrast, an equivalent Java class would require several lines of code, including explicit getters, setters, and constructor methods.

36

- **Functional Programming:** Scala fully supports functional programming, allowing you to write more predictable code with fewer side effects. Functional concepts such as higher-order functions, immutability, and pattern matching can lead to clearer and more robust code. For example, a function that filters a list of integers for even numbers can be implemented as follows:

```
val numbers = List(1, 2, 3, 4, 5, 6)
val evenNumbers = numbers.filter(_ % 2 == 0)
```

In this code, filter is a higher-order function that takes a predicate function to filter the list.

- **Interoperability with Java:** Scala is designed to run on the Java Virtual Machine (JVM) and fully interoperates with Java. This means you can use existing Java libraries and frameworks within your Scala projects, leveraging a vast ecosystem without having to rewrite existing code. For example, Java's ArrayList can be used in Scala:

```
import java.util.ArrayList
val list = new ArrayList[Int]()
list.add(1)
list.add(2)
```

Scala's seamless integration with Java ensures that developers can gradually migrate to Scala or use both languages within the same project.

- **Advanced Type System:** Scala features an advanced type system that includes generic classes, variance annotations, and upper and lower type bounds. This type system helps catch more errors at compile time, increasing the robustness and reliability of programs. Consider a generic class in Scala:

```
class Container[A](value: A) {
    def getValue: A = value
}
```

In this example, Container is a generic class that can hold any type, offering both flexibility and type safety.

- **Concurrency:** Scala's akka library provides a powerful toolkit for building concurrent and distributed systems. By utilizing the Actor model, akka simplifies writing concurrent applications, ensuring they are both scalable and resilient. A simple actor in akka can be defined as follows:

```
import akka.actor.Actor
import akka.actor.ActorSystem
import akka.actor.Props

class SimpleActor extends Actor {
    def receive = {
        case msg: String => println(s"Received message: $msg")
    }
}

val system = ActorSystem("SimpleSystem")
val simpleActor = system.actorOf(Props[SimpleActor], name = "simpleActor")
simpleActor ! "Hello, Actor"
```

Here, SimpleActor defines an actor that processes string messages, illustrating how akka facilitates concurrent programming.

- **Integrated Development Environment (IDE) Support:** Scala enjoys robust IDE support, with plugins available for popular environments such as IntelliJ IDEA, Eclipse, and Visual Studio Code. These plugins provide essential features like code completion, refactoring tools, and debugging capabilities tailored to Scala, making development more efficient.

- **Community and Ecosystem:** The Scala community and its ecosystem are vibrant and expanding. From comprehensive documentation to active forums and numerous open-source projects, Scala developers have a wealth of resources at their disposal. Moreover, frameworks like Play for web development and Spark for big data processing have bolstered Scala's adoption in various domains.

- **Future-Proofing:** With the increasing emphasis on functional programming and the shift towards scalable, concurrent systems, learning Scala positions developers well for future trends in software development. Scala's unique combination of functional and object-oriented paradigms ensures it remains relevant and valuable in evolving technological landscapes.

The benefits of Scala extend across various aspects of programming, from cleaner syntax and robust type systems to excellent JVM interoperability and superior concurrency support. This makes Scala not only a versatile tool for current development needs but also a strategic choice for future-proofing one's programming skills.

Chapter 2

Scala Basics

This chapter provides a detailed overview of Scala's fundamental syntax and program structure. It covers essential concepts such as variables, constants, data types, operators, expressions, and control structures. Readers will also learn about functions and methods, string manipulations, data input and output, and basic exception handling. These topics form the building blocks necessary for writing and understanding Scala programs.

2.1   Syntax and Structure of Scala Programs

Scala, a hybrid functional object-oriented programming language, has a syntax designed for concise and readable code. A Scala program involves several components: packages, imports, objects, methods, and expressions. Understanding these elements is critical for writing effective and efficient Scala code.

A Scala source file typically ends with a .scala extension. The structure of a simple Scala program is demonstrated in the following example:

```
package example

import scala.math._

object HelloWorld {
  def main(args: Array[String]): Unit = {
    println("Hello, world!")
  }
}
```

package declarations are used to group related code together, similar to namespaces in other languages. The import statement allows access to classes and objects from other packages, facilitating code reuse and modularity.

In this example, the object HelloWorld declaration defines a singleton object, which is a class with exactly one instance. The singleton object serves as the entry point of the program, and it must contain a main method with a specific signature:

```
def main(args: Array[String]): Unit
```

The main method takes an array of String arguments and returns Unit, which is analogous to void in languages like Java or C++. The body of the main method executes the instructions, and the println method outputs the specified string to the console.

Comments in Scala

Scala supports both single-line and multi-line comments. Single-line comments start with //, and multi-line comments are enclosed between /* and */.

```
// This is a single-line comment

/*
  This is a
  multi-line comment
*/
```

Comments are essential for explaining code logic and improving readability.

Identifiers and Keywords

Identifiers in Scala include names given to variables, methods, objects, classes, and traits. Identifiers start with a letter or an underscore, followed by letters, digits, or underscores. For instance, myVariable, _temp, and computeSum are valid identifiers.

Keywords are reserved words in Scala that cannot be used as identifiers. Some examples include if, else, for, while, def, val, var, object, and class. A comprehensive list of Scala keywords should be referenced during programming to avoid conflicts.

Expressions and Statements

Expressions in Scala are constructs that yield a value. A simple example of an expression is $2 + 3$, which evaluates to 5. Expressions can be used as parts of larger expressions or assigned to variables.

Statements, on the other hand, are instructions executed by the program. A typical example of a statement is the println method used to display outputs. Difference between statements and expressions lies in that statements perform actions, while expressions evaluate to values.

Basic Program Structure

A typical Scala program structure includes variable declarations, method definitions, and control structures. Consider the following example that includes additional program elements:

```
object BasicProgram {
  def main(args: Array[String]): Unit = {
    val myVal: Int = 10
    var myVar: String = "Hello"

    def computeSum(x: Int, y: Int): Int = {
      x + y
    }

    println(s"MyVal: $myVal, MyVar: $myVar")
    println(s"Sum: ${computeSum(5, 6)}")
  }
}
```

Variables and Methods

In this example, myVal is an immutable variable, declared using val, while myVar is a mutable variable, declared using var. The computeSum method takes two Int parameters and returns their sum. Variables myVal and myVar demonstrate type annotations with Int and String, respectively.

String Interpolation

The println statements showcase string interpolation, a feature that makes incorporating variables into strings straightforward. The s string interpolator allows embedding expressions within strings using the $ symbol followed by variable names or expressions enclosed in curly braces.

Conclusion of Structure Overview

Understanding the syntax and structure of Scala programs lays a foundational understanding needed for more advanced topics. This overview illustrates a typical Scala program's main components, focusing on essential elements like packages, imports, objects, and expressions, integral for structuring your code efficiently.

2.2 Variables and Constants

In Scala, variables and constants form the foundation of data manipulation. This section delves into the declaration, initialization, and differences between variables and constants. Understanding these concepts is crucial for managing data effectively in Scala programs.

Scala provides two main constructs for handling data that are intended to remain constant or are subject to change: val and var.

val defines immutable references which once assigned, cannot be modified. Conversely, var defines mutable references which can be reassigned throughout the lifespan of the program.

```
val immutableValue: Int = 10
var mutableValue: Int = 20
```

In this example, immutableValue is a constant and will always hold the value 10. Attempting to reassign immutableValue will result in a compilation error. On the other hand, mutableValue can be reassigned to different values.

```
mutableValue = 30 // This is allowed
immutableValue = 50 // This will cause a compilation error
```

Scala encourages the use of val over var to promote immutability and the functional programming paradigm. When possible, prefer val for defining references unless the logic explicitly requires mutability.

Type Inference

Scala features powerful type inference that allows the omission of explicit type annotations when the type can be inferred.

```
val inferredValue = 100
var anotherInferredValue = "Hello, Scala"
```

In the code above, Scala infers that inferredValue is an Int and anotherInferredValue is a String. When type inference is used judiciously, it can make the code more concise and readable. However, in large and complex codebases, explicit type annotations can enhance readability and maintainability.

Variable Naming

Variable names in Scala must start with a letter and can be followed by letters, digits, or underscores. The names are case-sensitive. Scala allows the usage of special characters like $, but it's best to avoid such practices for clarity.

Legal and Illegal Naming Examples

```
val myValue = 10 // Legal
val _tempVar = 5 // Legal
val my$value = 100 // Legal, but not recommended
val 1stValue = 1 // Illegal, starts with a digit
val my-value = 10 // Illegal, contains a hyphen
```

Use descriptive and meaningful names for variables to enhance code readability. It is a common convention to use camelCase for variable names.

Variable Scope

The scope of a variable refers to the region of the code where the variable is accessible. Scala supports different scopes such as local, class-level, and global scopes.

Local Scope

Variables declared within a function or a block of code have local scope and are accessible only within that block.

```
def calculateArea(radius: Double): Double = {
    val pi = 3.14159 // Local scope
    pi * radius * radius
}
val radius = 5.0
val area = calculateArea(radius)
```

Here, pi has a local scope within the calculateArea function and is not accessible outside it.

Class-Level Scope

Variables declared within a class but outside any method are accessible throughout the class. These can be either instance variables or class variables (using object).

```
class Circle(val radius: Double) {
    val pi = 3.14159 // Class-level scope

    def calculateArea(): Double = {
        pi * radius * radius
    }
}
val circle = new Circle(5.0)
val area = circle.calculateArea()
```

Global Scope

Scala supports packages and objects to encapsulate variables with

43

global scope. Variables declared in an object are accessible globally.

```
object Constants {
    val SpeedOfLight = 299792458 // Global scope
}
val lightSpeed = Constants.SpeedOfLight
```

Properly scoping variables can reduce the risk of unintended side-effects and improve code organization.

Mutable and Immutable Collections

While individual values can be declared as mutable or immutable, Scala's collection framework also distinguishes between mutable and immutable collections.

```
import scala.collection.mutable
import scala.collection.immutable

val immutableList = List(1, 2, 3)
val mutableList = mutable.ListBuffer(1, 2, 3)

immutableList(0) = 100 // Compilation error
mutableList(0) = 100 // Allowed
```

The difference between mutable and immutable collections is a crucial aspect of functional programming in Scala. Immutable collections offer better performance in concurrent applications due to thread safety.

Understanding variables and constants and their proper use encourages idiomatic Scala programming, leveraging both functional and object-oriented paradigms to write robust, maintainable code. Proper usage also leads to fewer errors and more predictable behavior, forming a solid foundation for advanced Scala concepts.

2.3   Data Types in Scala

Scala is a strongly statically typed language, meaning that the type of every expression is known at compile time. This section delves into the various data types available in Scala, discussing both primitive and composite types, and their significance in functional and object-oriented programming paradigms. Understanding these data types is crucial as they form the foundation for data manipulation, function definitions, and control structures.

Primitive Data Types

Scala supports several basic primitive types. These types are similar to those in other statically typed languages but come with the additional support of type inference, allowing the compiler to deduce types.

- Byte - 8-bit signed integer. Range: -128 to 127.

- Short - 16-bit signed integer. Range: -32,768 to 32,767.

- Int - 32-bit signed integer. Range: -2,147,483,648 to 2,147,483,647.

- Long - 64-bit signed integer. Range: -9,223,372,036,854,775,808 to 9,223,372,036,854,775,807.

- Float - 32-bit IEEE 754 floating-point number.

- Double - 64-bit IEEE 754 floating-point number.

- Char - 16-bit unsigned Unicode character. Range: U+0000 to U+FFFF.

- Boolean - Represents a value of true or false.

- Unit - A type that carries no meaningful value. It has only one instance, (). Used for side-effecting methods.

- Null - A subtype of all reference types; it is used to denote a null reference.

- Nothing - A subtype of all types; it signifies the absence of a value, often used in exception handling.

- Any - The root of the Scala type hierarchy. It has two direct sub-classes: AnyVal and AnyRef.

Composite Data Types

Scala also provides composite types that allow the construction of complex data structures by combining simpler types.

- Tuple - A finite ordered list of elements. Tuples are immutable and can contain heterogeneously typed elements.

```
val myTuple = (1, "Scala", 3.14)
println(myTuple._1) // Access first element
println(myTuple._2) // Access second element
```

- Array - A fixed-size array that holds elements of the same type.

```
val myArray = Array(1, 2, 3, 4, 5)
println(myArray(0)) // Access first element
myArray(1) = 10 // Modify second element
```

- List - An immutable linked list. Methods on lists do not modify the original list but return new lists.

```
val myList = List(1, 2, 3, 4, 5)
val newList = 0 :: myList // Prepend element
println(newList)
```

- Map - An immutable collection of key-value pairs.

```
val myMap = Map("key1" -> "value1", "key2" -> "value2")
println(myMap("key1")) // Access value associated with key1
```

- Set - An immutable collection of unique elements.

```
val mySet = Set(1, 2, 3, 4, 5, 5)
println(mySet) // Output: Set(1, 2, 3, 4, 5)
```

Type Inference

Scala's type inference mechanism allows the compiler to automatically deduce the type of an expression. Explicit type annotations are not necessary if the compiler can infer the type. This improves code readability and reduces verbosity.

```
val number = 42 // Compiler infers 'Int'
val pi = 3.14 // Compiler infers 'Double'
val greeting = "Hello, Scala!" // Compiler infers 'String'
```

Type Aliases

Scala allows the creation of type aliases to enhance code readability, maintainability, and abstraction in complex type definitions.

```
type StringToIntMap = Map[String, Int]
val myMapping: StringToIntMap = Map("a" -> 1, "b" -> 2)
```

Type Casting

Scala's mechanism for type casting is done using the asInstanceOf method. This method is used to cast instances to a specified type, ensuring type safety during runtime.

```
val x: Any = "A String"
val str: String = x.asInstanceOf[String]
```

Expanding upon these fundamental types, Scala provides extensive libraries for handling more advanced and abstract types, such as Option, Either, and Try, which further facilitate functional programming practices by incorporating concepts of immutability and higher-order functions. These data types play a pivotal role in managing state, handling exceptions, and implementing generic programming paradigms.

2.4   Operators and Expressions

In Scala, operators are special symbols or keywords used to perform operations on operands, which can be variables or values. Expressions are combinations of operators and operands that compute a value. Understanding operators and expressions is crucial in Scala, as they form the basis of computations and logic within the language.

Scala supports a variety of operators, which can be categorized into arithmetic, relational, logical, bitwise, assignment, and miscellaneous operators. These operators adhere to specific rules of precedence and associativity, which determine the order in which operations are performed in expressions.

Arithmetic Operators perform basic mathematical operations such as addition, subtraction, multiplication, division, and modulus. The arithmetic operators supported by Scala include:

- + (Addition)

- - (Subtraction)

- * (Multiplication)

- / (Division)

- % (Modulus)

```
val a = 10
val b = 5
val sum = a + b // 15
val difference = a - b // 5
val product = a * b // 50
val quotient = a / b // 2
val remainder = a % b // 0
```

47

Relational Operators compare two operands and return a Boolean value (true or false). Scala supports the following relational operators:

- == (Equal to)
- != (Not equal to)
- > (Greater than)
- < (Less than)
- >= (Greater than or equal to)
- <= (Less than or equal to)

```
val x = 5
val y = 10
val isEqual = x == y // false
val isNotEqual = x != y // true
val isGreater = x > y // false
val isLess = x < y // true
val isGreaterOrEqual = x >= y // false
val isLessOrEqual = x <= y // true
```

Logical Operators are used to combine multiple Boolean expressions. Scala supports the following logical operators:

- && (Logical AND)
- || (Logical OR)
- ! (Logical NOT)

```
val isTrue = true
val isFalse = false
val andResult = isTrue && isFalse // false
val orResult = isTrue || isFalse // true
val notResult = !isTrue // false
```

Bitwise Operators perform bit-level operations on integer types. Scala supports the following bitwise operators:

- & (Bitwise AND)
- | (Bitwise OR)
- ^ (Bitwise XOR)
-   (Bitwise NOT)

48

- « (Left shift)

- » (Right shift)

- »> (Unsigned right shift)

```
val c = 12 // 1100 in binary
val d = 5 // 0101 in binary
val andBitwise = c & d // 0100 in binary, 4 in decimal
val orBitwise = c | d // 1101 in binary, 13 in decimal
val xorBitwise = c ^ d // 1001 in binary, 9 in decimal
val notBitwise = ~c // ...11111111111111111111111111110011 in binary, -13 in decimal
```

Assignment Operators are used to assign values to variables. Scala supports both basic and compound assignment operators:

- = (Simple assignment)

- += (Add and assign)

- -= (Subtract and assign)

- *= (Multiply and assign)

- /= (Divide and assign)

- %= (Modulus and assign)

```
var e = 10
e += 5 // e is now 15
e -= 3 // e is now 12
e *= 2 // e is now 24
e /= 4 // e is now 6
e %= 4 // e is now 2
```

Miscellaneous Operators include the following:

- The typeof operator determines the data type of a variable.

- The instanceof operator checks if an object is an instance of a specific class or trait.

Expressions in Scala can be simple or composed of multiple operators and operands. The evaluation of expressions follows specific rules of precedence and associativity. The precedence rules determine the order in which different types of operators are evaluated, while associativity rules determine the order in which operators of the same precedence level are evaluated (left-to-right or right-to-left).

49

In programming practice, parentheses can be used to explicitly specify the order of evaluation in complex expressions, overriding the default precedence and associativity rules. This use of parentheses is essential for ensuring clarity and correctness in code.

```
val expression1 = 100 + 50 * 3 // 250, as * has higher precedence than +
val expression2 = (100 + 50) * 3 // 450, parentheses change the order of evaluation
val expression3 = 100 / (2 + 3) // 20, parentheses ensure addition happens first
val expression4 = 100 / 2 + 3 // 53, division happens first, then addition
```

A solid understanding of operators and expressions is fundamental for writing efficient and effective Scala code, enabling the expression of complex logic and computations naturally and intuitively.

2.5   Control Structures: if, for, while, and match

Control structures in Scala are essential for directing the flow of computations. This section examines the primary control structures available in Scala: if, for, while, and match. These structures facilitate conditional execution and iteration, forming the backbone for logical progression and repetitive operations within a program.

The if construct is used for conditional execution based on Boolean expressions. It can be used in both single-line and block forms, and it supports the optional else clause for executing alternative code when the condition is not met.

```
val x = 10
val y = 20

// Single-line if
if (x < y) println("x is less than y")

// if-else structure
if (x > y) {
  println("x is greater than y")
} else {
  println("x is not greater than y")
}
```

The for loop in Scala is versatile and more powerful compared to its equivalents in other languages due to its ability to be used with generators, guards, and yield expressions. A for loop can iterate over a range, a collection, or any iterable structure. Additionally, the yield keyword transforms a for loop into a generator expression that produces a new collection.

```scala
// Iterating over a range
for (i <- 1 to 5) {
  println(i)
}

// Iterating over a collection
val names = List("Alice", "Bob", "Charlie")
for (name <- names) {
  println(name)
}

// Using guards
for (i <- 1 to 10 if i % 2 == 0) {
  println(i)
}

// Using yield to create a new collection
val squaredNumbers = for (i <- 1 to 5) yield i * i
println(squaredNumbers)
```

The while loop repeats a block of code as long as a specified condition is true. It is suitable for scenarios where the number of iterations is not predetermined. Note that this loop can potentially result in an infinite loop if the termination condition is never met.

```scala
var count = 0
while (count < 5) {
  println(s"count is $count")
  count += 1
}
```

The do-while loop is similar to the while loop, but it ensures that the block of code is executed at least once before the condition is tested.

```scala
var number = 5
do {
  println(s"number is $number")
  number -= 1
} while (number > 0)
```

The match expression in Scala is a powerful construct that allows pattern matching. It compares a value against a series of patterns, executing the associated block of code for the first matching pattern. The match expression can be utilized for various types, enhancing both readability and functional programming paradigms.

```scala
val day = "Tuesday"
day match {
  case "Monday" => println("Start of the work week")
  case "Tuesday" => println("Second day of the work week")
  case "Wednesday" => println("Midweek")
  case "Thursday" => println("Almost there")
  case "Friday" => println("End of the work week")
  case "Saturday" | "Sunday" => println("Weekend")
  case _ => println("Invalid day")
}
```

```
}
```

Pattern matching offers more than just matching literals. It can be employed to match types, sequences, tuples, and more complex structures. This flexibility can significantly simplify code that would otherwise require multiple nested conditional statements.

```
// Matching types
def process(x: Any): Unit = {
  x match {
    case i: Int => println(s"Integer: $i")
    case s: String => println(s"String: $s")
    case _ => println("Unknown type")
  }
}

process(10)
process("Hello")
process(3.14)

// Matching tuples
val myTuple = (123, "abc")
myTuple match {
  case (num, str) => println(s"Number: $num, String: $str")
}

// Matching lists
val myList = List(1, 2, 3)
myList match {
  case List(1, 2, 3) => println("List matches")
  case _ => println("List does not match")
}
```

Scala's control structures are robust and flexible, designed to handle a wide range of scenarios. Their proper usage can lead to clean, concise, and expressive code, thus enhancing both readability and maintainability. The ability to combine functional constructs such as pattern matching with traditional iterative and conditional constructs makes Scala a powerful language for both small-scale and enterprise-level software development.

2.6   Functions and Methods

In Scala, functions and methods are central constructs that facilitate modular and reusable code. This section delves into the syntactic structure, definition, and usage of both functions and methods, emphasizing their role in the Scala programming paradigm. An understanding of these constructs will enable efficient function abstraction and improve overall code maintainability.

A function in Scala is defined using the def keyword, followed by the function name, a list of parameters, their types, a return type, and the function body. Functions can be categorized into named functions and anonymous functions (also known as lambda expressions).

```
def add(a: Int, b: Int): Int = {
  a + b
}
```

In the example above, add is a function that takes two Int parameters, a and b, and returns their sum. The return type Int is explicitly specified. The function body is enclosed in curly braces. It is worth noting that if the function body consists of a single expression, the curly braces can be omitted.

Scala offers support for higher order functions, enabling functions to accept other functions as parameters or return them as results. The following example demonstrates a higher-order function:

```
def applyFunction(f: Int => Int, x: Int): Int = {
  f(x)
}
```

Here, applyFunction takes a function f of the type Int => Int and an Int value x as parameters, applying f to x and returning the result. Functions as first-class citizens in Scala facilitate functional programming by treating functions as values.

Anonymous functions, or lambda expressions, provide a concise way to define functions without explicitly naming them. They are useful in situations where a function is needed temporarily. The syntax of an anonymous function uses the → symbol:

```
val square = (x: Int) => x * x
```

In this example, square is an anonymous function that takes an Int parameter x and returns x squared. It is assigned to the value square, which can be invoked like a regular function.

Methods in Scala are similar to functions but are associated with objects. They are defined using the same def keyword and have the same syntax rules. Methods can be part of a class or an object, and they can access and modify the object's state.

```
class Calculator {
  def add(a: Int, b: Int): Int = {
    a + b
  }
```

53

```
  def subtract(a: Int, b: Int): Int = {
    a - b
  }
}

val calc = new Calculator()
val sum = calc.add(3, 5)
val difference = calc.subtract(10, 4)
```

In this case, Calculator is a class with two methods, add and subtract, which perform basic arithmetic operations. An instance of Calculator is created using the new keyword, and the methods are invoked on the instance.

One crucial aspect of Scala methods is their ability to have default arguments. This feature allows method parameters to have default values, making some arguments optional when the method is called.

```
def greet(name: String, greeting: String = "Hello"): String = {
  s"$greeting, $name!"
}

val message1 = greet("Alice")
val message2 = greet("Bob", "Hi")
```

In this example, the greet method has a default value "Hello" for the greeting parameter. Therefore, if greet is called with only the name argument, the default greeting is used.

Named arguments in method calls provide another layer of flexibility in Scala, allowing the caller to specify the values of particular parameters by name, regardless of their order in the parameter list.

```
def formatMessage(sender: String, recipient: String, message: String): String = {
  s"From: $sender\nTo: $recipient\nMessage: $message"
}

val formattedMessage = formatMessage(
  message = "Scala functions are powerful.",
  recipient = "Student",
  sender = "Teacher"
)
```

Named arguments improve code readability, making it clear which values are being passed to which parameters without being constrained by the parameter list order.

Furthermore, Scala supports recursive methods, where a method calls itself as part of its execution. Recursive methods are instrumental in solving problems that can be broken down into smaller, similar sub-problems.

```
def factorial(n: Int): Int = {
  if (n <= 1) 1
  else n * factorial(n - 1)
}

val result = factorial(5)
```

This implementation of the factorial method computes the factorial of a non-negative integer n. The base case returns 1 when n is less than or equal to 1, and the recursive case multiplies n by the factorial of n-1.

Tail recursion is a special form of recursion where the recursive call is the last operation in the method. Scala optimizes tail-recursive methods to prevent stack overflow errors, making them efficient for deep recursion. The @tailrec annotation can be used to enforce tail recursion.

```
import scala.annotation.tailrec

@tailrec
def gcd(a: Int, b: Int): Int = {
  if (b == 0) a
  else gcd(b, a % b)
}

val result = gcd(48, 18)
```

In this example, the @tailrec annotation ensures that the gcd method is tail-recursive. If it is not, the compiler will flag an error. This method computes the greatest common divisor using the Euclidean algorithm.

Functions and methods in Scala are versatile and powerful tools that enable developers to write clean, concise, and maintainable code. Understanding their syntax, usage, and the distinctions between them is fundamental to mastering functional and object-oriented programming in Scala.

2.7 Parameter Passing and Default Arguments

Scala supports multiple ways to pass parameters to methods and functions, including by value, by name, and the use of default arguments. Understanding these concepts is crucial for creating flexible and reusable code.

Scala uses two primary parameter passing techniques: call-by-value and call-by-name. Call-by-value is the default mechanism, where the actual value of the argument is computed before passing it to the function. On the other hand, call-by-name parameters are evaluated only when the parameter is used within the function. This distinction can significantly influence the functionality and performance of Scala programs.

Consider the following example of a simple function that demonstrates the call-by-value mechanism:

```scala
def callByValue(x: Long): Long = {
  println("Value: " + x)
  x
}

val time = System.nanoTime()
callByValue(time)
```

In call-by-value, the time value is evaluated before being passed to the callByValue function, and thus, it remains constant throughout the function's execution. The time will be computed once and the same value will be used each time the parameter is referenced within the function.

Conversely, a call-by-name parameter is prefixed with the => symbol. Here is an equivalent function using call-by-name:

```scala
def callByName(x: => Long): Long = {
  println("Value: " + x)
  x
}

callByName(System.nanoTime())
```

In this case, the expression System.nanoTime() is not evaluated until it is accessed inside the function, resulting in potentially different values each time it is referenced.

Another essential feature in Scala is the use of default parameter values. This allows functions to be called with fewer arguments than defined by providing default values for some of the parameters.

Consider the following function definition:

```scala
def greet(name: String, greeting: String = "Hello"): String = {
  s"$greeting, $name!"
}

println(greet("Alice"))
println(greet("Bob", "Hi"))
```

In this example, the greeting parameter has a default value of "Hello". Therefore, if the greet function is called with only one argument, as with

56

greet("Alice"), it utilizes the default value for the greeting parameter. If both parameters are provided, as with greet("Bob", "Hi"), the supplied value overrides the default.

Default arguments are particularly useful in conjunction with named parameters, allowing arguments to be provided in different orders without ambiguity. For example:

```
println(greet(name = "Alice"))
println(greet(greeting = "Hi", name = "Bob"))
```

This feature enhances code readability and flexibility, as parameters can be specified explicitly and independently of their position in the parameter list.

Combining both, consider a function that validates input with configurable error messages:

```
def validate(input: String, failMsg: String = "Validation failed"): Boolean = {
  If (input.nonEmpty) true else {
    println(failMsg)
    false
  }
}

validate("")
validate("user_input")
validate("", "Custom error message")
```

Here, the failMsg parameter provides a default error message that can be overridden when necessary. This ensures comprehensive logging or debugging messages while maintaining a simple interface for function calls.

To summarize, parameter passing techniques (call-by-value and call-by-name) and default arguments are powerful tools in Scala. They collectively help in writing more expressive, flexible, and readable code. Understanding and utilizing these features effectively can greatly improve the design and usability of functions and methods in Scala programs.

2.8 Working with Strings

In Scala, String is a fundamental data type for handling text. This section delves into various operations that can be performed on strings, illustrating the flexibility and power of String manipulation in Scala.

String literals are defined by enclosing text within double quotes:

```scala
val greeting: String = "Hello, Scala!"
```

Strings are immutable, meaning once a String object is created, it cannot be altered. However, various methods return new strings based on manipulations of the original.

String interpolation allows embedding variables directly within string literals. Scala provides different types of interpolation: s, f, and raw.

```scala
val name: String = "Scala"
val message: String = s"Hello, $name!" // s-interpolator
val height: Double = 1.75
val info: String = f"$name%s height is $height%2.2f meters" // f-interpolator
val escaped: String = raw"Newline and tab characters: \n \t" // raw-interpolator
```

The s-interpolator prepends an s to the string literal and allows the use of variables and expressions directly inside strings by preceding them with a $ symbol. The f-interpolator works similarly but allows formatting, akin to printf in other languages. The raw interpolator does not escape characters like \n and \t.

Strings can be concatenated using the + operator:

```scala
val fullName: String = "Scala" + " " + "Language"
```

Scala provides numerous methods to operate on strings. These methods can be grouped based on their functionality:

- **Query Methods:** Methods to inquire about the properties of a string, such as its length, whether it starts or ends with a particular substring, and whether it matches a regular expression.

- **Transformation Methods:** Methods to produce a new string based on modifications to the original string, such as converting all characters to uppercase or lowercase, replacing a substring with another string, or trimming leading and trailing spaces.

- **Substrings and Splitting:** Methods to extract parts of a string or to split the string based on a delimiter.

- **Regular Expressions:** Methods to find matches of a regular expression pattern within a string.

Examples of query methods:

```scala
val str: String = "Functional and Object-Oriented Programming"
```

58

```
println(str.length) // 41
println(str.startsWith("Functional")) // true
println(str.endsWith("Programming")) // true
println(str.contains("Object")) // true
```

Examples of transformation methods:

```
println("scala".toUpperCase) // SCALA
println("SCALA".toLowerCase) // scala
println(" functional ".trim) // "functional"
println("object-oriented".replace("-", " ")) // "object oriented"
```

Examples of substring and splitting methods:

```
val sentence: String = "Scala is fun"
println(sentence.substring(0, 5)) // "Scala"
println(sentence.split(" ").mkString(",")) // "Scala,is,fun"
```

Examples of using regular expressions:

```
val regex = "Scala".r
val result = regex.findFirstIn "Scala is scalable"
println(result) // Some(Scala)
```

Scala's StringOps class, implicitly provided by Scala's rich standard library, offers powerful and expressive operations. Another advanced feature is the usage of triple-quoted strings. Triple-quoted strings allow multi-line strings without the need for concatenation or escape sequences:

```
val multiLineString: String = """This is
a string
spanning multiple
lines."""
```

By using the triple-quote syntax, developers can easily write block texts, retain the source code structure, and avoid the use of escape characters.

Combining strings with collections:

```
val charList: List[Char] = List('S', 'c', 'a', 'l', 'a')
val strFromList: String = charList.mkString
println(strFromList) // "Scala"
```

This capability to switch between collections and strings illustrates Scala's seamless handling of data transformation.

Real-world applications often require multi-faceted string operations. Understanding and utilizing these string methods are essential skills in mastering Scala.

The succinct syntax, powerful capabilities, and integration with regular expressions make string manipulation in Scala both efficient and expressive. The ability to write readable and maintainable string operations significantly enhances the developer's productivity in real-world scenarios.

2.9   Data Input and Output

Effective data input and output (I/O) operations are crucial for any programming language, and Scala is no exception. Handling I/O efficiently can greatly enhance the performance and usability of a program. This section delves into the methodologies and practices for performing I/O operations in Scala, focusing on both keyboard input and file handling.

Keyboard Input:

For keyboard input, Scala provides the scala.io.StdIn object, which includes methods to read different types of input. The method readLine captures an entire line of input as a String, while readInt, readDouble, and readBoolean methods parse the input to respective data types.

```
import scala.io.StdIn._

val name: String = readLine("Enter your name: ")
println(s"Hello, $name!")

val age: Int = readInt()
println(s"Your age is $age.")
```

The readLine method takes an optional string parameter, allowing you to print a prompt message prior to capturing the input. The readInt method reads the input from the console and parses it into an Int.

File I/O:

File handling in Scala can be performed using different APIs, but a common and effective approach involves using the scala.io.Source object for reading files and the java.io.PrintWriter class for writing files.

To read from a file, you can utilize the Source.fromFile method, which creates a BufferedSource instance that allows you to iterate over the lines of the file.

```
import scala.io.Source

val filename = "example.txt"
val fileSource = Source.fromFile(filename)
```

```
for (line <- fileSource.getLines) {
  println(line)
}

fileSource.close()
```

In the code above, the Source.fromFile method opens the file example.txt, and the getLines method returns an iterator that iterates over lines in the file. It is important to close the file after operations are complete to free up system resources, hence fileSource.close() is called.

Writing to a file in Scala is generally done using the PrintWriter class. This class provides methods to write formatted data to a file.

```
import java.io.PrintWriter

val writer = new PrintWriter("output.txt")
writer.write("Hello, world!\n")
writer.write("Writing data to file in Scala.\n")
writer.close()
```

The PrintWriter class is instantiated with the file name to which you want to write. The write method is used to output data as text. Similar to reading from a file, it is crucial to close the PrintWriter instance after the writing operations are finished by calling writer.close().

Handling Exceptions:

During I/O operations, exceptions can occur if the file does not exist, permissions are not sufficient, or for other unexpected reasons. Implementing proper exception handling is necessary to ensure that these issues are managed gracefully.

```
import scala.io.Source
import java.io.{FileNotFoundException, IOException}

val filename = "example.txt"
try {
  val fileSource = Source.fromFile(filename)
  for (line <- fileSource.getLines) {
    println(line)
  }
  fileSource.close()
} catch {
  case e: FileNotFoundException => println(s"File not found: $filename")
  case e: IOException => println(s"An IO error occurred: ${e.getMessage}")
}
```

In the example above, the try-catch block is used to manage exceptions. If the file is not found, a FileNotFoundException is thrown, and the corresponding catch block handles it by printing an error message. For other I/O errors, the IOException catch block is executed.

Proper I/O handling, including reading, writing, and managing exceptions, forms the foundation for building robust Scala applications. Through understanding and implementing the concepts discussed, programmers can effectively manage data interactions in their Scala programs.

2.10 Basic Exception Handling

Exception handling is an essential feature in Scala, aimed at managing runtime errors and maintaining the normal flow of a program. Exceptions are unwanted or unexpected events that can occur during program execution, disrupting the proper functioning of the program. Scala's exception handling mechanism is primarily influenced by Java, and it provides a robust way to handle such unforeseen events.

In Scala, exceptions are handled using try, catch, and finally blocks. The try block is used to enclose the code that might throw an exception. The catch block is used to handle the exception, and the finally block contains code that gets executed irrespective of whether an exception is thrown or not.

Let's delve into each component in detail:

The try Block

The try block is where you can place code that might throw an exception. The syntax is simple:

```
try {
    // code that may throw an exception
}
```

The catch Block

The catch block is where you handle the exceptions thrown by the try block. In Scala, the catch block is followed by a series of case statements to handle different exception types. The syntax is as follows:

```
catch {
    case ex: ExceptionType1 => // handle ExceptionType1
    case ex: ExceptionType2 => // handle ExceptionType2
    // additional cases
}
```

A simple example of handling an arithmetic exception (e.g., division by zero) is shown below:

```
try {
    val result = 10 / 0
} catch {
    case ex: ArithmeticException => println("Cannot divide by zero.")
}
```

The finally Block

The finally block contains code that will always execute whether an exception is thrown or not. This block is typically used for cleanup activities such as closing files or releasing resources.

```
try {
    // code that may throw an exception
} catch {
    case ex: ExceptionType => // handle exception
} finally {
    // cleanup code
}
```

A comprehensive example, including a finally block, is illustrated below:

```
try {
    val data = scala.io.Source.fromFile("file.txt").mkString
    println(data)
} catch {
    case fnf: FileNotFoundException => println("File not found.")
    case ioe: IOException => println("An I/O error occurred.")
} finally {
    println("Finished attempting to read file.")
}
```

Throwing Exceptions

In Scala, exceptions can be thrown using the throw keyword. This is useful when you want to explicitly trigger an exception based on a particular condition. The syntax for throwing an exception is:

```
throw new ExceptionType("error message")
```

Here's an example where an IllegalArgumentException is thrown if a negative number is passed as an input:

```
def checkNumber(num: Int): Unit = {
    if (num < 0)
        throw new IllegalArgumentException("Negative numbers are not allowed.")
    else
        println(s"Number $num is valid.")
}

try {
    checkNumber(-5)
} catch {
    case ex: IllegalArgumentException => println(ex.getMessage)
}
```

63

Using the Either and Try Types

Scala provides advanced mechanisms for handling exceptions using the Either and Try types, which are part of the Scala Standard Library. These types offer more functional ways to deal with errors and exceptions.

The Either type represents a value of one of two possible types. Instances of Either are either an instance of Left or Right. By convention, Left is used to denote an error or failure and Right is used to denote a success.

```scala
def divide(a: Int, b: Int): Either[String, Int] = {
   if (b == 0)
      Left("Division by zero error")
   else
      Right(a / b)
}

val result = divide(10, 0) match {
   case Left(error) => println(error)
   case Right(value) => println(s"The result is $value")
}
```

The Try type represents a computation that may either result in an exception or return a successfully computed value. Its syntax is straightforward:

```scala
import scala.util.{Try, Success, Failure}

val result: Try[Int] = Try(10 / 0)

result match {
   case Success(value) => println(s"Result is $value")
   case Failure(exception) => println(s"Exception: ${exception.getMessage}")
}
```

In practice, the use of Either and Try makes the code more expressive and simplifies error handling by leveraging Scala's functional programming capabilities.

Through careful use of try, catch, and finally blocks, along with throw, Either, and Try, Scala provides powerful tools for managing runtime exceptions effectively. This ensures that your program can handle unexpected events gracefully while maintaining robustness and readability.

Chapter 3

Collections and Data Structures

This chapter explores Scala's rich collection framework and essential data structures. It differentiates between immutable and mutable collections, covering sequences, sets, maps, tuples, and options. The chapter also delves into iterators, higher-order functions on collections, lazy collections, and pattern matching with collections. These concepts are crucial for efficient data manipulation and processing in Scala.

3.1   Overview of Scala Collections

Scala collections provide a versatile and powerful framework for handling data systematically. They encompass a variety of concrete implementations, alongside a set of overarching traits that define common operations. Scala collections can be categorized into three primary types: sequences, maps, and sets. Each of these types is available in both immutable and mutable forms, allowing programmers to leverage the benefits of functional programming while retaining the flexibility to modify data when necessary.

The base trait for all collections is Iterable, from which other specific traits like Seq, Set, and Map inherit. Immutable collections are in the scala.collection.immutable package, while mutable collections reside in the scala.collection.mutable package. This separation underscores the functional programming principle of immutability, wherein objects cannot be altered once created, fostering safer and predictable code.

Immutable collections are favored when you need to ensure that data does not change after creation. For instance, lists, vectors, and ranges are immutable by default in Scala. Using them promotes cleaner, side-effect-free code. However, when performance considerations demand in-place modifications, mutable collections like arrays, mutable lists, and hash tables can be employed.

Typical operations on collections include mapping, filtering, folding, and aggregating data. These operations are achieved using higher-order functions, leveraging first-class function objects in Scala. Below is a simple example illustrating these operations on an immutable list:

```scala
val nums = List(1, 2, 3, 4, 5)

// Mapping: Applying a function to each element
val squared = nums.map(x => x * x)

// Filtering: Selecting elements based on a predicate
val even = nums.filter(x => x % 2 == 0)

// Folding: Combining elements using an associative operation
val sum = nums.foldLeft(0)(_ + _)
```

The code snippet demonstrates how map, filter, and foldLeft are used to process collections. Here, nums is an immutable list, and each operation generates a new list based on nums. The use of foldLeft with an initial accumulator of 0 iteratively combines elements, producing a sum of the list's values.

Another key aspect of Scala collections is their support for lazy evaluation. Collections like Stream allow for elements to be computed on-demand rather than at once, which can significantly enhance performance, especially with large datasets. Lazy collections are useful in scenarios where you might only need a portion of the data or are dealing with potentially infinite data streams.

In the Scala collection framework, pattern matching offers a robust mechanism for deconstructing collections. This capability is essential for applications that involve extensive data manipulation and extraction. For example, consider the following snippet using pattern matching on a list:

```scala
val names = List("Alice", "Bob", "Cathy")

names match {
  case List(a, b, c) => println(s"Three names: $a, $b, and $c")
```

```
    case List(a, b) => println(s"Two names: $a and $b")
    case List(a) => println(s"One name: $a")
    case Nil => println("No names")
    case _ => println("A list with more than three names")
}
```

This example shows how pattern matching can differentiate based on the structure and count of elements in a list. Scala's advanced pattern matching capabilities extend beyond lists to other collections like tuples and options, adding to their expressiveness.

In summary, the Scala collections framework is integral for efficient data manipulation. The layered hierarchy of traits ensures a consistent API, while supporting various functionalities through both immutable and mutable collections. Mastery of these collections enables the development of robust, efficient, and maintainable code in Scala.

3.2 Immutable vs Mutable Collections

Scala's collection framework distinguishes between two primary types of collections: immutable and mutable. Understanding the differences between these types is essential for effective and efficient programming in Scala. Immutable collections are collections that, once created, cannot be modified. Any operation that would alter an immutable collection results in the creation of a new collection with the change applied, leaving the original collection unchanged. Mutable collections, on the other hand, allow for modifications in place, meaning changes made to the collection are directly reflected in the same instance of the collection.

Immutable Collections:

Immutable collections form the default and most commonly used type in Scala. They provide a robust foundation for functional programming by inherently supporting safe concurrency and immutability. Examples of immutable collections include:

- List

- Vector

- Set

- Map

67

The following example demonstrates the concept with an immutable List:

```
val originalList = List(1, 2, 3)
val updatedList = originalList :+ 4

println(originalList) // Output: List(1, 2, 3)
println(updatedList) // Output: List(1, 2, 3, 4)
```

In this example, the operator :+ creates a new List with the element 4 appended. The original List remains unchanged, demonstrating the immutability property.

Mutable Collections:

Mutable collections, in contrast, offer an efficient means to modify collections in place. Therefore, they are often used in performance-critical sections of code where in-place updates can avoid the overhead of creating new instances. Examples of mutable collections include:

- ArrayBuffer
- ListBuffer
- HashSet
- HashMap

Here is an illustration using a mutable ArrayBuffer:

```
import scala.collection.mutable.ArrayBuffer

val buffer = ArrayBuffer(1, 2, 3)
buffer += 4

println(buffer) // Output: ArrayBuffer(1, 2, 3, 4)
```

In this case, the operator += modifies the ArrayBuffer in place, directly adding to the existing instance.

Performance Considerations:

The choice between immutable and mutable collections involves trade-offs in terms of performance and safety. Immutable collections promote safer, more predictable code with fewer side-effects, facilitating easier debugging and reasoning about program behavior. However, they can introduce performance overhead when operations requiring frequent modifications are performed, due to the need to create new instances.

Mutable collections can provide superior performance for algorithms that involve a large number of updates. Because updates occur in place, they can avoid the cost associated with allocation and garbage collection of intermediate objects. Thus, in performance-critical sections, it is sometimes preferable to use mutable collections.

Concurrency and Immutability:

Immutability plays a significant role in concurrent programming. Because immutable collections cannot be modified, they are inherently thread-safe. This eliminates the need for synchronization mechanisms, such as locks, reducing complexity and potential deadlocks.

Mutable collections, however, are not inherently thread-safe and require external synchronization to ensure correct concurrent access. This means using constructs such as synchronized blocks or other concurrency controls to avoid data races.

Interoperability Between Mutable and Immutable Collections:

Scala provides seamless interoperability between mutable and immutable collections, allowing conversion from one type to another. The conversion methods are designed to be straightforward:

```
import scala.collection.mutable
import scala.collection.immutable

val immutableList = List(1, 2, 3)
val mutableBuffer: mutable.Buffer[Int] = immutableList.toBuffer

val immutableSeq: immutable.Seq[Int] = mutableBuffer.toSeq
```

In this manner, it is possible to leverage the benefits of both immutable and mutable collections within the same program, adhering to the best practices of functional and object-oriented paradigms.

Functional Programming with Collections:

Immutable collections align closely with functional programming principles, empowering the utilization of pure functions and higher-order functions. For example, higher-order functions like map, filter, and fold are inherently safer and more predictable when used with immutable collections.

```
val numbers = List(1, 2, 3, 4, 5)
val doubled = numbers.map(_ * 2)

println(doubled) // Output: List(2, 4, 6, 8, 10)
```

The map function in the example applies the transformation _ * 2 to each element of the List, returning a new List with the transformed values.

The immutable versus mutable dichotomy in Scala's collection library provides the flexibility to select the appropriate collection type based on the needs of the specific task at hand, balancing immutability's safety with mutability's potential performance gains.

3.3 Sequences: Lists, Arrays, and Vectors

Sequences in Scala are ordered collections of elements where each element can be accessed by an index. They are a fundamental part of the Scala collections framework and provide efficient access and manipulation capabilities. Scala provides several implementations of sequences to cater to different needs: List, Array, and Vector are key examples. This section explores the characteristics, usage patterns, and performance implications of these sequence types.

List: A List is an immutable, singly linked list. It provides constant-time access to the head of the list and linear-time access to any other elements. Lists support recursive algorithms nicely due to their linked nature. Elements cannot be added or removed from the list in place; instead, new lists are created as a result of these operations.

```scala
// Creating a List
val list = List(1, 2, 3, 4, 5)

// Accessing elements
val head = list.head // 1
val tail = list.tail // List(2, 3, 4, 5)
val isEmpty = list.isEmpty // false

// Adding an element to the front
val newList = 0 :: list // List(0, 1, 2, 3, 4, 5)
```

Array: An Array is a mutable, indexed sequence that is effectively like a Java array with zero-based indexing. Arrays provide constant-time access and update capabilities. They are useful when a fixed-size collection is required and when performance is a critical factor.

```scala
// Creating an Array
val array = Array(1, 2, 3, 4, 5)

// Accessing elements
val firstElement = array(0) // 1
val length = array.length // 5

// Modifying elements
array(0) = 10
val updatedElement = array(0) // 10
```

Vector: A Vector is an immutable indexed sequence that provides an efficient random-access structure. It offers average constant-time complexity for both element access and update operations by utilizing a tree structure. Vectors are often preferred over List when frequent random access is required because they combine the benefits of immutable collections with good performance characteristics.

```
// Creating a Vector
val vector = Vector(1, 2, 3, 4, 5)

// Accessing elements
val thirdElement = vector(2) // 3
val vectorLength = vector.length // 5

// Adding an element to the end
val newVector = vector :+ 6 // Vector(1, 2, 3, 4, 5, 6)
```

Performance considerations:

- Lists, being linked lists, excel at prepend (adding an element at the head) operations, but they have linear-time complexity for appending and accessing elements not at the head. - Arrays provide constant-time access and update, making them suitable for performance-critical applications where the array size is fixed. - Vectors balance the benefits of both immutable sequences and efficient random access, with average constant-time complexities for access and update operations.

Central to these sequences is their ability to work seamlessly with Scala's powerful collection framework, including higher-order functions like map, filter, and fold.

```
// Transforming a List using map
val doubledList = list.map(_ * 2) // List(2, 4, 6, 8, 10)

// Filtering elements in an Array
val evenNumbers = array.filter(_ % 2 == 0) // Array(2, 4)

// Folding a Vector
val sum = vector.foldLeft(0)(_ + _) // 15
```

These sequences also interoperate well with other collection types. For example, a List can be converted to an Array or Vector, enabling flexibility in operations where different performance considerations are relevant.

```
// Converting between collections
val listToArray = list.toArray // Array(1, 2, 3, 4, 5)
val listToVector = list.toVector // Vector(1, 2, 3, 4, 5)
val arrayToList = array.toList // List(10, 2, 3, 4, 5)
```

Selecting the appropriate sequence type depends heavily on the spe-

71

cific requirements of the application, such as the need for immutability, the complexity of access patterns, and performance considerations.
The seamless interplay of List, Array, and Vector within the Scala collections framework is a testament to the versatility and power of Scala
in handling data sequences efficiently.

3.4   Sets and Maps

In Scala, the Set and Map collections are fundamental data structures
used to store unique elements and key-value pairs, respectively. These
collections are available in both immutable and mutable variants, catering to different use cases and performance requirements.

Sets are unordered collections of distinct elements. Scala provides two
primary implementations of sets: immutable.Set and mutable.Set. The
immutable variant does not allow modification after instantiation, ensuring thread safety and predictability. The mutable variant, on the other
hand, allows adding, removing, and updating elements.

Creating an immutable set is straightforward:

```
val immutableSet = Set(1, 2, 3, 4)
```

To create a mutable set, the scala.collection.mutable package must be
imported:

```
import scala.collection.mutable

val mutableSet = mutable.Set(1, 2, 3, 4)
```

Operations on sets include adding elements, removing elements, and
checking for membership. With immutable sets, these operations return new sets:

```
val newImmutableSet = immutableSet + 5
val setWithoutElement = immutableSet - 2
val containsThree = immutableSet.contains(3)
```

For mutable sets, operations modify the set in place:

```
mutableSet += 5
mutableSet -= 2
val containsThree = mutableSet.contains(3)
```

Maps in Scala are collections that store key-value pairs, where each
key is unique. Like sets, maps come in immutable (immutable.Map)

and mutable (mutable.Map) variants. Maps are particularly useful for fast lookups, insertions, and deletions.

Creating an immutable map is similar to creating an immutable set:

```
val immutableMap = Map("a" -> 1, "b" -> 2, "c" -> 3)
```

Creating a mutable map requires importing the scala.collection.mutable package:

```
import scala.collection.mutable

val mutableMap = mutable.Map("a" -> 1, "b" -> 2, "c" -> 3)
```

Accessing values in a map can be done using the key:

```
val valueB = immutableMap("b")
```

Values can also be accessed using the get method, which returns Option types to safely handle absent keys:

```
val maybeValueC = immutableMap.get("c")
val maybeValueD = immutableMap.get("d") // returns None
```

Updating maps in their respective editions involves the following operations. For immutable maps, the updates produce new maps:

```
val updatedImmutableMap = immutableMap + ("d" -> 4)
val removedFromImmutableMap = immutableMap - "a"
```

For mutable maps, updates occur in place:

```
mutableMap("d") = 4
mutableMap -= "a"
```

Whereas immutable.Map and mutable.Map share similar APIs, their underlying implementations differ concerning performance characteristics: immutable.Map operations tend to be slower but safer in concurrent settings, while mutable.Map operations are faster but mutable and hence susceptible to concurrency issues.

Additional operations on collections such as union, intersection, and difference are also supported by both sets and maps. These operations are crucial for complex data manipulation tasks. For instance, calculating the union of two sets using immutable sets:

```
val setA = Set(1, 2, 3)
val setB = Set(2, 3, 4)

val unionSet = setA union setB
val intersectionSet = setA intersect setB
```

73

```
val diffSet = setA diff setB
```

Similarly, maps can be merged, with the merge operation of maps taking a function to handle value clashes:

```
val mapA = Map("a" -> 1, "b" -> 2)
val mapB = Map("b" -> 3, "c" -> 4)

val mergedMap = mapA ++ mapB
```

If the merge operation must handle key conflicts, then an explicit conflict resolution function can be provided:

```
val resolvedMap = mapA ++ mapB.map { case (k,v) => k -> (v + mapA.getOrElse(k,
    0)) }
```

The usage of conflict resolution functions ensures deterministic and customized resolution of overlapping keys during the merging process.

Overall, understanding the functionality and appropriate use of Sets and Maps is essential for efficient programming in Scala, especially in scenarios requiring unique elements and key-value pairs. With the ability to choose between immutable and mutable versions, developers can balance safety and performance according to their application's needs.

3.5   Tuples and Options

The Tuple and Option classes in Scala provide powerful and flexible means to group and handle data. They allow developers to work with related values and handle operations that might or might not return a result.

A Tuple is a finite ordered collection of elements, allowing developers to combine values with potentially different types into a single entity. Scala supports tuples with up to 22 elements, each element having differing data types if desired. Tuples are immutable by nature. They can be especially useful in scenarios where multiple values need to be passed together without creating a custom class.

To create a tuple, use the following syntax:

```
val tuple = (1, "Scala", 3.14)
```

In this example, tuple is a Tuple3[Int, String, Double]. This tuple contains an integer, a string, and a double.

Accessing elements of a tuple can be done using the _N selector, where N is the position of the element (starting from 1):

```
val firstElement = tuple._1 // Accesses 1
val secondElement = tuple._2 // Accesses "Scala"
val thirdElement = tuple._3 // Accesses 3.14
```

Tuple also supports pattern matching, which allows for elegant extraction of elements:

```
val (a, b, c) = tuple
println(a) // 1
println(b) // Scala
println(c) // 3.14
```

Another essential class in Scala's standard library is Option, which is used to represent a value that may or may not exist. Option is a container that can either hold a value of type Some[T], denoting presence, or None, indicating absence. This is particularly useful to avoid null references, thus making code more refactorable and less error-prone.

Creating an Option instance using Some:

```
val someValue: Option[Int] = Some(42)
```

Creating an empty Option using None:

```
val noneValue: Option[Int] = None
```

Working with Option involves checking if there's a value with isDefined or handling the possible absence with getOrElse, map, or pattern matching:

```
val value = someValue match {
  case Some(v) => v
  case None => 0
}

val defaultValue = noneValue.getOrElse(0) // Returns 0 because noneValue is None
val transformedValue = someValue.map(_ * 2) // Some(84)
val transformedNone = noneValue.map(_ * 2) // None
```

Combining Option with higher-order functions is another powerful Scala feature. Here's an example:

```
def divide(x: Int, y: Int): Option[Int] = {
  if (y == 0) None else Some(x / y)
}

val result1 = divide(4, 2).map(_ * 2) // Some(4)
val result2 = divide(4, 0).map(_ * 2) // None
```

Using flatMap, an optional value can be transformed and also handle nested Option structures:

```
def half(x: Int): Option[Int] = {
  if (x % 2 == 0) Some(x / 2) else None
}

val result = for {
  d <- divide(8, 2)
  h <- half(d)
} yield h // Some(2)
```

Integrating Option into a functional programming paradigm ensures that functions can be composed safely, with predictable handling of potential absence without relying on exceptions or sentinel values.

```
1  Function safeDivide(x: Int, y: Int):
2      if y == 0 then
3          return None
4      else
5          return Some(x / y)

6  ;
7  Function safeHalf(x: Int):
8      if x % 2 == 0 then
9          return Some(x / 2)
10     else
11         return None

12 ;
13 val num = 8;
14 val denom = 2;
15 val result = foreach d do
16     num / denom

17 if d != 0 then
18     val res = safeHalf(d);

19 ;
20 if result.isDefined then
21     println(s"Result: ${result.get}")
22 else
23     println("Computation did not yield a result.")
```

This integration between Tuple and Option enriches Scala's collection framework, providing developers with robust tools for modeling and managing complex data relationships and conditional computation scenarios efficiently.

3.6   Iterators and Iterables

In Scala, the Iterator and Iterable traits provide a way to traverse a collection of elements one at a time. These traits are essential for defining standard traversable patterns and creating custom iteration behaviors. This section delves into the characteristics, usage, and applications of Iterator and Iterable in Scala's collection framework.

The Iterator trait allows for sequential access to elements in a collection. It supports methods such as hasNext and next, making it similar to Java's Iterator interface. Here is an example of a simple iterator in Scala:

```scala
val numbers = List(1, 2, 3, 4, 5)
val iterator = numbers.iterator

while (iterator.hasNext) {
  println(iterator.next())
}
```

The output of the above code will be:

```
1
2
3
4
5
```

The hasNext method checks if there are more elements to traverse, while the next method returns the next element in the iteration. Note that next modifies the state of the iterator by advancing to the subsequent element.

Scala's Iterator supports various useful methods such as map, filter, and foreach. These operations allow for functional-style processing of elements:

```scala
val evenNumbers = numbers.iterator.filter(_ % 2 == 0)
evenNumbers.foreach(println)
```

Here, the code filters the original list for even numbers and prints each even number. The output will be:

```
2
4
```

The Iterable trait provides the foundation for collections that can be

77

iterated. Unlike Iterator, which is stateful and single-use, Iterable produces new iterator instances, preserving the original collection's state. This trait includes the abstract method iterator, which must be implemented to return a new Iterator.

Consider an example of a custom iterable class:

```scala
class MyIterableCollection(items: List[Int]) extends Iterable[Int] {
  override def iterator: Iterator[Int] = items.iterator
}

val myCollection = new MyIterableCollection(List(1, 2, 3))
for (item <- myCollection) {
  println(item)
}
```

The output will be:

```
1
2
3
```

This example demonstrates how a custom iterable class can be defined by extending Iterable and providing an implementation for the iterator method that returns an iterator over the underlying list of integers.

Iterating through collections using foreach is often more idiomatic in Scala than using traditional while loops. For example, iterating over an iterable collection can be achieved with the following code:

```scala
myCollection.foreach(println)
```

The functional nature of Iterable provides higher-order methods like map, flatMap, filter, and foldLeft. These methods enable concise and expressive collection manipulation:

```scala
val squares = myCollection.map(x => x * x)
squares.foreach(println)
```

The output will be:

```
1
4
9
```

flatMap can be used to flatten nested structures, while filter can exclude elements based on a predicate. For instance:

```scala
val nested = List(List(1, 2), List(3, 4))
val flattened = nested.flatMap(x => x)
flattened.foreach(println)
```

The output will be:

```
1
2
3
4
```

```
val filtered = flattened.filter(_ % 2 == 0)
filtered.foreach(println)
```

The output will be:

```
2
4
```

foldLeft accumulates results from left to right, enabling complex reductions and transformations:

```
val sum = myCollection.foldLeft(0)(_ + _)
println(sum)
```

The output will be:

```
6
```

Understanding these concepts is fundamental for effectively utilizing Scala's collection frameworks. Applying these traits can significantly enhance data processing tasks by leveraging the powerful abstractions of Iterator and Iterable.

3.7 Higher-Order Functions on Collections

The exploration of higher-order functions in Scala is essential for mastering functional programming paradigms. Higher-order functions are functions that can take other functions as parameters or return functions as results. This section will delve into the use of higher-order functions in the context of collections, highlighting their significance, usage, and application.

In Scala, collections such as List, Array, Vector, and others, provide a plethora of higher-order functions that facilitate operations on the elements of these collections. Common higher-order functions include map, flatMap, filter, fold, reduce, and foreach. These functions enable concise and expressive manipulation of data.

map applies a function to each element of a collection, transforming it into a new collection of the same type. The map function is defined as follows:

```
def map[B](f: A => B): List[B]
```

Here is an example of the map function in use:

```
val numbers = List(1, 2, 3)
val squaredNumbers = numbers.map(x => x * x)
println(squaredNumbers)

Output:
\begin{FittedVerbatim}
List(1, 4, 9)
\end{FittedVerbatim}
```

flatMap is similar to map but it applies a function that returns a collection for each element and then concatenates the resulting collections:

```
def flatMap[B](f: A => IterableOnce[B]): List[B]
```

An example of using flatMap:

```
val nestedNumbers = List(List(1, 2), List(3, 4))
val flatNumbers = nestedNumbers.flatMap(x => x)
println(flatNumbers)

Output:
\begin{FittedVerbatim}
List(1, 2, 3, 4)
\end{FittedVerbatim}
```

filter creates a new collection containing only those elements that satisfy a given predicate:

```
def filter(p: A => Boolean): List[A]
```

Example of the filter function:

```
val numbers = List(1, 2, 3, 4, 5)
val evenNumbers = numbers.filter(x => x % 2 == 0)
println(evenNumbers)

Output:
\begin{FittedVerbatim}
List(2, 4)
\end{FittedVerbatim}
```

fold and reduce are used for aggregating the elements of a collection. fold allows the accumulation to start with an initial value:

```
def fold[B](z: B)(op: (B, A) => B): B
```

The following example illustrates fold:

```
val numbers = List(1, 2, 3, 4)
val sum = numbers.fold(0)((acc, x) => acc + x)
println(sum)

Output:
\begin{FittedVerbatim}
```

```
10
\end{FittedVerbatim}
```

reduce, unlike fold, does not require an initial value and operates directly on pairs of elements within the collection. It is defined as:

```
def reduce[B >: A](op: (B, B) => B): B
```

An example of reduce usage:

```
val numbers = List(1, 2, 3, 4)
val product = numbers.reduce((x, y) => x * y)
println(product)

Output:
\begin{FittedVerbatim}
24
\end{FittedVerbatim}
```

foreach is used primarily for side effects, applying a function to each element of the collection without returning a new collection:

```
def foreach[U](f: A => U): Unit
```

Example of foreach:

```
val words = List("hello", "world")
words.foreach(println)

Output:
\begin{FittedVerbatim}
hello
world
\end{FittedVerbatim}
```

These higher-order functions are foundational for functional programming in Scala, providing versatile tools for transforming and aggregating collections efficiently and declaratively. Understanding and effectively utilizing these functions are critical for writing idiomatic and powerful Scala code.

3.8 Streams and Lazy Collections

Scala provides powerful abstractions for dealing with potentially infinite data structures through the use of Streams and lazy collections. These constructs are essential when working with large datasets or when the dataset is not fully defined at the time of consumption.

A Stream is a lazily evaluated linked list where elements are evaluated only as needed. This allows the creation of infinite sequences without causing memory overflows. The concept of laziness in collections is critical for performance optimization and efficient memory usage.

Here's a simple example demonstrating the use of a Stream to create an infinite list of natural numbers:

```
val naturalNumbers: Stream[Int] = Stream.from(1)
```

In this example, Stream.from(1) generates an infinite stream of integers starting at 1. The elements of the stream are computed lazily, meaning that the next element is only calculated when it is requested. This allows the handling of sequences that would otherwise be too large to store in memory.

Consider the following example where we take the first 10 natural numbers from our naturalNumbers stream:

```
val firstTenNumbers = naturalNumbers.take(10).toList
```

When executed, this code will produce the following output:

```
List(1, 2, 3, 4, 5, 6, 7, 8, 9, 10)
```

This illustrates how only the necessary elements of the Stream are evaluated and converted into a list. Streams support various standard collection operations like map, filter, foldLeft, and others.

For a concrete example, let's create a stream that generates the Fibonacci sequence:

```
def fibonacci(a: Int, b: Int): Stream[Int] = a #:: fibonacci(b, a + b)
val fibs = fibonacci(0, 1)

val firstTenFibs = fibs.take(10).toList
```

The #:: operator is used to prepend an element to a Stream. The fibonacci function defines a recursive stream where the next value is computed as the sum of the two preceding values. The first ten Fibonacci numbers are obtained by:

```
List(0, 1, 1, 2, 3, 5, 8, 13, 21, 34)
```

Streams are only one aspect of Scala's support for lazy collections. Lazy evaluation can also be applied to other collection types using views. A view is a lazy version of a collection where transformations are not immediately applied but are instead deferred until the collection is actually evaluated.

The following example demonstrates the use of a view to generate a

82

large list of numbers where each element is squared, but the squaring operation is deferred:

```scala
val largeList = (1 to 1000000).view.map(x => x * x)
```

Here, largeList is not an actual list but a view. The map function has been called, but the squaring operation won't be performed until the elements are accessed. If we take the first 10 elements:

```scala
val firstTenSquares = largeList.take(10).toList
```

The resulting output is:

```scala
List(1, 4, 9, 16, 25, 36, 49, 64, 81, 100)
```

This clearly demonstrates that the operations are delayed until absolutely necessary, providing significant performance benefits especially with computationally intensive operations or very large datasets.

Additionally, views can be composed to create pipelines of transformations that remain lazy until the final result is required. Consider the following chained operations:

```scala
val complexView = (1 to 1000000).view
  .map(_ * 2)
  .filter(_ % 5 == 0)
  .map(_ + 1)

val firstTenComplex = complexView.take(10).toList
```

This example showcases a series of operations (doubling, filtering, and incrementing) applied in a lazy manner. The result of taking the first 10 elements after all transformations is:

```scala
List(11, 21, 31, 41, 51, 61, 71, 81, 91, 101)
```

In cases where operations on collections are needed but immediate evaluation is either inefficient or infeasible, leveraging Stream and views can lead to more efficient and cleaner code. Understanding the underlying mechanics of laziness in Scala collections allows for better memory management and performance optimization, especially when dealing with potentially infinite or very large datasets.

3.9 Views and Their Applications

Scala's collection library includes a versatile feature known as view. A view in Scala allows you to create a lazy version of a collection, meaning

83

that all transformations applied to the collection will be delayed until it is evaluated. This can be particularly advantageous when working with large datasets where immediate evaluation would be costly in terms of performance.

A view does not store the data itself but provides a pathway to the data, ensuring efficient computation and memory usage until the final result is required. For instance, if you require a sequence of transformations but only need the end result, using a view can avoid the overhead of intermediate processing.

To create a view in Scala, we can call the view method on a collection. Here is an example that demonstrates the difference between a regular collection and a view.

```
val regularList = (1 to 1000000).filter(_ % 2 == 0).map(_ * 2)
val viewList = (1 to 1000000).view.filter(_ % 2 == 0).map(_ * 2)
```

In this example, regularList immediately filters even numbers and then maps each element to its double. Conversely, viewList only sets up the sequence of operations without executing them. The transformations (filter and map) are applied lazily and only computed when necessary.

To realize the values in viewList, we can convert the view back to a strict collection:

```
val resultList = viewList.toList
```

Until toList is called, no filtering or mapping occurs. This deferred evaluation model is particularly useful for optimizing performance when dealing with complex pipelines of operations.

Consider a more complex scenario where you combine several high-cost operations:

```
val complexProcessing = (1 to 1000000).view
  .filter(_ % 2 == 0)
  .map(_ * math.sqrt(2))
  .map(_ + 10)
  .map(_ / 2)
  .filter(_ > 5)
```

Here, each operation (filter, map, and so on) sets up a sequence of transformations. If this was a strict collection, Scala would eagerly evaluate each step. Instead, with a view, evaluation is deferred.

To process and collect the final results, invoke:

```
val processedResults = complexProcessing.take(100).toList
```

84

The take(100) method extracts the first 100 elements that meet the filtering criteria, ensuring only necessary operations are performed to fulfill this requirement. This minimizes computational overhead by avoiding unnecessary intermediate calculations.

For further clarification, let's measure the performance difference between using a strict collection and a view.

```
val largeRange = 1 to 1000000

def strictExecution(): List[Int] = {
  largeRange.filter(_ % 2 == 0)
          .map(_ * 2)
          .map(_ + 1)
          .map(_ / 3)
          .toList
}

def lazyExecution(): List[Int] = {
  largeRange.view
          .filter(_ % 2 == 0)
          .map(_ * 2)
          .map(_ + 1)
          .map(_ / 3)
          .toList
}

val strictStart = System.nanoTime
strictExecution()
val strictEnd = System.nanoTime
println("Strict execution time: " + (strictEnd - strictStart))

val lazyStart = System.nanoTime
lazyExecution()
val lazyEnd = System.nanoTime
println("Lazy execution time: " + (lazyEnd - lazyStart))
```

```
Strict execution time: 37304500
Lazy execution time: 25840000
```

The execution times for strict and lazy evaluations demonstrate that the view-based approach can often yield better performance, particularly when intermediate results are not required.

Furthermore, beyond performance optimization, views are invaluable in scenarios requiring non-strict evaluation models. For example, when working with infinite collections or streams, views enable working with potentially unbounded data without risking out-of-memory errors.

Consider generating an infinite series of Fibonacci numbers using a view:

```
def fibs: LazyList[BigInt] = {
  def next(a: BigInt, b: BigInt): LazyList[BigInt] =
    a #:: next(b, a + b)
  next(0, 1)
}
```

```
val fibView = fibs.view
val firstTenFibs = fibView.take(10).toList
println(firstTenFibs)
```

List(0, 1, 1, 2, 3, 5, 8, 13, 21, 34)

Here, LazyList generates an infinite sequence of Fibonacci numbers while fibView provides a lazy view over this sequence. The take(10) method limits the evaluation to the first ten elements, resulting in efficient processing and memory usage.

Through these applications, Scala's view mechanism proves to be a powerful tool in functional programming, enabling efficient and flexible data manipulation. This lazy evaluation approach allows for more elegant and performance-aware code, especially crucial when dealing with large or infinite datasets.

3.10   Using Pattern Matching with Collections

Pattern matching in Scala is a powerful feature that allows for the deconstruction and inspection of data in a concise and readable manner. It is particularly useful when working with collections, as it can greatly simplify the processing of elements. This section covers various ways to utilize pattern matching with Scala's collection framework, providing clear examples to illustrate each concept.

Pattern matching can be applied to several types of collections, including sequences, tuples, and options. When used with collection operations, it not only improves code readability but also enhances functionality by enabling more expressive and compact code.

Pattern Matching with Lists:

The List class in Scala is a commonly used sequence collection that supports pattern matching. Lists can be deconstructed into head and tail components, which can be matched against patterns. Here is a basic example:

```
// Matching a list with a head and tail
val list = List(1, 2, 3, 4)

list match {
  case Nil => println("Empty list")
  case head :: tail => println(s"Head: $head, Tail: $tail")
```

```
}
```

The above example checks if the list is empty (Nil) or if it has a head element followed by a tail (indicated by the :: operator). The output for the given input list would be:

Head: 1, Tail: List(2, 3, 4)

Pattern Matching with Arrays:

Arrays in Scala can also be decomposed using pattern matching. However, the syntax is slightly different:

```
// Matching an array with specific elements
val array = Array(1, 2, 3)

array match {
  case Array(1, x, y) => println(s"Matched: 1, $x, $y")
  case _ => println("No match")
}
```

In this example, the pattern $Array(1, x, y)$ expects an array with exactly three elements, where the first is 1. If the pattern matches, the variables x and y will capture the second and third elements of the array, respectively. The output is:

Matched: 1, 2, 3

Pattern Matching with Tuples:

Tuples are a way to group a fixed number of items together. They can be matched against patterns involving the specific number of elements and their types:

```
// Matching a tuple with two elements
val tuple = (10, "Scala")

tuple match {
  case (a, b) => println(s"First: $a, Second: $b")
  case _ => println("No match")
}
```

The pattern (a, b) matches any tuple with exactly two elements, assigning the first element to a and the second to b. For the given tuple, the output is:

First: 10, Second: Scala

Pattern Matching with Options:

Option is used in Scala to represent optional values that can either be Some(value) or None. Pattern matching on Option is straightforward:

87

```scala
// Matching an Option value
val option: Option[Int] = Some(5)

option match {
  case Some(value) => println(s"Got value: $value")
  case None => println("No value")
}
```

For the given Option, the output will be:

```
Got value: 5
```

Pattern Matching and Higher-Order Functions:

Pattern matching can also be integrated with higher-order functions on collections, such as map, filter, and flatMap. Here is an example using map:

```scala
// Using pattern matching within a higher-order function
val list = List(Some(1), None, Some(2), Some(3), None)

val filteredValues = list.map {
  case Some(value) => Some(value * 2)
  case None => None
}
```

This code will double the values wrapped in Some and leave None values unchanged. The resulting List will be:

```
List(Some(2), None, Some(4), Some(6), None)
```

Pattern Matching with Extractors:

Extractors are objects in Scala that define an unapply method used to extract values from objects. Extractors facilitate custom pattern matching on complex data types.

```scala
// Defining and using an extractor
object Twice {
  def unapply(x: Int): Option[Int] = if (x % 2 == 0) Some(x / 2) else None
}

val number = 20
number match {
  case Twice(n) => println(s"Twice of $n is $number")
  case _ => println("Not a twice")
}
```

The custom extractor Twice checks if a number is even and, if so, allows matching against half of that number. The output for the given number is:

```
Twice of 10 is 20
```

Understanding and utilizing pattern matching with collections in Scala

88

enables more expressive and concise code, allowing for efficient data processing and manipulation in a functional programming style.

3.11 Common Collection Operations

Scala collections offer a suite of operations that provide powerful methods for manipulating data. Understanding these operations is vital for leveraging the full potential of Scala's collections framework. This section explores key operations that can be applied to various collection types, including sequences, sets, and maps.

1. map **Operation**

The map function is a fundamental higher-order function that transforms each element of a collection using the provided function.

```
val numbers = List(1, 2, 3, 4, 5)
val squares = numbers.map(x => x * x)
// squares: List(1, 4, 9, 16, 25)
```

In this example, each element of the numbers list is transformed by squaring it. The resulting collection, squares, contains the squared values.

2. filter **Operation**

The filter method selects elements of a collection that satisfy a given predicate function. It produces a new collection containing only the elements that pass the test.

```
val numbers = List(1, 2, 3, 4, 5, 6)
val evenNumbers = numbers.filter(_ % 2 == 0)
// evenNumbers: List(2, 4, 6)
```

Here, the filter method extracts only the even numbers from the numbers list.

3. reduce **and** reduceLeft **/** reduceRight **Operations**

The reduce method combines all elements of a collection using a binary operation, producing a single result. The operations reduceLeft and reduceRight are variations that reduce the collection from the left or right, respectively.

```
val numbers = List(1, 2, 3, 4, 5)
val sum = numbers.reduce(_ + _)
// sum: 15
```

In this case, the reduce method adds all the elements of the numbers list. One can use reduceLeft and reduceRight for left-to-right or right-to-left reductions, respectively, when the operation is not associative.

4. fold **and** foldLeft **/** foldRight **Operations**

The fold method, like reduce, processes elements to yield a single result but with the advantage of a specified initial value. It also comes in left (foldLeft) and right (foldRight) variants.

```
val numbers = List(1, 2, 3, 4, 5)
val product = numbers.fold(1)(_ * _)
// product: 120
```

This example multiplies all elements of the numbers list, starting with an initial value of 1. This initial value can be particularly useful for operations like initialization of an accumulator.

5. flatMap **Operation**

The flatMap method is a combination of map and flatten. It applies a function that produces a collection for each element, then concatenates the resulting collections into a single collection.

```
val nestedNumbers = List(List(1, 2), List(3, 4), List(5))
val flattened = nestedNumbers.flatMap(identity)
// flattened: List(1, 2, 3, 4, 5)
```

Here, flatMap(identity) flattens the list of lists into a single list. This operation is particularly useful for dealing with nested collections.

6. groupBy **Operation**

The groupBy method partitions a collection into a map of collections based on a given classifier function.

```
val words = List("scala", "spark", "java", "javascript")
val grouped = words.groupBy(_.charAt(0))
// grouped: Map(s -> List(scala, spark), j -> List(java, javascript))
```

In this case, the groupBy method groups words by their starting character, resulting in a map where keys are characters and values are lists of words.

7. foreach **Operation**

The foreach method applies a given function to each element of the collection, primarily for side effects.

```
val numbers = List(1, 2, 3, 4, 5)
numbers.foreach(println)
```

This example prints each element of the numbers list to the standard output.

8. collect **Operation**

The collect method applies a partial function to all elements of the collection for which the partial function is defined, producing a new collection.

```
val numbers = List(1, 2, 3, 4, 5)
val doubled = numbers.collect {
  case x if x % 2 == 0 => x * 2
}
// doubled: List(4, 8)
```

Here, the collect method doubles only the even numbers in the list.

9. partition **Operation**

The partition method splits a collection into a tuple of two collections: one containing elements that satisfy a predicate and one that does not.

```
val numbers = List(1, 2, 3, 4, 5)
val (evens, odds) = numbers.partition(_ % 2 == 0)
// evens: List(2, 4)
// odds: List(1, 3, 5)
```

This example partitions the numbers list into even and odd numbers.

10. zip **and** zipWithIndex **Operations**

The zip method pairs corresponding elements from two collections into tuples, whereas zipWithIndex pairs each element with its index.

```
val numbers = List(1, 2, 3)
val letters = List('a', 'b', 'c')
val zipped = numbers.zip(letters)
// zipped: List((1, 'a'), (2, 'b'), (3, 'c'))

val numbered = numbers.zipWithIndex
// numbered: List((1, 0), (2, 1), (3, 2))
```

In these examples, zip creates a list of pairs combining numbers and letters, while zipWithIndex creates pairs of elements with their indices.

Understanding and proficiently applying these operations can significantly improve code efficiency and readability when working with Scala collections. The operations outlined above are merely a subset of the comprehensive methods available in Scala's collections library.

Chapter 4

Functional Programming in Scala

This chapter delves into the core principles of functional programming in Scala, including first-class and higher-order functions, immutability, and pure functions. Readers will learn about function literals, closures, currying, and recursion. Additionally, the chapter covers functional data structures, monads, for-comprehensions, and functional error handling, providing a comprehensive foundation for writing robust functional code in Scala.

4.1   Introduction to Functional Programming

Functional programming is a paradigm centered around the concept of mathematical functions, which provide a means of mapping inputs to outputs without altering the state of the system. This paradigm enforces a programming style that emphasizes immutability, pure functions, and declarative code. Scala, being a hybrid language, supports both functional and object-oriented programming, allowing the developers to leverage the advantages of both paradigms.

Functional programming in Scala revolves around the following core principles:

- Immutability

- First-class and Higher-order functions

- Pure functions

- Declarative code

Immutability refers to the inability to change an object once it has been created. In functional programming, data structures are immutable, and functions return new structures instead of modifying the existing ones. This practice leads to easier reasoning about code, avoidance of side effects, and improved concurrency safety.

First-class and Higher-order functions is another foundational concept. In Scala, functions are first-class citizens, meaning they can be assigned to variables, passed as arguments, and returned from other functions. Higher-order functions are functions that take other functions as parameters or return functions.

Pure functions are functions where the output value is determined only by its input values, and they produce no side effects. In other words, pure functions do not read from or write to any external state. This characteristic simplifies testing and reasoning about the code.

The declarative nature of functional programming involves describing *what* the program should accomplish rather than detailing the steps of *how* to achieve it. This is in contrast to imperative programming, where explicit instructions are given.

A simple example of a pure function in Scala:

```
// A pure function in Scala
def add(x: Int, y: Int): Int = {
  x + y
}

// Using the pure function
val sum = add(3, 4) // sum evaluates to 7
```

In the above example, the function add is pure because it solely relies on its input parameters x and y to compute the result and does not cause any side effects.

A higher-order function example in Scala:

```
// A higher-order function in Scala
def applyFunction(f: Int => Int, x: Int): Int = {
  f(x)
}

// Using the higher-order function
val increment: Int => Int = (x: Int) => x + 1
```

```
val result = applyFunction(increment, 5) // result evaluates to 6
```

In this case, the higher-order function applyFunction takes another function f and an integer x as its parameters. When called with increment and 5, it applies increment to 5, producing the result 6.

To further grasp the core principles of functional programming, consider the following algorithm for computing the factorial of a number. Here, recursion plays a fundamental role, eliminating the need for mutable state.

Algorithm 1: Recursive computation of factorial

Input: A non-negative integer n
Output: The factorial of n, denoted as $n!$
1 **if** $n == 0$ **then**
2 | **return** 1;
3 **else**
4 | **return** $n * $ factorial$(n-1)$;
5 **end**

In Scala, this algorithm can be implemented using a pure recursive function:

```
// Recursive factorial function in Scala
def factorial(n: Int): Int = {
  if (n == 0) 1
  else n * factorial(n - 1)
}

// Using the factorial function
val fact5 = factorial(5) // fact5 evaluates to 120
```

This function cleanly and efficiently computes the factorial of a given number without relying on any mutable state or side effects. Although simple, this example encapsulates many attributes of functional programming: immutability, recursion, and pure functions.

To illustrate the power of higher-order functions, consider a scenario where we need to apply a list of functions to a single value. Higher-order functions allow us to elegantly express such operations.

```
// List of functions to apply
val functions: List[Int => Int] = List(
  (x: Int) => x + 1,
  (x: Int) => x * 2,
  (x: Int) => x - 3
)

// Function to apply all functions in the list to a value
def applyAll(functions: List[Int => Int], x: Int): Int = {
```

```
  functions.foldLeft(x)((acc, func) => func(acc))
}

// Using the applyAll function
val result = applyAll(functions, 5) // result evaluates to 9
```

In this example, the applyAll function uses foldLeft to cumulatively apply each function in the functions list to the initial value 5, resulting in the final value 9. This demonstrates the expressive power of functional programming in Scala, highlighting the use of higher-order functions and functional patterns to write concise and readable code.

Understanding the core tenets of functional programming lays a solid foundation for delving deeper into Scala's functional constructs. The principles of immutability, pure functions, and higher-order functions are not merely theoretical; they offer practical advantages in writing robust, maintainable, and concurrent applications.

4.2 First-Class and Higher-Order Functions

In Scala, functions are first-class citizens, meaning they can be treated like any other values. This attribute enables developers to pass functions as arguments, return them from other functions, and assign them to variables. A clear understanding of first-class and higher-order functions is crucial for mastering functional programming in Scala.

First-class functions can be illustrated by assigning a function to a variable:

```
val square = (x: Int) => x * x
```

Here, square is a function that takes an integer and returns its square. The function is assigned to the variable square, demonstrating that functions can be values.

Higher-order functions are functions that take other functions as parameters or return functions as results. Consider the following example of a higher-order function that takes a function and an integer as arguments and applies that function to the integer:

```
def applyFunction(f: Int => Int, x: Int): Int = f(x)
```

This definition uses a higher-order function applyFunction, which takes a function f and an integer x, then applies f to x.

The power of higher-order functions can be observed in functional abstraction. Functions such as map, filter, and reduce are commonly used in functional programming to operate on collections. They accept functions as arguments, applying them to each element of the collection.

To gain practical understanding, consider the following example that squares each element in a list:

```
val numbers = List(1, 2, 3, 4)
val squaredNumbers = numbers.map(x => x * x)
```

In this case, map is a higher-order function that takes the anonymous function x => x * x and applies it to each element of numbers, resulting in squaredNumbers as List(1, 4, 9, 16).

Higher-order functions also enable partial application and function composition. Partial application allows for fixing a few arguments of a function and generating a new function. Considering a standard addition function:

```
def add(a: Int, b: Int): Int = a + b
```

A partially applied version fixing one argument:

```
val addFive = add(5, _: Int)
val result = addFive(3) // Result is 8
```

Function composition uses two or more functions to create a new function. Scala provides the compose and andThen methods for this purpose. For two functions f and g, f.compose(g) creates a new function that applies g first and then f, whereas f.andThen(g) applies f first and then g.

```
val f = (x: Int) => x + 2
val g = (x: Int) => x * 3
val h = f compose g // equivalent to f(g(x))
val i = f andThen g // equivalent to g(f(x))

val resultH = h(4) // Result is 14
val resultI = i(4) // Result is 18
```

f and g are simple functions; h applies g first, then f, and i applies f first, then g. The results 14 and 18 substantiate the defined compositions.

Realizing higher-order functions' potential, developers can abstract recurrent patterns of computation and make code modular and reusable, enhancing readability and maintainability. Higher-order functions form a fundamental part of functional programming in Scala, enabling sophisticated operations through simple compositions.

4.3 Immutability and Its Importance

In functional programming, immutability is a cornerstone principle that significantly enhances the reliability, scalability, and simplicity of code. Immutability refers to the practice of ensuring that data structures and variables, once created, cannot be modified. Instead of altering the existing data, functions produce new data structures with the modified values, leaving the original data untouched.

Consider a simple example where we define an immutable list in Scala:

```
val immutableList = List(1, 2, 3)
val newList = immutableList :+ 4
println(immutableList) // Output: List(1, 2, 3)
println(newList) // Output: List(1, 2, 3, 4)
```

In the above code snippet, `immutableList` remains unchanged after the operation. Instead, a new list `newList` is created with the additional element. This fundamental nature of immutability offers several advantages:

- **Thread Safety**: Since immutable data cannot be modified, concurrent operations on the same data do not lead to race conditions, making immutability inherently thread-safe.

- **Simplified Reasoning**: With immutable data, understanding the flow and changes in the program becomes more straightforward because the data dependencies are explicit and each state of the data is preserved.

- **Predictability**: Functions with immutable data are typically pure, meaning they have no side effects. This predictability facilitates debugging, testing, and reasoning about code as functions will always yield the same output for the same input.

In a concurrent context, immutability eliminates the need for complex locking mechanisms. Consider the following example using concurrency with immutable data structures:

```
import scala.concurrent._
import ExecutionContext.Implicits.global

val immutableMap = Map("a" -> 1, "b" -> 2)

val future1 = Future {
  immutableMap + ("c" -> 3)
}
```

```
val future2 = Future {
  immutableMap + ("d" -> 4)
}

for {
  result1 <- future1
  result2 <- future2
} yield {
  println(result1)
  println(result2)
  println(immutableMap)
}
```

```
Output:
Map(a -> 1, b -> 2, c -> 3)
Map(a -> 1, b -> 2, d -> 4)
Map(a -> 1, b -> 2)
```

In this example, the immutable nature of immutableMap ensures that concurrent modifications do not conflict. Each future operation generates a new map, thus preserving the original map's state.

Scala also provides various immutable collections such as List, Map, Set, and Vector. These collections facilitate the development of functional code by encouraging immutability. Below is an example demonstrating the immutability of a Vector:

```
val vector = Vector(1, 2, 3, 4)
val newVector = vector.updated(2, 5)
println(vector) // Output: Vector(1, 2, 3, 4)
println(newVector) // Output: Vector(1, 2, 5, 4)
```

When applying transformations to immutable collections, it is crucial to understand the concept of structural sharing. Structural sharing enables efficient memory usage by reusing parts of the existing data structure rather than copying elements. This ensures that immutability does not incur significant performance overhead.

For instance, consider the following transformation on a List:

```
val originalList = List(1, 2, 3)
val extendedList = 0 :: originalList
println(originalList) // Output: List(1, 2, 3)
println(extendedList) // Output: List(0, 1, 2, 3)
```

Here, extendedList and originalList share the tail portion of the list, which optimizes the memory usage. Such techniques are fundamental in functional programming to maintain performance efficiency while adhering to immutability principles.

Understanding and effectively utilizing immutability in Scala empowers developers to write robust, maintainable, and clear code.

4.4   Pure Functions and Referential Transparency

Pure functions are fundamental to functional programming and play a significant role in enabling referential transparency. A function is considered pure if it satisfies two key properties: 1. The function's return value is determined only by its input values, with no observable side effects. 2. The function does not alter any state or interact with the outside world, such as modifying a global variable or performing I/O operations.

These properties ensure that pure functions are predictable and easy to reason about, as any function call's outcome remains consistent given the same input parameters.

Referential transparency is a concept that follows naturally from pure functions. An expression is referentially transparent if it can be replaced with its corresponding value without changing the program's behavior. Referential transparency offers several practical benefits, including easier reasoning about code, simplified debugging, and more robust optimization opportunities by the compiler.

```
def add(x: Int, y: Int): Int = x + y

// The function 'add' is pure because its result is determined solely by its inputs 'x'
        and 'y', with no side effects.
```

In the example above, the function add is a pure function. Invoking $add(2, 3)$ will always yield the result 5, regardless of any external state or context. This consistency is a hallmark of pure functions.

To illustrate the importance of referential transparency, consider the following example:

```
val result = add(2, 3)
// The expression 'add(2, 3)' can be replaced with '5' without altering the program's
        behavior.
val expected = 5
```

In this case, the expression $add(2, 3)$ can be substituted with 5 without changing the result's meaning or behavior. This substitution property is crucial for various functional programming techniques, such as equational reasoning and optimizing computations.

Most importantly, pure functions and referential transparency enable more reliable and straightforward testing. Since pure functions always produce the same output given the same inputs, they can be tested in isolation without considering external state or side effects.

However, achieving pure functions in real-world scenarios often involves handling side effects in a controlled manner. One common approach in functional programming is to push side effects to the boundaries of a system, making the core logic purely functional. Techniques such as using monads (e.g., Option, Either, Future) can help encapsulate effects, thereby maintaining purity in most of the codebase.

Consider the following example of an impure function:

```scala
var counter = 0

def increment(): Unit = {
  counter += 1
}
```

In this case, the function increment is impure because it modifies the external variable counter. The function's behavior depends on the state of counter, making it less predictable and harder to reason about.

To refactor this into a pure function, the state can be passed and returned explicitly:

```scala
def increment(counter: Int): Int = counter + 1

val newCounter = increment(0) // newCounter is 1
```

In the refactored version, increment becomes pure by taking counter as an input and returning a new value without altering any external state. This change restores referential transparency, making the function's behavior purely dependent on its input argument.

The combined power of pure functions and referential transparency facilitates advanced functional programming techniques like lazy evaluation and memoization. For instance, memoization—caching the results of expensive function calls—relies on the consistency of function outputs for identical inputs, which is guaranteed by purity.

By understanding and employing these concepts, developers can write more predictable, maintainable, and testable code in Scala, leveraging the strengths of functional programming to build reliable systems.

101

4.5 Function Literals and Anonymous Functions

In Scala, function literals and anonymous functions play a significant role in functional programming. These concepts allow for the concise declaration and utilization of functions directly within expressions, providing a powerful tool for developers to create more readable and efficient code.

Function literals in Scala are syntactic constructs that denote unnamed or anonymous functions. They are a cornerstone of functional programming because they enable the passing of functions as arguments and the assignment of functions to variables. Function literals are defined using the $\Rightarrow$ operator, which separates the function's parameter list from its body.

Consider a simple example of a function literal:

```
val add = (x: Int, y: Int) => x + y
```

In this example, add is a function literal that takes two parameters, x and y, both of type Int, and returns their sum. This function can be invoked like any other named function:

```
val result = add(5, 3)
println(result) // Output: 8
```

Anonymous Functions

Anonymous functions, also known as lambda expressions, are function literals that do not have a name. These functions are typically used when a function is needed only once or in a limited scope, such as within higher-order functions. Scala's syntax for anonymous functions prioritizes brevity and readability.

A function literal can be transformed into an anonymous function. For example, the above add function can be rewritten as an anonymous function and passed directly to another function:

```
val result = List(1, 2, 3, 4).reduce((x, y) => x + y)
println(result) // Output: 10
```

In this case, the anonymous function $(x, y) => x + y$ is passed to the reduce method of List, which combines the elements of the list using the specified binary operation.

Type Inference with Function Literals

Scala provides robust type inference capabilities, reducing the verbosity associated with explicitly specifying types. When the compiler can infer the types of the parameters in a function literal, you may omit the type annotations for simplicity.

For instance, the previous example can be further simplified:

```
val result = List(1, 2, 3, 4).reduce(_ + _)
println(result) // Output: 10
```

Here, the underscore (_) is a placeholder for parameters whose types are inferred by the compiler. This concise notation is particularly useful when working with simple operations.

Higher-Order Functions and Function Literals

Function literals are often employed in the context of higher-order functions, which are functions that take other functions as parameters or return functions as results. The seamless integration of function literals and higher-order functions enables a functional style of programming that promotes code reuse and modularity.

For instance, consider the map method for collections. It transforms each element of a collection using a specified function:

```
val numbers = List(1, 2, 3, 4)
val doubled = numbers.map(x => x * 2)
println(doubled) // Output: List(2, 4, 6, 8)
```

In this example, an anonymous function x => x * 2 is passed to the map method, which doubles each element of the list.

Closures

Closures represent a powerful aspect of anonymous functions. A closure is a function literal that captures free variables from its environment. These captured variables are closed over, meaning the function retains access to their values even when the function is executed outside their original scope.

Consider the following example demonstrating closures:

```
var factor = 3
val multiplier = (i: Int) => i * factor

val res1 = multiplier(2) // Output: 6
factor = 5
val res2 = multiplier(2) // Output: 10
```

The function multiplier defines a closure over the variable factor. Changes to factor outside the function's scope impact the function's behavior when it is executed.

Practical Example: Sorting with Function Literals

To illustrate the practical application of function literals, consider using them to sort a list of tuples by their second element:

```
val tuples = List((1, 2), (3, 4), (2, 1))
val sortedTuples = tuples.sortWith((a, b) => a._2 < b._2)
println(sortedTuples) // Output: List((2, 1), (1, 2), (3, 4))
```

The anonymous function (a, b) => a._2 < b._2 specifies the sorting order based on the second element of each tuple, demonstrating how succinct and expressive Scala's function literals can be.

4.6   Closures and Partial Functions

Closures and partial functions are fundamental concepts in functional programming that enable powerful abstraction, code reuse, and modularity. Understanding closures and partial functions is essential for mastering more advanced functional programming techniques in Scala.

A closure is a function that captures the bindings of free variables in its lexical context. Free variables are those that are not defined within the function but are taken from its environment. Closures retain references to these external variables, thus allowing the function to access them even when the context in which they were defined is no longer active.

For example, consider the following Scala code snippet:

```
var factor = 3
val multiplier = (i: Int) => i * factor
```

Here, factor is a free variable within the multiplier function. When multiplier is called, it references factor from its defining environment, forming a closure. To observe this, execute:

```
factor = 5
println(multiplier(2)) // Output: 10
```

10

The function multiplier retains a reference to the variable factor, even after its value changes. This example illustrates the power of closures, enabling a function to access and manipulate variables outside its immediate scope.

In contrast, a partial function is a function that is defined only for a subset of its input domain. Partial functions in Scala are instances of the PartialFunction trait, which is defined as follows:

```
trait PartialFunction[-A, +B] extends (A => B) {
    def isDefinedAt(x: A): Boolean
}
```

A partial function must implement the isDefinedAt method, which checks whether the function is defined for a particular input. If isDefinedAt returns true, the function can be safely applied to that input. Consider the following example:

```
val squareRoot: PartialFunction[Double, Double] = {
    case x if x >= 0 => Math.sqrt(x)
}
```

Here, squareRoot is a partial function that computes the square root of a non-negative number. It is defined only for non-negative inputs. To verify which inputs the partial function supports, use:

```
println(squareRoot.isDefinedAt(-1)) // Output: false
println(squareRoot.isDefinedAt(4)) // Output: true
```

false
true

Applying a partial function to an undefined input will throw a MatchError. To safely handle inputs that may not be defined, use the collect method, passing a collection of elements and the partial function:

```
val numbers = List(-3.0, 4.0, 9.0)
val results = numbers.collect(squareRoot)
println(results) // Output: List(2.0, 3.0)
```

List(2.0, 3.0)

The collect method filters elements on which the partial function is defined and applies the function to these elements.

105

Understanding closures and partial functions provides a foundation for developing more advanced functional programming techniques. These concepts facilitate the encapsulation of state and the definition of functions over a constrained domain, enabling flexible and expressive code design.

Closures allow developers to create functions that maintain state between invocations, promoting reusable and modular code. Partial functions, on the other hand, enable the creation of functions that operate over specific domains, supporting safe and predictable error handling. These advanced functional programming constructs form the basis for building robust and scalable software systems.

4.7   Currying and Partially Applied Functions

Currying is a technique in functional programming where a function that takes multiple arguments is transformed into a sequence of functions, each taking a single argument. In Scala, currying allows for the creation of simpler, reusable, and more abstract functions by breaking down the functions into smaller parts. This technique not only aids in enhancing code readability but also in fostering function composition.

To understand currying in Scala, let's consider a basic example without currying:

```scala
def add(x: Int, y: Int): Int = x + y
```

In the above example, the add function takes two arguments, x and y, returning their sum. Now, we will transform this function into a curried function:

```scala
def add(x: Int)(y: Int): Int = x + y
```

With the curried version of add, the function add takes an integer x and returns another function that takes an integer y.

Using the curried function is straightforward. Here is how you can call it:

```scala
val add5 = add(5) _ // partially applying the first argument
val result = add5(10) // applying the second argument
```

Currying enables partially applied functions. The expression add(5) _ creates a new function by applying the first argument 5 and leaving the second argument y to be specified later. At this point, add5 is a function that takes a single integer argument and adds 5 to it. Hence, calling add5(10) returns 15.

Partially applied functions are a powerful abstraction mechanism in functional programming, permitting the creation of more specialized functions from general ones. This utility can be further explained with another example:

```
def multiply(x: Int)(y: Int): Int = x * y

val multiplyBy2 = multiply(2) _
val result2 = multiplyBy2(5) // result2 will be 10
```

Here, multiplyBy2 is a partially applied function created by fixing the first argument of the multiply function. When multiplyBy2(5) is called, it returns the product of 2 and 5, which is 10.

Currying and partially applied functions complement the concept of higher-order functions, allowing for more modular and flexible code. By breaking down arguments into a sequence of functions, currying facilitates the use of functions as first-class citizens, enabling their use as values that can be passed and returned within other functions.

Consider a more advanced example that demonstrates how currying can integrate with function composition:

```
def concatenate(a: String)(b: String): String = a + b

val greet = concatenate("Hello, ")
val greetingMessage = greet("World!") // adds "World!" to "Hello, "
```

In this snippet, greet is a curried function obtained by partially applying the concatenate function with the string "Hello, ". Subsequently, invoking greet("World!") produces "Hello, World!".

The flexibility of currying is not limited to simple examples. It becomes very impactful when dealing with more complex transformations and functional programming paradigms. Functional libraries often utilize currying to create highly abstract and reusable code components.

Another significant advantage of currying is its alignment with function composition, heavily used in functional programming. Function composition allows us to build complex functions by combining simpler ones. Through currying, you can easily compose functions to achieve sophisticated behaviors without the need for deeply nested or complex function calls.

```
val addCurried: Int => Int => Int = (x: Int) => (y: Int) => x + y

def applyAndCompose(f: Int => Int, g: Int => Int, x: Int): Int = f(g(x))
```

```
val add5Compose = addCurried(5)
val resultCompose = applyAndCompose(add5Compose, multiplyBy2, 5) // (2 * 5) + 5
```

This example highlights the confluence of currying and function composition. The applyAndCompose function takes two functions, f and g, and composes them with the argument x. Using the curried add5Compose and multiplyBy2, applyAndCompose(add5Compose, multiplyBy2, 5) first computes $(2 * 5)$ and then applies add5Compose to the result, yielding 15.

By using currying and partially applied functions, Scala provides a sophisticated and powerful mechanism for functional programming, crucially influencing code reusability, modularity, and abstraction. Currying transforms the approach to function creation and invocation, enhancing both simplicity and expressiveness in writing functional programs.

4.8   Recursion and Tail-Recursion

One of the foundational concepts in functional programming is recursion. In Scala, recursion is a method where a function calls itself to solve a problem. This technique is essential for breaking down complex problems into simpler subproblems, which can be solved more easily. Let's explore recursion with an example:

```
def factorial(n: Int): Int = {
  if (n == 0) 1
  else n * factorial(n - 1)
}
```

In this factorial function, the base case is when n is zero, returning 1. For all other values, the function multiplies n by the result of calling itself with n - 1. While recursion simplifies problem-solving, it is crucial to be aware of stack overflow issues that may arise when dealing with large inputs, as each recursive call consumes stack space.

Scala introduces tail recursion as a mechanism to optimize recursive functions and mitigate stack overflow problems. A function is tail-recursive if the recursive call is the last operation in the function. This form allows the compiler to optimize the recursion by reusing the current stack frame, effectively transforming it into an iterative process.

Here is the tail-recursive version of the factorial function:

```
@annotation.tailrec
def factorialTailRec(n: Int, acc: Int = 1): Int = {
  if (n == 0) acc
  else factorialTailRec(n - 1, n * acc)
}
```

Notice the changes made:

- The function includes an accumulator acc to store the result of intermediate calculations.

- The recursive call at the end of the function uses updated parameters $n - 1$ and $n * acc$, ensuring that it is the last operation.

- The @annotation.tailrec annotation is used to inform the compiler to perform tail-call optimization. If the function is not tail-recursive, the compiler will issue an error.

To further solidify the understanding of tail recursion, consider another example: computing the greatest common divisor (GCD) using the Euclidean algorithm.

```
@annotation.tailrec
def gcd(a: Int, b: Int): Int = {
  if (b == 0) a
  else gcd(b, a % b)
}
```

Here, the gcd function calculates the GCD of two integers a and b. The base case returns a when b is zero. Otherwise, it recursively calls itself with b and the remainder of a divided by b. This recursive call is in tail position, allowing the compiler to optimize it.

Tail recursion is a powerful tool in functional programming, enabling efficient recursion without compromising stack space. To integrate tail recursion in your solutions, ensure that recursive calls appear in the tail position. Leveraging the @annotation.tailrec annotation provides an additional layer of safety, prompting the compiler to validate tail recursion. These techniques ensure that your recursive functions are both elegant and performant.

4.9 Functional Data Structures

Functional data structures in Scala are built on the principles of immutability and pure functions, allowing for concurrent and predictable programming. This section explores key functional data structures, such as lists, trees, and more specialized constructs, examining their implementation and usage in the context of functional programming.

Immutable Lists

The List is one of the most fundamental data structures in functional programming. In Scala, lists are immutable by default. Immutable lists provide structural sharing, allowing operations such as cons (construct) to be performed in constant time.

```
val numbers: List[Int] = List(1, 2, 3, 4, 5)
val prependedList: List[Int] = 0 :: numbers // Prepends 0 to the list
```

The colon-colon operator (::) is used to prepend an element to a list. This operation reuses the tail of the list, enhancing performance through structural sharing.

Pattern Matching with Lists

Pattern matching is a powerful feature in Scala, enabling concise and readable destructuring of lists.

```
numbers match {
  case Nil => println("Empty list")
  case head :: tail => println(s"Head: $head, Tail: $tail")
}
```

The Nil case handles the empty list, while the head :: tail pattern matches a non-empty list, binding the first element to head and the rest to tail.

Trees

Trees are another essential functional data structure. Immutable binary trees can be represented using algebraic data types (ADTs).

```
sealed trait Tree[+A]
case class Leaf[A](value: A) extends Tree[A]
case class Branch[A](left: Tree[A], right: Tree[A]) extends Tree[A]
```

Tree is a sealed trait, meaning all implementations must be within the same file. A Leaf holds a single value, while a Branch contains two subtrees.

Tree Operations

Functional programming emphasizes recursive operations on data structures like trees. Consider a function to calculate the size of a tree.

```
def size[A](tree: Tree[A]): Int = tree match {
  case Leaf(_) => 1
```

```
    case Branch(left, right) => 1 + size(left) + size(right)
}
```

Each Leaf contributes a size of 1, and each Branch contributes one plus the sizes of its subtrees.

Mapping Over Trees

Similar to lists, we can apply a function to every element in a tree using map.

```
def map[A, B](tree: Tree[A])(f: A => B): Tree[B] = tree match {
  case Leaf(value) => Leaf(f(value))
  case Branch(left, right) => Branch(map(left)(f), map(right)(f))
}
```

The function f is applied to each Leaf, transforming values of type A to type B. Branches support the structure, maintaining the tree's form.

Balanced Trees and Performance

The balance of a tree influences its performance. An unbalanced tree can degrade to a list, affecting operations negatively. Keeping trees balanced ensures logarithmic time complexity for operations. AVL trees and red-black trees are common examples of self-balancing trees.

Functional Queues

Queues, unlike lists, follow a first-in-first-out (FIFO) order. They can be implemented functionally with two lists: an in list for enqueuing elements and an out list for dequeuing them.

```
case class Queue[+A](in: List[A], out: List[A]) {
  def enqueue[B >: A](element: B): Queue[B] = Queue(element :: in, out)
  def dequeue: Option[(A, Queue[A])] = out match {
    case Nil if in.isEmpty => None
    case Nil => Queue(Nil, in.reverse).dequeue
    case head :: tail => Some((head, Queue(in, tail)))
  }
}
```

The enqueue operation always prepends the element to the in list. The dequeue operation checks the out list; if empty, it reverses the in list to maintain order.

Persistent Data Structures

Persistent data structures allow previous versions of the data structure to remain available after modifications. This feature is crucial for functional programming, where immutability is a key concept. List and tree structures in Scala benefit from persistence, enabling efficient updates with minimal overhead.

The functional approach to data structures emphasizes immutability, enabling safe parallel execution and simplifying reasoning about code. Understanding the implementation and manipulation of these structures lays a foundation for effective functional programming in Scala.

4.10   Monads and For-Comprehensions

In Scala, monads provide a powerful abstraction for managing computations. They encapsulate values along with a set of operations that can be applied to these values, abstracting away details like error handling and state management. Monads follow three fundamental laws: left identity, right identity, and associativity.

The essence of a monad lies in its ability to chain operations while maintaining context. This chaining is generally facilitated by the flatMap method, which is defined for monadic types.

```
trait Monad[M[_]] {
  def flatMap[A, B](ma: M[A])(f: A => M[B]): M[B]
  def unit[A](a: => A): M[A]
}
```

The unit operation wraps a value into a monadic context, while flatMap takes a monadic value ma and a function f, applying f to the value inside ma and returning a new monad.

Consider the Option type in Scala, which represents a value that may or may not be present. The Option type is a monad. Let's illustrate this with a simple example:

```
val maybeNumber: Option[Int] = Some(10)
val maybeString: Option[String] = Some("Scala")

def addAndStringify(optNum: Option[Int], optStr: Option[String]): Option[String] = {
  optNum.flatMap(num =>
    optStr.map(str =>
      num.toString + str))
}
```

In this example, maybeNumber and maybeString are both Option types. The function addAndStringify combines these options into another Option, containing a concatenated string of the number and the string, if both are present.

Monads often require nested flatMap and map calls, which can become cumbersome. Scala addresses this complexity with for-comprehensions, providing a syntactic sugar that simplifies

112

monadic operations.

Using for-comprehensions, the previous example can be rewritten as:

```
def addAndStringify(optNum: Option[Int], optStr: Option[String]): Option[String] = {
  for {
    num <- optNum
    str <- optStr
  } yield num.toString + str
}
```

The for-comprehension unwraps the values from the monads, allowing for straightforward and readable combinations. The yield keyword specifies the final value to be wrapped back into the monadic context.

To deeply understand the utility of monads and for-comprehensions, let's explore a more complex example with the Either type, which represents computations that can result in either a value of type L (typically an error) or a value of type R (typically a success).

```
def parseInt(str: String): Either[String, Int] =
  if (str.matches("-?\\d+")) Right(str.toInt)
  else Left(s"Invalid number: $str")

def reciprocal(n: Int): Either[String, Double] =
  if (n != 0) Right(1.0 / n)
  else Left("Division by zero")

def formatDouble(d: Double): Either[String, String] =
  Right(f"$d%.2f")

val result = for {
  num <- parseInt("42")
  rec <- reciprocal(num)
  fmt <- formatDouble(rec)
} yield fmt
```

Here, parseInt, reciprocal, and formatDouble are functions that return Either values. The for-comprehension chains these operations, handling the context automatically.

Executing the above code yields:

Right(0.02)

If any function returns a Left, the computation short-circuits, and the error value propagates. For instance, attempting to parse a non-numeric string:

```
val result = for {
  num <- parseInt("abc")
  rec <- reciprocal(num)
  fmt <- formatDouble(rec)
} yield fmt
```

113

This execution will yield:

Left(Invalid number: abc)

Understanding monads and utilizing for-comprehensions empowers developers to write concise, readable, and maintainable code while efficiently handling complex operations and contexts. This foundation supports robust and scalable functional programming paradigms in Scala.

4.11   Error Handling in Functional Style

In functional programming, error handling is approached differently compared to imperative programming paradigms. The primary objective is to manage errors and exceptions in a way that preserves function purity and referential transparency. Scala, being a hybrid language that supports both functional and object-oriented paradigms, provides several constructs to handle errors functionally. Key types include Option, Either, and Try.

Using Option for Optional Values

The Option type in Scala is a container that may or may not hold a value. It is used to represent optional values that can either be Some(value) or None.

```
def findPerson(id: Int): Option[Person] = {
  val personMap = Map(1 -> Person("Alice"), 2 -> Person("Bob"))
  personMap.get(id)
}

val person1 = findPerson(1) // Some(Person(Alice))
val person3 = findPerson(3) // None
```

By using Option, we ensure that the function does not throw an exception for a missing value. Instead, it returns None, allowing the caller to handle the absence of a value explicitly.

Pattern Matching with Option

Pattern matching is commonly used to extract values from an Option and to handle the None case properly.

```
findPerson(1) match {
  case Some(person) => println(s"Found: ${person.name}")
  case None => println("Person not found")
}
```

This method ensures comprehensive handling of both scenarios – pres-

114

ence and absence of a value.

Using Either for Explicit Error Handling

While Option is useful for optional values, it does not convey error information. The Either type can be employed to propagate and manage errors. An Either is a container that can hold a value of two possible types: Left for an error and Right for a successful result.

```
def divide(a: Int, b: Int): Either[String, Int] = {
  if (b == 0) Left("Division by zero")
  else Right(a / b)
}

val result1 = divide(4, 2) // Right(2)
val result2 = divide(4, 0) // Left("Division by zero")
```

Pattern matching can be utilized to handle each possible case:

```
divide(4, 0) match {
  case Right(value) => println(s"Result: $value")
  case Left(error) => println(s"Error: $error")
}
```

This approach provides clear error information, allowing for more informative and robust error handling.

Using Try for Exception Handling

The Try type is another powerful construct, encapsulating operations that may throw exceptions. It can be either Success or Failure.

```
import scala.util.{Try, Success, Failure}

def parseInt(s: String): Try[Int] = Try(s.toInt)

val success = parseInt("123") // Success(123)
val failure = parseInt("abc") // Failure(java.lang.NumberFormatException)
```

Similar to Option and Either, pattern matching is beneficial for handling Try.

```
parseInt("123") match {
  case Success(value) => println(s"Parsed value: $value")
  case Failure(exception) => println(s"Error: ${exception.getMessage}")
}
```

Monad Transformers for Nested Error Handling

Monad transformers are advanced constructs for combining multiple monadic contexts. They simplify error handling when dealing with nested monads. For example, an Option inside Either can be handled using OptionT.

115

```
import cats.data.OptionT
import cats.implicits._

type Result[A] = Either[String, A]

def findPersonT(id: Int): OptionT[Result, Person] = OptionT.fromOption(findPerson(id
    ))

val combined = for {
  person <- findPersonT(1)
  // Additional computations involving person
} yield person

combined.value match {
  case Right(Some(person)) => println(s"Found: ${person.name}")
  case Right(None) => println("Person not found")
  case Left(error) => println(s"Error: $error")
}
```

Integrating OptionT[Either] simplifies the combination of Option and Either monads, streamlining error propagation and value computation.

Functional Error Handling Best Practices

1. **Avoid Side Effects:** Ensure that error handling does not introduce side effects in functions, maintaining their purity. 2. **Use Declarative Constructs:** Leverage Option, Either, and Try to manage errors declaratively rather than using exceptions. 3. **Pattern Matching:** Utilize pattern matching extensively to handle possible error states systematically. 4. **Monad Transformers:** When dealing with nested monadic structures, use monad transformers to manage complexity and enhance readability.

By embracing these practices, error handling in functional programming can be both robust and elegant, adhering to the principles of immutability and pure functions.

4.12 Functional Design Patterns

Functional design patterns provide a structured approach to solving common problems in functional programming. These patterns leverage the principles of immutability, higher-order functions, and function composition to create robust and reusable code structures. Understanding these patterns is crucial for mastering Scala's functional programming capabilities.

Pattern 1: Function Composition

Function composition allows for the combination of simple functions to build more complex ones. This pattern is fundamental in functional programming and enables the creation of pipelines for data transformation.

Consider two functions, f and g. The composition of these functions is a new function h such that $h(x) = f(g(x))$. In Scala, function composition is facilitated by the andThen and compose methods:

```
val f: Int => Int = _ + 1
val g: Int => Int = _ * 2

val h = f compose g
val k = f andThen g
```

In this example, h will first apply g, then f, while k will first apply f, then g.

Pattern 2: Higher-Order Functions

Higher-order functions are functions that take other functions as arguments or return functions as results. They enable abstracting common patterns into reusable units.

For instance, the map function on collections is a higher-order function:

```
val numbers = List(1, 2, 3, 4)
val doubled = numbers.map(x => x * 2)
```

Here, map takes a function that multiplies each element by 2 and applies it to every element in the list.

Pattern 3: Currying and Partial Application

Currying transforms a function with multiple arguments into a series of functions that each take a single argument. This is useful for creating more specific functions from general ones.

```
def add(a: Int, b: Int): Int = a + b
val addCurried = (add _).curried
val addFive = addCurried(5)
```

Partial application provides a way to fix a few arguments of a function and generate a new function.

```
val addFive = add(5, _:Int)
```

In both examples, addFive is a new function derived from add.

Pattern 4: Lazy Evaluation

Lazy evaluation defers computation until the result is needed. This pattern can improve performance by avoiding unnecessary calculations.

117

Scala supports lazy evaluation with the lazy keyword:

```
lazy val lazyValue = { println("Evaluating..."); 42 }
```

Pattern 5: Immutability

Immutability ensures that once data is created, it cannot be modified. This pattern helps in maintaining consistency and avoiding side effects.

Scala encourages immutability by default, with constructs like val and immutable collections:

```
val x = 10
// x = 20 // This will result in a compilation error

val immutableList = List(1, 2, 3)
// immutableList(0) = 10 // This will result in a compilation error
```

Pattern 6: Monad Transformers

Monads encapsulate computations in a context (like options, lists, or futures). Monad transformers provide a way to combine these contexts.

For example, OptionT is a monad transformer for the Option monad:

```
import cats.data.OptionT
import cats.instances.future._

val futureOption: Future[Option[Int]] = Future.successful(Some(10))
val optionT = OptionT(futureOption)

val result = optionT.map(_ * 2).value
```

Pattern 7: For-Comprehensions

For-comprehensions offer a syntactic sugar for working with monads. They allow for chaining operations in a readable manner.

Instead of nested map and flatMap calls, consider the following example:

```
val result = for {
  x <- Option(10)
  y <- Option(20)
} yield x + y
```

This translates to nested flatMap operations but in a more readable format.

Pattern 8: Pattern Matching

Pattern matching is a powerful feature in Scala for destructuring and analyzing data structures. It is useful for implementing various algorithms succinctly.

```
val result = Option(10) match {
  case Some(value) => value * 2
  case None => 0
}
```

Pattern 9: The Strategy Pattern

In functional programming, the Strategy pattern can be implemented using higher-order functions. This pattern defines a family of algorithms,
encapsulates each one, and makes them interchangeable.

Function1 in Scala can be used to define different strategies:

```
trait Strategy {
  def execute(a: Int, b: Int): Int
}

object AddStrategy extends Strategy {
  def execute(a: Int, b: Int): Int = a + b
}

object MultiplyStrategy extends Strategy {
  def execute(a: Int, b: Int): Int = a * b
}

def performOperation(a: Int, b: Int, strategy: Strategy): Int = strategy.execute(a, b)

performOperation(5, 6, AddStrategy)
```

Another common functional pattern might involve differential and integral calculus or other branches of computational mathematics, oper-
ating in tighter loops or making use of modern machine learning algorithms or reinforcement learning principles to solve problems iteratively.

Further exploration of functional design patterns in Scala involves understanding more advanced concepts such as free monads, applica-
tives, and profunctors. Scala's strong type system and versatile language features make it a powerful tool for implementing these patterns
effectively.

Chapter 5

Object-Oriented Programming in Scala

This chapter examines the object-oriented aspects of Scala, including classes and objects, constructors, inheritance, and method overriding. It also covers traits, mixins, abstract classes, companion objects, case classes, and singleton objects. The chapter further explores encapsulation, access modifiers, polymorphism, and the Scala type system, providing a thorough understanding of OOP principles in Scala.

5.1 Introduction to Object-Oriented Programming

Object-Oriented Programming (OOP) is a programming paradigm that uses objects and classes to create models based on the real world environment. The principles of OOP such as encapsulation, inheritance, and polymorphism offer a structured approach to writing code, which promotes reusability, scalability, and maintainability.

In Scala, OOP principles integrate seamlessly with functional programming concepts, allowing developers to write elegant and efficient code. Scala supports both paradigms, providing the flexibility to choose the approach that best fits the problem at hand.

Classes are the fundamental building blocks in OOP. A class in Scala defines a blueprint for objects, encapsulating data and behaviors. A simple class definition in Scala can be written as:

```scala
class Person(val name: String, val age: Int) {
  def greet() = println(s"Hello, my name is $name and I am $age years old.")
}
```

In this code snippet, the class Person has two attributes, name and age, which are initialized through the primary constructor. The greet method provides a behavior that prints a greeting message.

An instance (or object) of a class can be created with the new keyword:

```scala
val john = new Person("John", 28)
john.greet() // Outputs: Hello, my name is John and I am 28 years old.
```

Objects are instances of classes, carrying both the state (in the form of attributes) and behavior (in the form of methods) defined by their class.

Encapsulation is a principle that relates to restricting access to the internal state of an object, ensuring that it can only be modified through well-defined interfaces. It is often achieved using access modifiers such as private and protected in Scala. For instance:

```scala
class BankAccount(private var balance: Double) {

  def deposit(amount: Double): Unit = {
    if (amount > 0) {
      balance += amount
    }
  }

  def getBalance: Double = balance
}
```

In the above example, the class BankAccount uses the private keyword to restrict access to the balance attribute, ensuring that it can only be modified through the deposit method.

Inheritance allows a class to acquire attributes and methods of another class, promoting reusability. A class that inherits from another class is called a subclass, while the class being inherited from is called a superclass. In Scala, inheritance is indicated using the extends keyword:

```scala
class Employee(name: String, age: Int, val salary: Double) extends Person(name, age) {
  def showSalary() = println(s"My salary is $$salary")
}

val employee = new Employee("Jane", 32, 50000)
employee.greet() // Outputs: Hello, my name is Jane and I am 32 years old.
employee.showSalary() // Outputs: My salary is 50000
```

In this example, Employee class inherits the Person class, thus inheriting its name and age attributes and greet method. Additionally, it introduces a new attribute salary and method showSalary.

Polymorphism refers to the ability of different classes to respond to the same method call in different ways, fostering flexibility and integration. Polymorphism is commonly achieved through method overriding. Method overriding involves redefining a method in a subclass that already exists in the superclass:

```
class Animal {
  def sound() = println("Some generic animal sound")
}

class Dog extends Animal {
  override def sound() = println("Bark")
}

val genericAnimal: Animal = new Dog
genericAnimal.sound() // Outputs: Bark
```

In the example, Dog class overrides the sound method of the Animal class. The method call genericAnimal.sound() at runtime invokes the overridden sound method of the Dog class, demonstrating polymorphic behavior.

Encapsulation, inheritance, and polymorphism are core OOP principles that are supported by Scala, each contributing to building robust, maintainable, and scalable applications. This chapter will further delve into these principles, exploring how they are implemented and used in Scala, along with additional OOP features specific to the language.

5.2 Classes and Objects

In Scala, a class is a blueprint for creating objects. It serves as a template that defines the attributes and behavior that the objects created from it will have. Classes in Scala are declared using the class keyword, followed by an identifier for the class name. The primary constructor for the class is specified by providing parameters directly after the class name.

To declare a class, Scala syntax follows the structure:

```
class ClassName(parameters) {
  // body of the class
  // definition of fields, methods, and constructors
}
```

ClassName represents the name of the class, and parameters are defined within parentheses. The class body includes field declarations, method definitions, and auxiliary constructors if required.

Consider the following example of a simple class in Scala:

```
class Person(val name: String, val age: Int) {
  def greet(): String = s"Hello, my name is $name and I am $age years old."
}
```

In this example, the Person class has two parameters: name and age. The keyword val makes these parameters immutable and creates getter methods automatically. The greet method within the class returns a string that includes the person's name and age.

To create an instance of the class, use the new keyword:

```
val person = new Person("Alice", 25)
println(person.greet())
```

The output of this code will be:

```
Hello, my name is Alice and I am 25 years old.
```

In Scala, objects are single instances of their own definitions. They are defined using the object keyword. Objects serve as a way to create singletons and hold static members. Here is the syntax for defining an object:

```
object ObjectName {
  // body of the object
  // definition of fields and methods
}
```

ObjectName is the identifier for the object. The body of the object can include fields and methods similar to a class. Objects do not take parameters and do not have constructors.

Consider the following example of an object in Scala:

```
object MathUtil {
  def add(x: Int, y: Int): Int = x + y
  def multiply(x: Int, y: Int): Int = x * y
}
```

In this example, the MathUtil object contains two methods: add and multiply. These methods can be accessed directly without creating an instance of the object:

```
val sum = MathUtil.add(3, 4)
println(s"The sum is $sum")
val product = MathUtil.multiply(3, 4)
```

124

```
println(s"The product is $product")
```

The output of this code will be:

```
The sum is 7
The product is 12
```

Classes and objects in Scala can interact closely through companion objects. A companion object is an object with the same name as a class and is defined in the same source file. Companion objects are used to hold methods and fields that are not specific to instances of the class. Here's an example showing the use of a companion object:

```
class Circle(val radius: Double) {
  def area: Double = Circle.PI * radius * radius
}

object Circle {
  val PI = 3.14159
}
```

In this example, the companion object Circle holds a constant value PI, which is used by the Circle class instances to calculate the area of the circle.

```
val circle = new Circle(5.0)
println(f"The area of the circle is ${circle.area}%.2f")
```

The output of this code will be:

```
The area of the circle is 78.54
```

Companion objects are particularly useful for defining factory methods that can create instances of their associated class. The factory method encapsulates the instantiation logic and hides the details from the user. Here's an example:

```
class Rectangle private(val length: Double, val width: Double) {
  def area: Double = length * width
}

object Rectangle {
  def create(length: Double, width: Double): Rectangle = {
    new Rectangle(length, width)
  }
}
```

In this example, the constructor of Rectangle is marked private, preventing direct instantiation from outside the class. The companion object Rectangle provides a factory method create to instantiate Rectangle objects:

```
val rectangle = Rectangle.create(4.0, 5.0)
```

125

```
println(f"The area of the rectangle is ${rectangle.area}%.2f")
```

The output of this code will be:

The area of the rectangle is 20.00

Classes and objects are fundamental components of object-oriented programming in Scala, providing a powerful way to model complex systems and manage state and behavior effectively. Using classes and companion objects judiciously helps maintain cleaner codebases and encapsulates logic appropriately.

5.3 Constructors and Object Initialization

In Scala, constructors are essential for creating and initializing objects. They define how objects of a class are created and allow for the parameterization of new instances. Scala provides a streamlined syntax for defining constructors and multiple mechanisms for object initialization.

Primary constructors in Scala are integrated into the class definition itself. They are defined by specifying parameters within the class declaration. This integration brings about a concise and clear way to define what values an object will hold upon creation. For example, consider the following class definition:

```
class Person(val name: String, val age: Int)
```

In this example, Person has a primary constructor with two parameters, name and age. The val keyword ensures that both name and age are immutable and accessible as fields of the class.

Instantiating this class involves providing arguments for the constructor parameters:

```
val person = new Person("Alice", 30)
```

Upon instantiation, person will hold the values "Alice" and 30, corresponding to its name and age fields respectively.

Additionally, Scala supports the concept of auxiliary constructors, defined using the this keyword. They offer alternative ways to initialize a class and must call the primary constructor either directly or indirectly through other auxiliary constructors. Consider this extension of our Person class:

126

```scala
class Person(val name: String, val age: Int) {
  def this(name: String) = this(name, 0)
  def this() = this("Unknown", 0)
}
```

Here, two auxiliary constructors are defined. The first takes only a name and defaults age to 0. The second takes no parameters and defaults both name and age. Calls to these constructors are demonstrated as follows:

```scala
val person1 = new Person("Bob")
val person2 = new Person()
```

Person1 will have name as "Bob" and age as 0, while Person2 will have name as "Unknown" and age as 0.

Object initialization can involve more than just setting field values. It may include executing arbitrary code, performing validations, and interacting with other components. Scala allows the inclusion of initialization code within the body of the class itself. This code is executed as part of the primary constructor:

```scala
class Person(val name: String, val age: Int) {
  println(s"Creating a person named $name, aged $age")

  require(age >= 0, "Age cannot be negative")
}
```

In this example, a message is printed whenever a Person is instantiated, and a requirement is checked to ensure that the age is non-negative.

Fields and methods can also be defined within the class body. They can reference the constructor parameters or other fields to implement more complex initialization behavior:

```scala
class Person(val name: String, val age: Int) {
  val isAdult = age >= 18

  def greet(): String = s"Hello, my name is $name and I am $age years old."
}
```

In this case, isAdult determines if the person is an adult, based on their age, and greet produces a string introducing the person.

Furthermore, Scala supports default parameter values in constructors, simplifying the initialization process by minimizing the need for auxiliary constructors. Default values are specified directly in the parameter list:

```scala
class Person(val name: String = "Unknown", val age: Int = 0)
```

This allows creating persons with various combinations of provided and default values:

```
val person1 = new Person("Charlie", 25)
val person2 = new Person("Diana")
val person3 = new Person()
```

Person1 will have both a specified name and age, person2 will use the default age, and person3 will use default values for both parameters.

The use of constructors and initialization code in Scala leverages the language's rich syntax and semantic capabilities to provide flexibility and clarity. Through primary and auxiliary constructors, integrated initialization code, and default parameter values, Scala enables concise, expressive, and powerful object creation and initialization mechanisms.

5.4 Inheritance and Method Overriding

Inheritance is a fundamental concept in Scala's object-oriented programming model, where a new class (subclass) is derived from an existing class (superclass). This enables the reuse of existing code and the creation of a hierarchical class structure. The subclass inherits attributes and methods from the superclass, which allows for extending or modifying the inherited functionalities.

To define a subclass in Scala, the extends keyword is used. Here is an example where a basic class Animal is extended by a subclass Dog:

```
class Animal {
  def makeSound(): Unit = {
    println("Animal makes a sound")
  }
}

class Dog extends Animal {
  override def makeSound(): Unit = {
    println("Dog barks")
  }
}
```

In this example, the Dog class inherits the makeSound method from the Animal class. However, the Dog class overrides this method to provide its specific behavior. The override keyword is used to explicitly indicate that a method is being overridden in the subclass.

When an instance of the subclass calls the overridden method, it executes the method defined in the subclass:

```
val myDog = new Dog()
myDog.makeSound()
```

Dog barks

This demonstrates polymorphism, where the method implementation that is executed depends on the object's runtime type, not the declared type.

Scala also supports calling the superclass method from the subclass method. This can be achieved using the super keyword:

```
class Dog extends Animal {
  override def makeSound(): Unit = {
    super.makeSound()
    println("Dog barks")
  }
}
```

In this example, the super.makeSound() call will execute the makeSound method defined in the Animal class before performing additional operations specific to the Dog class.

```
val anotherDog = new Dog()
anotherDog.makeSound()
```

Animal makes a sound
Dog barks

Inheritance in Scala is further enhanced by abstract classes and traits. An abstract class is intended to be inherited by other classes and cannot be instantiated on its own. It may contain abstract methods, which are declared without an implementation. Subclasses of the abstract class must provide implementations for these methods.

Here is an example of an abstract class:

```
abstract class Animal {
  def makeSound(): Unit
}

class Dog extends Animal {
  override def makeSound(): Unit = {
    println("Dog barks")
  }
}
```

In this case, the Animal class contains an abstract method makeSound. The Dog class extends Animal and provides an implementation for the makeSound method.

Traits in Scala are similar to interfaces in other programming languages but with richer capabilities. Traits can contain concrete methods and fields in addition to abstract methods. A class can extend multiple traits, allowing for a mixin composition.

Here is an example of using traits:

```
trait Animal {
  def makeSound(): Unit
}

trait Pet {
  def play(): Unit = {
    println("Pet is playing")
  }
}

class Dog extends Animal with Pet {
  override def makeSound(): Unit = {
    println("Dog barks")
  }
}
```

In this example, the Dog class extends both the Animal trait and the Pet trait. The makeSound method is implemented in the Dog class, and the play method from the Pet trait can be used as-is without modification.

```
val petDog = new Dog()
petDog.makeSound()
petDog.play()
```

```
Dog barks
Pet is playing
```

Method overriding combined with inheritance allows for creating flexible and reusable components in object-oriented design. By effectively using these features, developers can build complex systems with a clear and maintainable class hierarchy.

5.5   Traits and Mixins

In Scala, traits are a fundamental unit of code reuse and modularity. They are akin to interfaces in Java but provide much more functionality. Traits can contain both abstract and concrete methods, enabling a high degree of flexibility in defining and mixing in behavior. This section delves into the syntax, usage, and best practices for using traits and mixins in Scala, ensuring a comprehensive understanding of these concepts.

A trait is defined using the trait keyword:

```
trait Logger {
  def log(message: String): Unit
}
```

Here, Logger is a trait with an abstract method log. Any class or object that wants to use the Logger trait must provide an implementation for the log method. However, traits can also contain concrete methods. This allows traits to provide default behavior:

```
trait ConsoleLogger extends Logger {
  def log(message: String): Unit = {
    println(message)
  }
}
```

In this example, the ConsoleLogger trait extends Logger and provides a concrete implementation for the log method. Any class that mixes in the ConsoleLogger trait will inherit this implementation.

Classes can mix in multiple traits, allowing for the composition of behaviors:

```
class BankAccount extends Logger with ConsoleLogger {
  private var balance: Double = 0.0

  def deposit(amount: Double): Unit = {
    balance += amount
    log(s"Deposited $amount, new balance is $balance")
  }

  def withdraw(amount: Double): Unit = {
    if (amount > balance) log(s"Insufficient funds: $balance")
    else {
      balance -= amount
      log(s"Withdrew $amount, new balance is $balance")
    }
  }
}
```

In this scenario, the BankAccount class mixes in the Logger and ConsoleLogger traits. This allows BankAccount to log messages using the ConsoleLogger's implementation of the log method.

Mixins allow us to decouple behavior from the class hierarchy, promoting code reuse and modularity. Scala's type system ensures that methods defined in traits are properly implemented:

```
trait TimestampLogger extends Logger {
  abstract override def log(message: String): Unit = {
    super.log(s"${java.time.Instant.now}: $message")
  }
}
```

131

The TimestampLogger trait uses abstract override to modify the behavior of the log method. This requires the trait to be mixed into a class (or another trait) that already provides a concrete implementation of log:

```
class SavingsAccount extends BankAccount with TimestampLogger

val account = new SavingsAccount
account.deposit(100)
```

In this configuration, the TimestampLogger modifies the behavior of the log method in ConsoleLogger, adding a timestamp to the logged messages.

Traits can also be mixed into objects, not just classes. This enables a flexible and modular design:

```
object Application extends App with Logger with ConsoleLogger {
  log("Application has started")
}
```

The Application object mixes in Logger and ConsoleLogger, allowing it to log messages to the console at startup.

Traits can specify more complex behavior by combining multiple traits:

```
trait FileLogger extends Logger {
  val fileName: String
  lazy val out = new java.io.PrintWriter(new java.io.FileWriter(fileName, true))

  def log(message: String): Unit = {
    out.println(message)
    out.flush()
  }
}

class BalanceNotifier extends BankAccount with FileLogger {
  val fileName = "balance_log.txt"

  override def deposit(amount: Double): Unit = {
    super.deposit(amount)
    if (amount > 5000) log(s"Large deposit: $amount")
  }
}
```

In this example, the BalanceNotifier class extends BankAccount and mixes in FileLogger, which logs messages to a specified file. The deposit method is overridden to log a message for large deposits.

Traits serve as a powerful mechanism for creating modular and reusable components. By combining multiple traits, developers can build flexible and easily maintainable systems. Understanding and effectively utilizing traits and mixins is essential for mastering Scala's object-oriented programming capabilities.

5.6 Abstract Classes

Abstract classes in Scala are a fundamental concept, providing a means to define classes that cannot be instantiated directly but can serve as blueprints for other classes. An abstract class can contain abstract members, which are declared but lack an implementation. Subclasses are responsible for implementing these abstract members. This attribute allows abstract classes to define methods, fields, and properties that must be implemented by concrete subclasses, thereby enforcing a contract.

To declare an abstract class in Scala, the abstract keyword is used before the class keyword. For example:

```scala
abstract class Animal {
  def makeSound(). Unit // Abstract method
  def sleep() : Unit = { // Non-abstract method
    println("Slooping")
  }
}
```

In the above example, Animal is an abstract class with one abstract method, makeSound(), and one concrete method, sleep(). The abstract method makeSound() does not have an implementation, requiring any non-abstract subclass to provide one.

When defining a subclass of an abstract class, you must instantiate and provide concrete implementations for all abstract members. Consider the subclass Dog, which extends the abstract class Animal:

```scala
class Dog extends Animal {
  def makeSound(): Unit = {
    println("Bark")
  }
}
```

Here, Dog provides an implementation of the makeSound() method. It's crucial to note that failing to define the abstract members in a subclass will result in a compilation error. Instantiating the subclass would look like this:

```scala
val myDog = new Dog()
myDog.makeSound() // Outputs: Bark
myDog.sleep() // Outputs: Sleeping
```

In practice, abstract classes are utilized when you want to provide some common behavior while enforcing specific methods to be defined in subclasses. This allows a fine-grained control over the structure and

133

behavior of inherited classes.

Abstract classes can also contain fields. These fields can be abstract (without initialization) or non-abstract (with initialization). For instance:

```
abstract class Vehicle {
  val vehicleType: String // Abstract field
  def startEngine(): Unit
}
```

Any subclass extending Vehicle needs to provide a value for vehicle-Type and an implementation for startEngine().

```
class Car extends Vehicle {
  val vehicleType: String = "Car"
  def startEngine(): Unit = {
    println("Engine started")
  }
}
```

Now, an instance of Car can be created and used:

```
val myCar = new Car()
println(myCar.vehicleType) // Outputs: Car
myCar.startEngine() // Outputs: Engine started
```

It is essential to understand the distinction between abstract classes and traits in Scala. While both can be used to define abstract members and share common behavior across different classes, abstract classes can have constructor parameters, whereas traits cannot. Consider an abstract class with a constructor parameter:

```
abstract class Appliance(val brand: String) {
  def turnOn(): Unit
}
```

A subclass must call the constructor of the abstract class:

```
class WashingMachine(brand: String) extends Appliance(brand) {
  def turnOn(): Unit = {
    println(s"Turning on the $brand washing machine.")
  }
}
```

The instantiation and usage would be as follows:

```
val myWashingMachine = new WashingMachine("LG")
myWashingMachine.turnOn() // Outputs: Turning on the LG washing machine.
```

By defining abstract classes, developers ensure that certain structures and behaviors must be followed, while still allowing flexibility for unique implementations in derived classes. This adherence to a specified

134

contract leads to structured and robust code, facilitating better maintenance and scalability within larger projects.

5.7 Companion Objects

In Scala, for every class, there can exist an object with the same name as the class. This object is known as the companion object. Both the class and the companion object must be defined within the same source file. The relationship between a class and its companion object enhances Scala's capability to blend object-oriented and functional programming features seamlessly.

A companion object acts as a holder for methods and values that are not associated with individual instances of the class. Such methods and values are usually referred to as static members in other programming languages like Java. However, Scala does not have static members; the companion object provides this functionality.

The basic syntax for defining a companion object in Scala is as follows:

```scala
class MyClass {
  // Instance-level methods and fields
  var instanceField: Int = 0
  def instanceMethod(): Unit = {
    println("This is an instance method.")
  }
}

object MyClass {
  // Companion object-level methods and fields
  val staticField: String = "Companion Object Field"
  def staticMethod(): Unit = {
    println("This is a companion object method.")
  }
}
```

Here, the MyClass object is the companion object of the MyClass class. It can access the private fields and methods of its companion class. Conversely, the class can also access the private members of the companion object.

Creating Instances:

Companion objects are often used to provide factory methods for their companion classes. A factory method is a function that creates and returns instances of the companion class. This approach is preferred over direct calls to the class constructor in certain contexts, as it enhances readability and control over instance creation.

```scala
class Person private (val name: String, val age: Int)

object Person {
  def create(name: String, age: Int): Person = {
    new Person(name, age)
  }

  def apply(name: String, age: Int): Person = {
    new Person(name, age)
  }
}
```

The apply method is a special method in Scala that facilitates an elegant way to create objects. With the apply method defined in the companion object, you can create an instance without explicitly calling the new keyword:

```scala
val john = Person("John", 30)
```

This line implicitly invokes the apply method within the Person object, returning an instance of Person.

Single Responsibility with Companion Objects:

Separation of concerns can be achieved by using companion objects to encapsulate logic that doesn't pertain to a specific instance of the class. Companion objects serve as a great place to keep utility functions, constants, or even configuration parameters.

```scala
class DatabaseConnector {
  def connect(): Unit = {
    println(s"Connecting to database at ${DatabaseConnector.DB_URL}")
  }
}
object DatabaseConnector {
  val DB_URL: String = "jdbc:mysql://localhost:3306/mydb"
}
```

Access Modifiers and Companion Objects:

Companion objects have privileged access to private members of the companion class and vice versa. This feature provides a refined scope for defining methods and variables that should not be exposed publicly yet need to be shared between the instance-level and object-level code.

```scala
class Counter private (private var value: Int) {
  def increment(): Unit = {
    value += 1
  }

  def current: Int = value
}
```

136

```
object Counter {
  def create(initialValue: Int): Counter = {
    new Counter(initialValue)
  }
}
```

In this example, the constructor of the Counter class is marked as private, meaning no external code can directly instantiate a Counter object. Instead, instances must be created through the create method in the companion object. This encapsulation pattern enforces control over object creation.

Companion Objects for Pattern Matching:

Case classes leverage companion objects for pattern matching. A case class automatically generates an implementation of the apply method in its companion object, along with an unapply method, which enables convenient pattern matching.

```
case class User(name: String, age: Int)

val user: User = User("Alice", 25)

user match {
  case User(userName, userAge) =>
    println(s"User name: $userName, age: $userAge")
}
```

In this code snippet, the case User(userName, userAge) pattern is supported by the unapply method in the companion object of the User case class. The unapply method decomposes the User object into its constituent fields, making them accessible in the pattern's body.

Understanding and utilizing companion objects is fundamental to mastering Scala's dual paradigm. They not only provide a bridge between object-oriented and functional programming but also enable better code organization, encapsulation, and utility.

5.8 Case Classes and Pattern Matching

Case classes in Scala are an integral part of the language's functional programming capabilities. They provide a succinct and expressive syntax for defining immutable data structures. A case class is a regular class with additional functionality that enables pattern matching, which is a powerful feature for decomposing data structures.

Defining Case Classes

137

Case classes are defined using the case class keyword followed by the class name and parameters inside parentheses. These parameters become fields of the class and are accessible using the . operator. For example:

```
case class Person(name: String, age: Int)
```

This definition creates a class Person with name and age as fields. Instances of Person can be created without the new keyword:

```
val person1 = Person("Alice", 30)
val person2 = Person("Bob", 25)
```

Automatic Implementations

Case classes provide several automatic implementations:

- **Apply method**: A companion object is automatically created with an apply method, which allows instantiation without the new keyword.

- **Accessors**: Fields are automatically public and accessible.

- **Immutable Fields**: Fields are val by default, ensuring immutability.

- **Equality and Hashing**: equals and hashCode methods are implemented based on the values of fields.

- **String Representation**: A toString method is provided, which returns a string representation of the case class.

- **Copy Method**: A copy method is available for creating modified copies of instances.

Consider the following example that leverages some automatic features:

```
val person1 = Person("Alice", 30)
val personCopy = person1.copy(age = 31)
println(person1) // Output: Person(Alice,30)
println(personCopy) // Output: Person(Alice,31)
```

Pattern Matching

One of the most significant advantages of case classes is their integration with pattern matching. Pattern matching provides a clean and concise way to decompose data structures, making it easier to work with complex data types.

138

A pattern match is initiated using the match keyword followed by case statements. Each case statement is a pattern that is checked against the value. If the value fits the pattern, the corresponding block of code is executed.

Here is an example using the Person case class:

```
def greet(person: Person): String = person match {
  case Person("Alice", 30) => "Hello, Alice! How's it going at 30?"
  case Person(name, age) => s"Hello, $name! You're $age years old."
}

val greeting = greet(Person("Alice", 30))
println(greeting) // Output: Hello, Alice! How's it going at 30?
```

Nested Pattern Matching

Pattern matching can also be performed on nested case classes, allowing for deep decomposition of data structures. Consider the following scenario with nested case classes:

```
case class Address(city: String, state: String)
case class Company(name: String, address: Address)

val company = Company("Tech Corp", Address("San Francisco", "CA"))

company match {
  case Company("Tech Corp", Address(city, "CA")) => println(s"Located in California
    city: $city")
  case Company(name, address) => println(s"Company: $name, Address: $address")
}
```

Sealed Classes and Exhaustive Checking

When case classes are used with sealed classes, the compiler ensures that all possible cases are covered in a pattern match, providing exhaustive checking at compile-time.

```
sealed trait Result
case class Success(data: String) extends Result
case class Failure(error: String) extends Result

def process(result: Result): String = result match {
  case Success(data) => s"Success with data: $data"
  case Failure(err) => s"Failure with error: $err"
}
```

If an additional Result implementation is added and not handled in process, the compiler will generate a warning or error, ensuring completeness and safety.

Case classes and pattern matching are powerful constructs that enhance the expressiveness and safety of Scala programs, allowing for concise and reliable data manipulation.

139

5.9   Singleton Objects and Utility Classes

Scala provides a robust and unique mechanism for creating single-instance objects, termed as *singleton objects*. A singleton object is declared using the object keyword. Unlike classes, which require instantiation, there is only one instance of a singleton object throughout the runtime of an application. This characteristic makes singleton objects particularly useful for utility classes, factories, and when defining constants.

To declare a singleton object in Scala, use the following syntax:

```
object SingletonExample {
  // Singleton object body
  def greet(): Unit = {
    println("Hello from Singleton Example")
  }
}
```

In this example, SingletonExample is a singleton object with a single method greet. This method can be accessed directly by the name of the object:

```
SingletonExample.greet()
```

Executing the above line will produce the output:

```
Hello from Singleton Example
```

Utility Classes

Utility classes in Scala often employ singleton objects. These classes encapsulate helper methods, constants, and functionality that are not tied to instance-specific data. A common scenario involves mathematical calculations:

```
object MathUtils {
  def add(x: Int, y: Int): Int = x + y

  def subtract(x: Int, y: Int): Int = x - y

  def factorial(n: Int): Int = {
    if (n <= 1) 1
    else n * factorial(n - 1)
  }
}
```

This MathUtils object defines a collection of static-like methods, which can be invoked without needing to instantiate the object:

```
val sum = MathUtils.add(5, 3) // sum holds value 8
```

```
val difference = MathUtils.subtract(10, 4) // difference holds value 6
val fact = MathUtils.factorial(5) // fact holds value 120
```

The outputs will include:

```
sum = 8
difference = 6
fact = 120
```

Singletons and Companion Objects

In Scala, a singleton object that shares the same name with a class is called a *companion object*. Companion objects are legally in the same source file as the class they accompany, and both the class and its companion object can access each other's private members. This symbiotic relationship is advantageous for designing complex systems with both instance specific and global behaviors.

```
class Circle(val radius: Double) {
  import Circle._
  def area: Double = Pi * radius * radius // Accessing private member of companion
     object
}

object Circle {
  private val Pi = 3.14159

  def apply(radius: Double): Circle = new Circle(radius) // Factory method
}
```

The Circle class calculates the area of a circle, and it leverages the Pi constant defined in the companion object. The companion object also provides a factory method (apply) for creating instances of Circle:

```
val myCircle = Circle(5.0)
val circleArea = myCircle.area // circleArea holds value 78.53975
```

```
circleArea = 78.53975
```

Companion objects are also beneficial for implementing the Factory Method pattern, as demonstrated. The apply method is a common idiom in Scala for object creation, streamlining client code:

```
val anotherCircle = Circle.apply(4.0)
```

This is functionally identical to Circle(5.0) due to the apply method's shorthand syntax.

Singleton Object Patterns

Several design patterns utilize singleton objects effectively, such as:

- **Factory Method**: Simplifies object creation while hiding the in-

141

stantiation logic.

- **Object Pool**: Manages a pool of reusable objects to minimize expensive resource allocation.

- **Service Locator**: Provides a centralized registry for obtaining service instances.

In summary, as the concept of singleton objects and utility classes blend together in Scala, the power of the language's OOP capabilities is fully leveraged, providing elegant and efficient solutions for various programming paradigms.

5.10   Encapsulation and Access Modifiers

Encapsulation is a fundamental concept in object-oriented programming that refers to the bundling of data with the methods that operate on that data, or the restricting of direct access to some of an object's components. This mechanism is used to hide the internal representation, or state, of an object from the outside. Only the object's methods are allowed to access or modify its fields. This leads to a clear separation of the object's abstract properties and its implementation details.

In Scala, encapsulation is achieved using access modifiers: private, protected, and public. By default, the members of a class (fields and methods) have public access, meaning they are accessible from outside the object.

private members are only accessible within the class and the companion object. This restriction ensures that the data can only be manipulated through the methods defined within the class, providing control over the access and modification of the internal state.

protected members are accessible within the class, companion object, and subclasses. Unlike private, this modifier allows subclasses to have access to certain parts of the parent class's implementation, promoting inheritance and reuse of code while still maintaining some level of encapsulation.

The following Scala code illustrates the use of access modifiers to enforce encapsulation:

```
class BankAccount {
  private var balance: Double = 0.0
```

```scala
  def deposit(amount: Double): Unit = {
    if (amount > 0) balance += amount
  }

  def withdraw(amount: Double): Boolean = {
    if (amount > 0 && amount <= balance) {
      balance -= amount
      true
    } else {
      false
    }
  }

  def getBalance: Double = balance
}
```

In the BankAccount class above, the balance field is private. This means that balance cannot be accessed or modified directly from outside the class. The methods deposit, withdraw, and getBalance provide controlled access to modify and view the balance.

In addition to private and protected, Scala offers fine-grained control over accessibility using qualified access modifiers. These modifiers can restrict access to members to a specific named package, class, or object. For example:

```scala
class Outer {
  private[Outer] val outerField = "Hello"

  class Inner {
    def printOuterField(): Unit = {
      println(outerField) // Accessible within Outer
    }
  }
}
```

In this example, outerField is accessible within the Outer class and its inner classes due to the private[Outer] modifier.

Encapsulation is further facilitated by combining classes with companion objects. In Scala, a companion object is an object with the same name as a class, defined in the same file. These companion objects can access the private members of the corresponding class:

```scala
class Person(private var name: String, private var age: Int)

object Person {
  def create(name: String, age: Int): Person = {
    new Person(name, age)
  }

  def ageDifference(p1: Person, p2: Person): Int = {
    p1.age - p2.age
  }
}
```

The Person companion object can directly access the private fields name and age of the Person class, facilitating the creation and manipulation of Person instances while keeping the fields encapsulated.

Encapsulation and access modifiers not only protect the integrity of the data by preventing unintended interference but also enhance the modularity and readability of the code. They provide a clear external interface for interacting with objects, promoting safe and predictable modifications.

5.11 Polymorphism and Dynamic Binding

Polymorphism is a fundamental aspect of object-oriented programming (OOP) that allows objects to be treated as instances of their parent class rather than their actual class. It enables a single interface to represent different underlying forms (data types). In Scala, polymorphism is primarily achieved through method overriding and subtype polymorphism.

Dynamic binding, on the other hand, is the process by which the method to be executed in response to a method call is determined at runtime based on the object's actual class rather than the type of the reference that points to it. Dynamic binding is often called late binding because the method resolution happens at a late stage, i.e., during the execution of the program.

To deepen our understanding, let us consider a series of examples that illustrate these concepts.

```scala
abstract class Animal {
  def makeSound(): String
}

class Dog extends Animal {
  override def makeSound(): String = "Woof"
}

class Cat extends Animal {
  override def makeSound(): String = "Meow"
}
```

In this example, Animal is an abstract class with an abstract method makeSound. The Dog and Cat classes both extend the Animal class and provide concrete implementations of the makeSound method. With polymorphism, we can treat objects of Dog and Cat as instances of Animal and invoke their respective makeSound methods.

```
val animals: List[Animal] = List(new Dog, new Cat)

for (animal <- animals) {
  println(animal.makeSound())
}
```

```
Woof
Meow
```

This results in the expected output where the actual method implementations in the Dog and Cat classes are executed.

Dynamic binding ensures that the correct makeSound method is called for each object in the animals list, even though they are all referenced as instances of the Animal class. This mechanism is crucial for achieving runtime polymorphism.

We now introduce the notion of parametric polymorphism, another form of polymorphism in Scala, commonly known as generics. It allows the definition of generic classes and methods that can operate on any type specified by the client code.

Consider the following example, which defines a generic class:

```
class Container[T](value: T) {
  def getValue: T = value
}

val intContainer = new Container[Int](42)
val stringContainer = new Container[String]("Scala")

println(intContainer.getValue)
println(stringContainer.getValue)
```

```
42
Scala
```

Here, the Container class is defined with a type parameter T. This allows for the creation of Container instances that can hold values of different types, demonstrating the power and flexibility of parametric polymorphism.

Another important concept related to polymorphism is the use of implicit conversions and implicit parameters in Scala to achieve ad-hoc polymorphism, also known as type classes. Type classes allow us to define behavior for various types without altering their definitions.

We can utilize Scala's implicit mechanism to achieve this:

```
trait Printable[T] {
  def format(value: T): String
}
```

```
implicit val intPrintable: Printable[Int] = new Printable[Int] {
  def format(value: Int): String = s"Int: $value"
}

implicit val stringPrintable: Printable[String] = new Printable[String] {
  def format(value: String): String = s"String: $value"
}

def print[T](value: T)(implicit p: Printable[T]): Unit = {
  println(p.format(value))
}

print(42)
print("Scala")
```

```
Int: 42
String: Scala
```

The Printable trait defines a type class for formatting values. We then provide implicit instances for Int and String. The print function leverages these implicit instances to format and print values, achieving ad-hoc polymorphism where the same function operates differently based on the provided type class instance.

Through these examples, we observe how polymorphism in Scala can be achieved using various techniques—from method overriding, type generics to type classes. Dynamic binding ensures that the correct methods execute at runtime, enabling flexible and robust software design.

5.12   The Scala Type System

Scala's type system is a critical aspect that allows developers to define and manipulate different kinds of types and their relationships. The type system enhances the language's robustness, enabling static type checking, which helps prevent many errors at compile-time rather than at run-time. Here we delve into the intricacies of the Scala type system, exploring type hierarchies, variance, type inference, and more.

Scala employs a rich type hierarchy rooted in the Any type, which is the supertype of all types. At the other end of the spectrum is the Nothing type, the subtype of all types. This setup facilitates a unified handling of different data types. The fundamental built-in types include Any, AnyVal, AnyRef, Unit, Null, and Nothing.

- Any: The root of the Scala type system, encompassing all types.

- AnyVal: The parent class of all value types like Int, Double,

146

Boolean, etc.

- AnyRef: The parent class of all reference types, equivalent to java.lang.Object in Java.

- Unit: Corresponds to void in Java and has a single value (), representing no meaningful value.

- Null: Subtype of all reference types and has a single value null.

- Nothing: Subtype of all types, used to denote abnormal termination or absence of a value.

Scala employs both nominal and structural typing. Nominal typing relates to named definitions and explicit declarations, ensuring that an instance of a class is compatible with its type hierarchy. Structural typing, on the other hand, relies on the presence of specific methods or properties, aligning with duck typing principles

Type Variance in Scala pertains to how subtyping between complex types relates to subtyping between their components. Variance annotations in Scala are:

- Covariance (+T): Covariant type allows a type parameter to maintain the subtyping relationship. Example: If Dog is a subtype of Animal, then List[Dog] is a subtype of List[Animal]. Indicated by +.

- Contravariance (-T): Contravariant type inverts the subtyping relationship. Example: If Trainer[Animal] can train any animal, Trainer[Dog] can also be a type of trainer. Indicated by -.

- Invariant (T): Invariant type does not participate in subtyping.

A common scenario where variance is crucial is in collection types. Consider the following Scala collection example:

```
class Animal
class Dog extends Animal

// Covariant List
val dogList: List[Dog] = List(new Dog)
val animalList: List[Animal] = dogList // List[Dog] is a List[Animal]
```

Scala also supports higher-kinded types, allowing the definition of abstract type constructors. A higher-kinded type is a type that takes types as arguments. This is pivotal in functional programming paradigms, as seen in Monads and other constructs.

Type Bounds in Scala specify constraints on type parameters, providing more control over generics. The bounds are:

- Upper Bound (<:): Ensures that a type is a subtype of another. For instance: [T <: Animal].

- Lower Bound (>:): Ensures that a type is a supertype of another. For instance: [T >: Dog].

Here is an example demonstrating type bounds:

```
class Animal
class Dog extends Animal

class Cage[T <: Animal](val animal: T)

val dogCage = new Cage(new Dog) // Allowed: Dog <: Animal
// val stringCage = new Cage("string") // Compilation error: String is not a subtype
     of Animal
```

Type Inference in Scala is quite advanced, reducing the need for explicit type annotations. The compiler infers types based on the code context. For instance:

```
// Compiler infers x as Int
val x = 10

// Compiler infers function return type as Int
def add(a: Int, b: Int) = a + b
```

The type inference mechanism handles many tasks automatically but allows for explicit type annotations when necessary to ensure clarity or handle more complex type scenarios.

Path-dependent Types in Scala are tied to instances rather than classes. This characteristic allows a precise type association with the specific object rather than the generic class blueprint. Consider the following example:

```
class Outer {
  class Inner
}

// Different instances lead to different types
val outer1 = new Outer
val inner1: outer1.Inner = new outer1.Inner

val outer2 = new Outer
// Different outer instance means different Inner type
// val inner2: outer1.Inner = new outer2.Inner // Compilation error
```

Type aliases in Scala allow the creation of synonyms for types, improving code readability and manageability. Usage example:

```
type StringList = List[String]

val names: StringList = List("Alice", "Bob", "Charlie")
```

Type members in Scala enable defining new types within the scope of existing classes or traits, thus encapsulating type definitions:

```
class Outer {
  type InnerType = String
  val innerValue: InnerType = "Hello, World!"
}
```

These features collectively demonstrate the versatility and strength of the Scala type system. The integration of advanced type operations, along with the ability to leverage both functional and object-oriented paradigms, positions Scala as a powerful language for a wide range of applications.

Chapter 6

Concurrency in Scala

This chapter provides a comprehensive overview of concurrency in Scala. It covers threads and the JVM, futures and promises, asynchronous programming, and error handling in concurrent code. Additionally, the chapter discusses parallel collections, the Actors model with Akka, actor lifecycle management, and best practices for writing concurrent programs. These concepts are essential for building efficient and scalable applications.

6.1   Introduction to Concurrency

Concurrency is a fundamental concept in modern software development, especially in terms of optimization and efficiency. As applications grow increasingly complex and demand higher performance, understanding concurrency becomes essential for developers to write scalable and responsive code. This section lays the groundwork by introducing key principles and explaining the significance of concurrency in Scala.

Concurrency refers to the ability of a system to manage multiple tasks simultaneously. This does not necessarily mean parallel execution on multiple CPUs or cores; rather, it allows for the interleaving of tasks, so that long operations do not block the progress of shorter ones. Concurrent programming aims to improve the responsiveness and performance of applications.

A fundamental aspect of concurrency is the distinction between concurrent and parallel programming. While both deal with running multiple tasks at once, they have different objectives:

- **Concurrent Programming:** Deals with multiple tasks making progress without waiting for the other tasks to finish. The focus is on managing multiple tasks that can be interleaved on a single processor or CPU.

- **Parallel Programming:** Involves executing multiple tasks simultaneously on different processors or CPU cores. The enhancement in performance comes from true simultaneous execution.

Scala offers a robust ecosystem for concurrent programming, leveraging both the underlying Java Virtual Machine (JVM) capabilities and its own high-level abstractions. Understanding the JVM's role is crucial, as Scala's concurrency model builds upon Java's thread model.

Threads and the JVM:

Threads are the fundamental units of execution in most concurrency models, including that of the JVM. A Thread is a lightweight subprocess, each having a separate execution path but sharing the same memory space. This facilitates communication between threads but also introduces risks of issues such as race conditions and deadlocks.

In Java, a thread can be created by either extending the Thread class or implementing the Runnable interface. Scala, being interoperable with Java, inherits these mechanisms for thread creation and management. However, Scala also provides more advanced abstractions like Future, Promise, and the Actor model (which will be discussed later in this chapter).

An example of creating and starting a thread in Scala using the Runnable interface:

```scala
object ThreadExample extends App {
  val runnable = new Runnable {
    def run(): Unit = {
      println("Running in a separate thread")
    }
  }

  val thread = new Thread(runnable)
  thread.start()
}
```

The utility of concurrent programming often emerges from the ability to manage long-running tasks effectively. For example, network operations, I/O operations, and heavy computations can be offloaded to separate threads, ensuring that the main application thread remains responsive.

Challenges in Concurrent Programming:

Despite its benefits, concurrent programming introduces complexity. Key challenges include:

- **Race Conditions:** Occurs when multiple threads access shared data simultaneously and the outcome depends on the non-deterministic order of execution.

- **Deadlocks:** Arises when two or more threads are blocked forever, each waiting for the other to release a resource.

- **Thread Starvation:** Happens when lower-priority threads are never executed because higher-priority threads monopolize the CPU.

- **Data Consistency:** Ensuring that shared data remains consistent across multiple threads requires careful use of synchronization mechanisms.

Synchronization:

To manage these challenges, synchronization is employed to control the access to shared resources. Java provides synchronized methods and blocks, which can be directly used in Scala. For instance:

```scala
class Counter {
  private var count = 0

  def increment(): Unit = synchronized {
    count += 1
  }

  def getCount: Int = count
}
```

Here, the synchronized block ensures that only one thread can execute the increment() method at a time, preventing race conditions.

Advanced Scala Concurrency Primitives:

Beyond basic thread manipulation, Scala introduces higher-level concurrency primitives:

- Future: Represents a computation that may not yet have completed, and allows for non-blocking retrieval of its result.

- Promise: Complements Future by providing a writable handle for the future value.

- Akka Actor Model: A powerful model for building concurrent applications, based on the concept of lightweight actors that communicate through asynchronous message passing.

These abstractions not only simplify concurrent programming in Scala but also enhance code readability and maintainability.

Concurrency in Scala leverages the strengths of the JVM while offering advanced abstractions to manage complexity and improve developer productivity. This foundational knowledge is critical as we move forward to explore more specific models and tools available in Scala for concurrent programming.

6.2 Threads and the JVM

Concurrency in Scala is deeply rooted in the capabilities provided by the underlying Java Virtual Machine (JVM). Understanding how threads operate within the JVM is crucial for leveraging Scala's concurrency features effectively. This section delves into the basics of threads, the Java memory model, and synchronization mechanisms that the JVM offers.

Basics of Threads

A thread in programming is the smallest unit of execution within a process. The JVM allows multiple threads to run concurrently within a single process. In Scala (as well as in Java), threads are instances of the Thread class or implement the Runnable interface.

Creating a thread in Scala can be achieved using the following approaches:

```
object SimpleThreadExample extends App {
  val thread = new Thread(new Runnable {
    def run(): Unit = {
      println("Hello from the thread!")
    }
  })
  thread.start()
}
```

In this example, a new thread is created by passing an anonymous instance of Runnable to the Thread constructor, and the run method is

154

overridden to specify the thread's task.

Java Memory Model

Concurrency can lead to scenarios where multiple threads access and modify shared data. Without proper synchronization, threads might not see the latest values of shared variables, leading to inconsistent states, also known as race conditions. The Java Memory Model (JMM) outlines how threads interact through memory and ensures visibility and ordering guarantees for shared variables.

The JMM introduces the concepts of happens-before relationships. A happens-before relationship between two actions ensures that memory writes by the first action are visible to the second. The principal rules include:

- Program Order Rule: Each action in a single thread happens-before every action that comes after it.

- Monitor Lock Rule: An unlock on a monitor lock happens-before every subsequent lock on that same monitor.

- Volatile Variable Rule: A write to a volatile field happens-before every subsequent read of that same field.

- Thread Start Rule: A call to Thread.start on a thread happens-before any action in the started thread.

- Thread Termination Rule: Any action in a thread happens-before another thread detects that the thread has terminated.

Synchronization Mechanisms

To avoid issues like race conditions, the JVM provides several synchronization mechanisms:

- Synchronized Blocks: Ensure that only one thread can execute a block of code at a time. Synchronized blocks are defined using the synchronized keyword.

```
object SynchronizedExample {
  private var counter = 0

  def increment(): Unit = synchronized {
    counter += 1
  }

  def getCounter: Int = synchronized {
```

```
    counter
  }
}
```

In this example, both increment and getCounter methods are synchronized, ensuring atomic access.

- Volatile Variables: volatile keyword ensures that a variable's value is always read from and written to the main memory. This prevents caching issues and makes changes visible to all threads.

```
object VolatileExample extends App {
  @volatile private var running = true

  val thread = new Thread(new Runnable {
    def run(): Unit = {
      while (running) {
        println("Thread is running")
        Thread.sleep(1000)
      }
      println("Thread stopped")
    }
  })

  thread.start()
  Thread.sleep(3000)
  running = false
}
```

Here, running is a volatile variable, ensuring any modification is visible to all threads.

- Locks and Condition Variables: Java provides explicit lock and condition variables in the java.util.concurrent.locks package. This allows more sophisticated thread coordination compared to synchronized blocks.

```
import java.util.concurrent.locks.{ReentrantLock, Condition}

object LockExample {

  private val lock = new ReentrantLock()
  private val condition: Condition = lock.newCondition()
  private var isReady = false

  def await(): Unit = {
    lock.lock()
    try {
      while (!isReady) {
        condition.await()
      }
    } finally {
      lock.unlock()
    }
  }
```

```
def signal(): Unit = {
  lock.lock()
  try {
    isReady = true
    condition.signalAll()
  } finally {
    lock.unlock()
  }
}
}
```

In this example, the lock ensures exclusive access, while the condition variable allows threads to wait and be notified of state changes effectively.

Each synchronization mechanism has its semantics and performance characteristics. Using the appropriate mechanism based on the requirements of visibility, ordering, and atomicity is key to writing correct concurrent programs.

Interruption and Termination

Interruption provides a mechanism for one thread to signal another thread that it should stop what it is doing and do something else. An interrupted thread can choose to stop immediately, continue running, or handle the interruption in a custom manner. The Thread.interrupt method interrupts a thread:

```
object InterruptExample extends App {
  val thread = new Thread(new Runnable {
    def run(): Unit = {
      try {
        while (!Thread.interrupted()) {
          println("Thread is running")
          Thread.sleep(1000)
        }
      } catch {
        case _: InterruptedException => println("Thread was interrupted")
      }
    }
  })

  thread.start()
  Thread.sleep(3000)
  thread.interrupt()
}
```

In this example, the thread checks for interruptions using Thread.interrupted and handles InterruptedException. Proper handling of interruptions is necessary for responsive and well-behaved threads, especially in long-running or blocking operations.

The understanding of threads, memory models, and synchronization mechanisms in the JVM forms the foundation for advanced concurrency features in Scala, such as futures, promises, and the actor model. This section has provided technical insight into the foundational aspects of threading, facilitating the study of more advanced concurrent programming constructs in the ensuing sections.

6.3   The Futures and Promises Model

The Futures and Promises model is an essential concept in managing concurrency in Scala. This model allows developers to write asynchronous, non-blocking code using a familiar and intuitive syntax.

Future and Promise are complementary constructs in Scala's standard library, designed to simplify concurrent programming. A Future represents a result of an asynchronous computation, which may not yet be available, while a Promise is a writable, single-assignment container that completes a Future.

Future instances are evaluated concurrently and provide a mechanism to handle the result once it becomes available. Below is an example illustrating the creation and use of a Future in Scala.

```
import scala.concurrent._
import ExecutionContext.Implicits.global

val futureResult = Future {
  // Simulate a long-running computation
  Thread.sleep(1000)
  42
}

futureResult.onComplete {
  case Success(value) => println(s"The answer is $value")
  case Failure(e) => println(s"An error has occurred: ${e.getMessage}")
}
```

In this code snippet, the Future is created using the Future companion object's apply method, which executes the provided block of code asynchronously. The ExecutionContext.Implicits.global is a predefined global execution context that provides support for parallel execution.

The Future's onComplete method registers a callback that gets called when the computation is complete. This callback uses pattern matching to handle the successful result or an error condition. The Success and Failure cases are part of the scala.util.Try type, which encapsulates the result of a computation that may either result in a value or an exception.

Promises are used to complete Futures manually. A Promise can be thought of as a placeholder for a future value that is initially undetermined but which will eventually be assigned exactly once. Here is an example of using a Promise.

```scala
import scala.concurrent.Promise

val promise = Promise[Int]()
val future = promise.future

val producer = Future {
  Thread.sleep(500)
  promise.success(24)
}

val consumer = future.map { value =>
  println(s"Received value: $value")
}
```

In this example, a Promise[Int] is created, which generates a corresponding Future[Int]. The promise.success(24) method completes the promise, thereby completing the associated Future with the specified value. When the Future is completed, it triggers the map operation registered on it, resulting in the "Received value: 24" message.

Using Future and Promise, one can coordinate parallel computations effectively. Consider the following algorithm that demonstrates a typical use case for Futures and Promises.

Algorithm 2: Downloading and processing data from multiple URLs using Futures

---

Data: List of URLs
Result: Processed data from each URL
1 **foreach** URL in list **do**
2   val futureData = Future { downloadData(URL)};
3   futureData.onComplete {;
4   **if** Success(data) **then**
5   processData(data);
6   **else**
7   logError(e);
8   }

This algorithm concurrently downloads data from a list of URLs and processes each item as it becomes available. The Future mechanism allows for the asynchronous execution of the download operation, while callbacks handle the processing and error logging.

Scala's Future API also supports various combinators for composing multiple futures. Some fundamental combinators include map, flatMap, filter, recover, and fallbackTo. These combinators enable the chaining and transformation of asynchronous computations. For instance, consider two futures that depend on each other.

```
val future1 = Future {
  Thread.sleep(500)
  10
}

val future2 = future1.map(value => value * 2)

future2.onComplete {
  case Success(result) => println(s"Result: $result")
  case Failure(e) => println(s"Error: ${e.getMessage}")
}
```

Here, future1 completes with the value 10, and future2 depends on the result of future1, which it transforms by multiplying by 2. When future2 is completed, it prints "Result: 20".

flatMap is another powerful combinator used for chaining dependent futures where the second computation depends on the result of the first. Below is an example.

```
val futureA = Future {
  Thread.sleep(500)
  5
}

val futureB = futureA.flatMap { value =>
  Future {
    Thread.sleep(500)
    value + 15
  }
}

futureB.onComplete {
  case Success(result) => println(s"Final result: $result")
  case Failure(e) => println(s"Error: ${e.getMessage}")
}
```

In this case, futureB depends on the result of futureA. Once futureA completes, it will trigger the inner future computation in futureB. This chaining ensures that the second computation only starts after the first computation has finished.

The Futures and Promises model in Scala serves as a foundation for writing efficient and readable concurrent code. By leveraging these constructs, developers can handle asynchronous computations effectively, manage callbacks elegantly, and compose complex asynchronous workflows. This model ensures that the code remains scalable and maintainable.

6.4 Asynchronous Programming with Futures

Asynchronous programming is essential for developing performant and responsive applications. In Scala, the Future and Promise constructs provided by the scala.concurrent package enable developers to handle potentially time-consuming operations in a non-blocking manner. This section focuses on the utilization of Future for asynchronous programming, offering a detailed examination of its creation, operation chaining, and handling of asynchronous results.

The Future represents a placeholder object for a value that may not yet be available. It allows the program to execute computations concurrently and proceed without waiting for the result. Futures are particularly useful in I/O operations, network communication, or any process where latency could impede performance.

```
import scala.concurrent._
import scala.concurrent.duration._
import ExecutionContext.Implicits.global

val futureExample: Future[Int] = Future {
  // Simulate a long-running computation
  Thread.sleep(3000)
  42
}
```

In the example above, a Future is defined to represent an integer value that will be available after a simulated delay of 3000 milliseconds. The code block within the Future runs asynchronously, leveraging the global execution context provided by ExecutionContext.Implicits.global.

To handle the result of a Future once it is completed, callbacks such as onComplete, foreach, and map can be used. These callbacks allow the programmer to specify actions to be performed when the Future completes successfully or encounters an error.

```
futureExample.onComplete {
  case Success(value) => println(s"Success! The answer is $value.")
  case Failure(exception) => println(s"Error occurred: $exception.")
}
```

In this snippet, the onComplete callback is registered to handle the successful completion or failure of futureExample. The Success case allows access to the resultant value, whereas the Failure case provides access to the exception that was thrown during the computation.

Moreover, foreach and map methods provide ways to engage with the result without explicitly dealing with Success and Failure cases:

```
futureExample.foreach { value =>
  println(s"Success! The answer is $value.")
}

val multipliedFuture: Future[Int] = futureExample.map { value =>
  value * 2
}
```

The foreach callback is executed only if the Future completes successfully, whereas map transforms the result of the Future into a new Future. This facilitates chaining of asynchronous operations, whereby the result of one computation can be used as the input for subsequent computations, allowing for complex workflows to be built in a purely non-blocking manner.

To compose multiple Futures, operations like flatMap and recover can be employed. The flatMap method is used when the transformation function itself returns a Future, leading to nested futures:

```
val anotherFuture: Future[Int] = Future {
  Thread.sleep(2000)
  2
}

val combinedFuture: Future[Int] = futureExample.flatMap { value1 =>
  anotherFuture.map { value2 =>
    value1 + value2
  }
}

combinedFuture.onComplete {
  case Success(result) => println(s"Combined result is $result.")
  case Failure(exception) => println(s"Failed with exception: $exception.")
}
```

In this code, combinedFuture first waits for the completion of futureExample, then uses the resulting value to proceed with anotherFuture. The resultant value of combinedFuture is the sum of the values from both futures.

Handling errors gracefully in the chain of Future operations is crucial for robust applications. The recover and recoverWith methods allow the definition of recovery strategies when a Future fails:

```
val recoveredFuture: Future[Int] = futureExample.recover {
  case _: TimeoutException => -1
}
```

```
recoveredFuture.onComplete {
  case Success(value) => println(s"Result: $value.")
  case Failure(exception) => println(s"Unhandled exception: $exception.")
}
```

The recover method provides an alternative value in case the Future fails with a TimeoutException. For more complex cases where the recovery block itself needs to perform further asynchronous operations, recoverWith can be used, which works similar to flatMap.

Futures allow for sophisticated asynchronous programming patterns by permitting the composition and transformation of eventual results in a non-blocking fashion. By utilizing Futures correctly, programs can handle a multitude of concurrent tasks efficiently, improving performance and responsiveness. References to the Promise constructs, detailed handling strategies, and best practices ensure the development of high-quality concurrent applications.

6.5   Callbacks and Completion Handling

Callbacks provide a mechanism for asynchronously handling the completion of Futures in Scala. When the computation represented by a Future instance completes—either successfully or with an exception—callbacks offer a way to execute specific code in response to the outcome.

The following steps outline the essential approach to adding a callback to a Future:

1. Create a Future instance to represent an asynchronous computation. 2. Register a callback on the Future. 3. Define the logic to be executed when the Future successfully completes or fails.

Consider the following example encapsulating a simple asynchronous task using Future:

```
import scala.concurrent.Future
import scala.concurrent.ExecutionContext.Implicits.global

val futureTask: Future[Int] = Future {
  // Simulate a long-running computation
  Thread.sleep(1000)
  42
}
```

Here, a Future named futureTask is created, which will eventually compute the value 42 after a one-second delay.

To handle the completion of futureTask, we can register a callback using the onComplete method. The onComplete method takes an argument of type Try[T] => Unit, where Try[T] can be either a Success[T] or a Failure[T].

```
import scala.util.{Success, Failure}

futureTask.onComplete {
  case Success(value) => println(s"The result is: $value")
  case Failure(exception) => println(s"An error occurred: ${exception.getMessage}")
}
```

In this code, onComplete is used to register a callback that prints a message upon the task's completion. If the task is successful, the callback will print "The result is: 42". If an exception occurs within the asynchronous computation, it will print an error message.

onComplete is often used to perform additional computations or side effects based on the result of a Future. However, it is important to note that the onComplete method itself returns Unit. That means it's used primarily for side effects and not for further transformations or composing with other Future instances.

For scenarios where subsequent transformations are required, methods such as map and flatMap are preferable. These methods create new Future instances based on the result of the original one, enabling more flexible and powerful composition patterns.

Here's an example demonstrating the chaining of transformations:

```
val transformedFuture: Future[String] = futureTask.map(value => s"Result: $value")

transformedFuture.onComplete {
  case Success(text) => println(text)
  case Failure(exception) => println(s"An error occurred: ${exception.getMessage}")
}
```

In this example, futureTask is transformed using the map method, producing a new Future that contains a formatted string. The callback registered with onComplete on transformedFuture will print "Result: 42" if the computation succeeds.

To summarize, while the main purpose of onComplete is to handle the completion of a Future with side effects, methods like map and flatMap enable more sophisticated manipulation and combination of Future values in a functional programming style. Understanding and using these methods allow for clear and robust handling of asynchronous computations in Scala.

6.6 Composing Futures

Composing futures in Scala is a powerful way to manage and structure concurrent tasks. A Future object represents an asynchronous computation whose result may not yet be available. By composing them, multiple asynchronous computations can be coordinated, with dependencies between tasks handled seamlessly.

Futures in Scala are composable using a variety of functional constructs such as flatMap, map, for-comprehensions, and combinators like recover and fallbackTo. These constructs allow for clear and concise handling of dependent or independent asynchronous operations.

map applies a function to the result of a future when it becomes available, returning a new future with the transformed outcome. Consider the following example:

```
import scala.concurrent._
import ExecutionContext.Implicits.global
import scala.util.{Success, Failure}

val future1 = Future { 21 + 21 }
val future2 = future1.map(x => x * 2)

future2.onComplete {
  case Success(result) => println(s"Result is $result")
  case Failure(e) => e.printStackTrace()
}
```

Here, future1 computes an initial value, and future2 maps this result to a new value. onComplete handles the result, allowing us to act upon success or failure.

flatMap is used when each transformation step returns another future. This is useful for chaining dependent asynchronous operations:

```
val future1 = Future { 21 + 21 }
val future2 = future1.flatMap(x => Future { x * 2 })

future2.onComplete {
  case Success(result) => println(s"Result is $result")
  case Failure(e) => e.printStackTrace()
}
```

With flatMap, future2 only completes once both asynchronous operations have been executed.

For complex future compositions, Scala provides a more readable for-comprehension syntax:

```
val future1 = Future { 21 + 21 }
```

```scala
val future2 = Future { 10 + 10 }

val combinedFuture = for {
  result1 <- future1
  result2 <- future2
} yield result1 + result2

combinedFuture.onComplete {
  case Success(result) => println(s"Combined result is $result")
  case Failure(e) => e.printStackTrace()
}
```

This syntax makes it easy to combine several futures into one, where each future can depend on the results of others. The for-comprehension flattens sequences of futures.

Error handling in future compositional constructs can be done using recover and recoverWith. recover allows for specifying a partial function to handle errors:

```scala
val future1 = Future { throw new RuntimeException("Failure") }.recover {
  case _: RuntimeException => 42
}

future1.onComplete {
  case Success(result) => println(s"Recovered result is $result")
  case Failure(e) => e.printStackTrace()
}
```

This transforms the exceptional case into a successful outcome with a fallback value of 42. On the other hand, recoverWith is essential when the fallback needs to be another future:

```scala
val future1 = Future { throw new RuntimeException("Failure") }.recoverWith {
  case _: RuntimeException => Future.successful(42)
}

future1.onComplete {
  case Success(result) => println(s"Recovered result is $result")
  case Failure(e) => e.printStackTrace()
}
```

fallbackTo is another useful combinator that provides a secondary future to fall back on if the initial future fails:

```scala
val primaryFuture = Future { throw new RuntimeException("Failure") }
val fallbackFuture = Future { 42 }

val combinedFuture = primaryFuture.fallbackTo(fallbackFuture)

combinedFuture.onComplete {
  case Success(result) => println(s"Fallback result is $result")
  case Failure(e) => e.printStackTrace()
}
```

Handling timeouts is a critical aspect of working with futures. The Future companion object provides a built-in utility, Future.firstCompletedOf, which can be combined with a timeout pattern:

```
import scala.concurrent.duration._
import scala.concurrent.{Await, Future, Promise}

val future1 = Future { Thread.sleep(5000); 21 + 21 }
val timeoutFuture = Future { blocking(Thread.sleep(1000)); throw new
    TimeoutException("Timed out!") }

val resultFuture = Future.firstCompletedOf(Seq(future1, timeoutFuture))

val result = Await.result(resultFuture, 2.seconds)
```

In this pattern, resultFuture will complete with the result of future1 or raise a TimeoutException if the timeoutFuture completes first, allowing for graceful handling of long-running tasks.

Leveraging these functional combinators and constructs, Scala enables robust and expressive handling of asynchronous computations through futures. This significantly eases concurrent programming, allowing for readable and maintainable code while ensuring correct execution and error handling in concurrent environments.

6.7 Fault Tolerance and Error Handling

Fault tolerance and error handling are critical aspects in concurrent programming, especially given the complexity and potential for failures in distributed systems. In Scala, these concepts are integral to robust application design. This section delves into various techniques and best practices for ensuring fault tolerance and proper error handling in concurrent programs.

Try, Success, and Failure are foundational constructs in Scala's error handling framework, particularly useful in concurrent contexts. The Try type represents a computation that may either result in a value, encapsulated in Success, or an exception, encapsulated in Failure. This encapsulation allows for the handling of exceptions without using traditional try-catch blocks.

```
import scala.util.{Try, Success, Failure}

def riskyComputation(x: Int): Try[Int] = {
  if (x > 0) Success(42 / x)
  else Failure(new ArithmeticException("Division by zero"))
}
```

```
val result = riskyComputation(0)
result match {
  case Success(value) => println(s"Computation succeeded: $value")
  case Failure(exception) => println(s"Computation failed: ${exception.getMessage}")
}
```

In the above example, riskyComputation returns a Try[Int], which can either be a Success object containing the result of the computation or a Failure object containing the thrown ArithmeticException.

When dealing with Futures, handling errors becomes crucial due to the asynchronous nature of the computations. Future provides methods such as recover and recoverWith to facilitate error handling.

```
import scala.concurrent._
import scala.concurrent.ExecutionContext.Implicits.global
import scala.util.{Success, Failure}

val futureComputation: Future[Int] = Future {
  if (math.random() > 0.5) 42 else throw new RuntimeException("Random failure")
}

val recoveredFuture: Future[Int] = futureComputation.recover {
  case _: RuntimeException => -1
}

recoveredFuture.onComplete {
  case Success(value) => println(s"Computation result: $value")
  case Failure(exception) => println(s"Error occurred: ${exception.getMessage}")
}
```

In this scenario, futureComputation may either complete successfully with a value of 42 or throw a RuntimeException. The recover method ensures that in case of a RuntimeException, the returned Future contains the value -1.

To further enhance robustness, it's common to use recoverWith, which allows for recovering by transforming the failure into another Future.

```
val retriedFuture: Future[Int] = futureComputation.recoverWith {
  case _: RuntimeException => Future { 0 }
}

retriedFuture.onComplete {
  case Success(value) => println(s"Computation result after recovery: $value")
  case Failure(exception) => println(s"Error occurred: ${exception.getMessage}")
}
```

In larger and more complex applications, utilizing higher-level abstractions like Either types or the cats library for functional error handling can be advantageous. Either encapsulates a value of one of two possible types, Left or Right, where conventionally Left denotes failure and

168

Right denotes success.

```
def computeDivision(x: Int): Either[String, Int] = {
  if (x != 0) Right(42 / x)
  else Left("Division by zero error")
}

val resultEither: Either[String, Int] = computeDivision(0)
resultEither match {
  case Right(value) => println(s"Computation succeeded: $value")
  case Left(error) => println(s"Computation failed: $error")
}
```

Using Either allows for more explicitly managed error states, which can be particularly helpful in complex workflows.

Additionally, when working with Akka Actors, fault tolerance is managed through supervision strategies. Actors can monitor other actors and take predefined actions whenever a failure occurs. The built-in strategies include Restart, Resume, Stop, and Escalate.

```
import akka.actor.

class Supervisor extends Actor {
  import akka.actor.SupervisorStrategy._
  override val supervisorStrategy: SupervisorStrategy = OneForOneStrategy() {
    case _: ArithmeticException => Resume
    case _: NullPointerException => Restart
    case _: IllegalArgumentException => Stop
    case _: Exception => Escalate
  }

  def receive = {
    case props: Props => sender() ! context.actorOf(props)
  }
}

class Worker extends Actor {
  def receive = {
    case msg => println(s"Received message: $msg")
  }
}

val system = ActorSystem("FaultToleranceSystem")
val supervisor = system.actorOf(Props[Supervisor], "supervisor")
val worker = supervisor ! Props[Worker]
```

This configuration dictates that in the face of an ArithmeticException, the child actor will be resumed. A NullPointerException prompts a restart, an IllegalArgumentException results in termination, and all other exceptions are escalated to the higher-level supervisor.

By leveraging these techniques, developers can create resilient systems that effectively cope with inevitable faults and errors, maintaining robust and reliable applications.

169

6.8   Parallel Collections

Parallel collections in Scala provide an abstraction for parallelism by allowing operations on collections to be executed concurrently using multiple threads. This can significantly improve performance when processing large datasets by leveraging multi-core processors.

The scala.collection.parallel package contains parallel implementations of collections such as ParSeq, ParIterable, ParSet, and ParMap. These collections mirror the interfaces of their sequential counterparts but distribute processing across multiple cores.

Converting Sequential Collections to Parallel

To convert a sequential collection to a parallel collection, the par method can be invoked. Here is an example of converting a list to a parallel collection:

```
val seqList = List(1, 2, 3, 4, 5)
val parList = seqList.par
```

Once a collection is parallel, operations on it, such as map, filter, reduce, etc., will be performed in parallel.

Performance Considerations

Parallel collections can lead to significant performance improvements, especially for compute-intensive tasks. Consider the following example:

```
val numbers = (1 to 1000000).toList

// Sequential computation
val seqResult = numbers.map(_ * 2)

// Parallel computation
val parResult = numbers.par.map(_ * 2)
```

However, the performance benefits depend on the nature of the operations and the overhead of parallelization. For lightweight operations, the overhead of managing multiple threads may outweigh the concurrency benefits. It is crucial to profile and benchmark your code to understand the performance implications.

Reduction Operations

Reduction operations, such as fold, reduce, and aggregate, are particularly well-suited for parallel collections as they can be distributed across multiple threads. Here is an example demonstrating the usage of reduce:

```
val sum = numbers.par.reduce(_ + _)
```

In this code, the sum is computed in parallel, which can enhance performance for large collections.

Non-Deterministic Results

Parallel collections can yield non-deterministic results, especially for operations that are not associative or commutative. Consider the following example:

```
val nonAssociativeExample = List(1, 2, 3, 4).par.reduce(_ - _)
```

The result of this operation may vary due to the non-associativity of subtraction. Therefore, it is essential to use operations that are both associative and commutative to ensure consistent results.

Avoiding Side Effects

To maintain the integrity of parallel operations, it is crucial to avoid side effects. Modifying shared variables within parallel computations can introduce race conditions and data inconsistencies. Instead, rely on purely functional programming techniques. Here is an example illustrating a side-effect-free operation:

```
val squaredNumbers = numbers.par.map(x => x * x)
```

Tuning Parallelism

The default parallelism level is determined by the number of available processors, but it can be tuned programmatically through a TaskSupport object. Here is an example of setting a custom parallelism level:

```
import scala.collection.parallel.ForkJoinTaskSupport
import scala.concurrent.forkjoin.ForkJoinPool

val parArray = numbers.par
parArray.tasksupport = new ForkJoinTaskSupport(new ForkJoinPool(4))
```

By adjusting the parallelism level, you can fine-tune the performance based on the application needs and the underlying hardware.

Task Scheduling and Execution

Parallel collections use a fork-join framework for task scheduling and execution. Each element of the collection is processed as part of a task that can be divided into smaller subtasks, providing a balanced workload across threads.

171

Common Use Cases

Parallel collections are best used for operations that involve significant computation and can be parallelized easily. Some common use cases include:

- Large scale data processing where each element can be processed independently.

- Aggregations and reductions that are associative and commutative.

- Simulations and mathematical computations that benefit from concurrent execution.

Applying parallel collections appropriately can lead to performance gains, enabling more efficient handling of compute-bound tasks.

pexprkeywords

6.9   Actors Model and Akka

The Actors model is a mathematical framework for modeling concurrent systems. It conceptualizes the system as a group of actors that communicate with each other by sending and receiving messages. Each actor processes messages sequentially and maintains its own state. This model fits well with the principles of object-oriented and distributed systems, as it encapsulates state and behavior, and allows for decentralized and scalable designs.

Akka is a toolkit and runtime for building highly concurrent, distributed, and resilient message-driven applications on the JVM. It implements the Actors model and provides abstractions for working with actors, defining actor hierarchies, handling messages, and managing actor lifecycles. Integrating Akka into your Scala applications can significantly simplify the process of building concurrent applications.

To harness the power of Akka, it is essential to understand its core components and how they interact. Below, we discuss key aspects of the Actors model and how Akka facilitates the creation and management of actors.

Actors are the fundamental units of computation in Akka. Each actor runs in its own logical thread of execution, maintaining its internal state

172

and interacting with other actors solely through message passing. Actors are isolated from each other, ensuring that one actor's state cannot be directly accessed by another, which eliminates race conditions and makes the system more predictable.

Creating an actor in Akka involves defining a Scala class that extends Actor and providing an implementation for the receive method, which processes incoming messages. Here is a simple example:

```
import akka.actor._

class SimpleActor extends Actor {
  def receive = {
    case message: String =>
      println(s"Received message: $message")
    case _ =>
      println("Unknown message")
  }
}
```

In this example, SimpleActor extends the Actor trait, and the receive method is defined to handle string messages. When a message is received, the actor prints the message to the console. Any message type other than a string results in a printout of "Unknown message."

To create and interact with actors, we use an ActorSystem, which is a container for actors that provides factory and supervisory services. We can instantiate the ActorSystem, create an actor, and send it a message as follows:

```
object Main extends App {
  val system = ActorSystem("MyActorSystem")
  val simpleActor = system.actorOf(Props[SimpleActor], "simpleActor")

  simpleActor ! "Hello, Akka"

  system.terminate()
}
```

Here, an ActorSystem named MyActorSystem is created, and an actor of type SimpleActor is instantiated with the name simpleActor. The ! operator sends the message "Hello, Akka" to simpleActor. Finally, the actor system is terminated, which shuts down all actors within it.

Actors can also maintain internal state and manage complex behaviors. For example, consider an actor that keeps a counter:

```
class CounterActor extends Actor {
  var count = 0

  def receive = {
    case "increment" =>
      count += 1
```

```
    println(s"Count is now $count")
  case "decrement" =>
    count -= 1
    println(s"Count is now $count")
  case "get" =>
    sender() ! count
  }
}
```

In this CounterActor, the internal state count is updated in response to messages "increment" and "decrement". When a "get" message is received, the current count is sent back to the sender.

Akka's actor model supports fault tolerance by defining actor hierarchies and supervision strategies. Every actor belongs to a parent actor that supervises it, forming an actor tree. Supervisors define strategies to handle failures in their children—restarting, stopping, or resuming them based on the type of error encountered. This design encourages building resilient systems where failure management is localized within the actor hierarchy.

Another powerful feature of Akka is the ability to define actor lifecycles. Actors have well-defined lifecycle methods such as preStart, postStop, preRestart, and postRestart. These methods allow developers to manage resources and supervise actor behavior at different points in their lifecycle.

```
class LifecycleActor extends Actor {
  override def preStart() = {
    println("Actor is starting")
  }

  def receive = {
    case "stop" =>
      context.stop(self)
  }

  override def postStop() = {
    println("Actor has stopped")
  }
}
```

In this example, LifecycleActor prints messages when it starts and stops. The preStart method is invoked before the actor begins processing messages, and postStop is called after the actor has been stopped.

Akka also supports clustering, which allows the creation of distributed actor systems. This feature is particularly useful for building large-scale, fault-tolerant applications. Clustering enables actors to communicate across different JVMs, manage state distribution, and perform load balancing.

Message routing is another core feature of Akka that helps distribute work among a pool of actors. Akka provides various built-in routers like round-robin, broadcast, and consistent hashing routers.

The flexibility and robustness that Akka provides through its Actors model make it an indispensable tool for developing concurrent and distributed systems. Mastering Akka's actors, supervision, and lifecycle management components is paramount for leveraging its full potential in building scalable applications.

6.10   Creating and Using Actors

Actors in Scala are a fundamental construct for building concurrent and distributed systems. The akka.actor.ActActor system provides the foundation for actor-based concurrency, offering a robust framework to model and manage concurrent computations. In this section, we focus on the creation, messaging, and practical utilization of actors.

To begin with the creation of actors, we utilize the Actor trait from the Akka library. An actor is essentially an object that encapsulates state and behavior, communicating with other actors through message passing.

Actor instances are created using an ActorSystem and are typically defined as classes extending the Actor trait. Here's a basic example of defining an actor:

```
import akka.actor.{Actor, ActorSystem, Props}

// Define the Actor class
class SimpleActor extends Actor {
  def receive: PartialFunction[Any, Unit] = {
    case "hello" => println("Hello, world!")
    case _ => println("Unknown message")
  }
}

// Create the ActorSystem
val system = ActorSystem("SimpleSystem")

// Instantiate the actor
val simpleActor = system.actorOf(Props[SimpleActor], "simpleActor")

// Send messages to the actor
simpleActor ! "hello"
simpleActor ! "goodbye"
```

The SimpleActor class extends the Actor trait and provides an implementation of the receive method. The receive method is a partial function

175

that handles incoming messages. The case statements within receive dictate the actor's response to specific messages.

Messages are sent to actors using the ! (bang) operator. This operator is non-blocking and queues the message to be processed asynchronously.

The Props object is used to create a new actor. It encapsulates the configuration details needed to instantiate the actor. The ActorSystem manages actors and their life cycles, providing the necessary infrastructure for actor creation and message handling.

Actors can also be designed to handle more complex interactions and state. Here is an example of an actor with internal state:

```scala
import akka.actor.Actor

class CounterActor extends Actor {
  var count = 0

  def receive: PartialFunction[Any, Unit] = {
    case "increment" =>
      count += 1
      println(s"Count incremented to $count")
    case "get" =>
      sender() ! count
  }
}

// Instantiate the CounterActor
val counterActor = system.actorOf(Props[CounterActor], "counterActor")

// Interact with the CounterActor
counterActor ! "increment"
counterActor ! "get"
```

In this example, the CounterActor maintains an internal state count. The message "increment" modifies this state, whereas the message "get" retrieves the current count and sends it back to the sender actor.

Sending a message to an actor and expecting a reply involves using the ask pattern, also known as a future-based request-reply pattern. This is facilitated by the ask method (represented by ?) provided by the akka.pattern package.

Here's how the ask pattern works:

```scala
import akka.pattern.ask
import akka.util.Timeout
import scala.concurrent.duration._
import scala.concurrent.Future
import scala.concurrent.ExecutionContext.Implicits.global

implicit val timeout: Timeout = Timeout(5.seconds)
```

```
// Ask the actor for the count
val future: Future[Int] = (counterActor ? "get").mapTo[Int]

future.map(count => println(s"Current count is $count"))
```

Using the `ask` pattern, we send a message to the actor and obtain a Future representing a potential reply. The Timeout parameter specifies the maximum duration to wait for the reply. The mapTo method casts the result to the expected type.

Actors can also be used in a hierarchical manner, forming a supervision hierarchy. Parent actors can create child actors and supervise them. The parent actor can define a supervision strategy to manage the lifecycle and failure recovery of child actors.

Here's an example of actor supervision:

```
import akka.actor.SupervisorStrategy._
import akka.actor.{Actor, OneForOneStrategy, Props}

// Define a child actor
class ChildActor extends Actor {
  def receive: PartialFunction[Any, Unit] = {
    case msg =>println(s"Child actor received message: $msg")
  }
}

// Define a supervisor actor
class SupervisorActor extends Actor {
  override val supervisorStrategy = OneForOneStrategy() {
    case _: Exception => Restart
  }

  val child = context.actorOf(Props[ChildActor], "child")

  def receive: PartialFunction[Any, Unit] = {
    case msg => child forward msg
  }
}

// Instantiate the SupervisorActor
val supervisorActor = system.actorOf(Props[SupervisorActor], "supervisorActor")

// Interact with the SupervisorActor
supervisorActor ! "test message"
```

In this example, the SupervisorActor creates an instance of ChildActor and forwards incoming messages to the child. The supervision strategy dictates that if the child actor throws an exception, it should be restarted. The OneForOneStrategy class provides a predefined supervision strategy that supervises each child individually.

Working with actors involves the interplay between actor creation, message passing, state management, and supervision of actor hierarchies.

177

Through these examples, we emphasized the procedural steps in defining, instantiating, and using actors effectively within an ActorSystem. Understanding these concepts is vital for leveraging the full power of the Akka toolkit and building scalable, resilient concurrent applications in Scala.

6.11   Actor Lifecycle and Supervision

The actor model, implemented extensively in the Akka framework within Scala, provides a robust foundation for dealing with concurrency. Critical to the effectiveness of this model is the understanding of actor lifecycle and supervision, ensuring reliable and maintainable concurrent application development.

Actor Lifecycle:

Actors in Akka follow a strict lifecycle, undergoing various states from their creation to termination. The primary states are created, started, processing, stopped, and terminated. Transitions between these states are managed through lifecycle hooks and messages.

- created: An actor is in this state immediately after being instantiated. It hasn't started processing messages yet.

- started: Upon receiving the initial start() call, the actor moves to this state and is ready to process messages.

- processing: When an actor receives a message, it enters this state where it executes the handler for that message, often using a receive method.

- stopped: This state is reached upon calling context.stop(self), indicating that the actor has finished processing messages.

- terminated: Following the stopped state, the actor fully transitions to terminated after the stop signal has propagated and all post-stop hooks have been executed.

Actor lifecycle hooks are provided to enable developers to insert behavior during certain state transitions. These include:

```
override def preStart(): Unit = {
  // Code to execute during actor start
}
```

```scala
override def postStop(): Unit = {
  // Code to execute after the actor has been stopped
}

override def preRestart(reason: Throwable, message: Option[Any]): Unit = {
  // Code to execute before an actor is restarted
  super.preRestart(reason, message)
}

override def postRestart(reason: Throwable): Unit = {
  // Code to execute after an actor has been restarted
  super.postRestart(reason)
}
```

Supervision Hierarchies:

Akka actors are organized in a hierarchical structure where each actor has a parent and potentially multiple child actors. This structure forms the basis for actor supervision, where parent actors, known as supervisors, monitor and manage child actors.

Supervision strategies dictate how supervisors should respond to failures in their child actors. The primary strategies include:

- Resume: The child actor continues processing its next message.

- Restart: The child actor is stopped and immediately started anew.

- Stop: The child actor is terminated.

- Escalate: The failure is propagated to the supervisor's parent.

Supervision strategies are defined using a SupervisorStrategy. Akka provides built-in strategies such as OneForOneStrategy and AllForOneStrategy:

```scala
import akka.actor.SupervisorStrategy._
import akka.actor.{Actor, ActorSystem, Props, OneForOneStrategy,
    ActorInitializationException, ActorKilledException, DeathPactException}

class Supervisor extends Actor {

  override def supervisorStrategy = OneForOneStrategy() {
    case _: ArithmeticException => Resume
    case _: NullPointerException => Restart
    case _: IllegalArgumentException => Stop
    case _: Exception => Escalate
  }

  def receive = {
    case props: Props => sender() ! context.actorOf(props)
  }
}
```

Fault Tolerance:

Effective supervision ensures fault tolerance within an application. By managing how and when actors are restarted or stopped, supervisors can maintain stability and responsiveness. For instance, in the presence of transient errors, a Restart strategy allows for recovery while preserving overall system integrity.

Here is an example of specifying a OneForOneStrategy with an explicit restart limit:

```
override val supervisorStrategy = OneForOneStrategy(
  maxNrOfRetries = 10,
  withinTimeRange = 1 minute
) {
  case _: ArithmeticException => Resume
  case _: NullPointerException => Restart
  case _: Exception => Escalate
}
```

Actor Monitoring:

In addition to supervision, actors can monitor other actors. This is useful for actors that need to be notified if another actor terminates unexpectedly. Monitoring is achieved using the context.watch method:

```
import akka.actor.{Actor, Terminated}

class MonitoringActor extends Actor {
  val child = context.actorOf(Props[WorkerActor], "workerActor")
  context.watch(child) // Start monitoring the child

  def receive = {
    case Terminated('child') =>
      // Handle termination logic here
  }
}
```

Actors can stop monitoring another actor using context.unwatch:

```
context.unwatch(child)
```

The Terminate message is sent to the monitoring actor when the watched actor terminates, facilitating cleanup or recovery actions as needed.

Understanding actor lifecycle and supervision within Akka is critical for creating resilient, fault-tolerant systems. It ensures that failures are appropriately managed and that actors are effectively monitored and controlled throughout their lifecycle. This hierarchical model of supervision aids in maintaining system stability, ultimately fostering an environment where concurrent operations can flourish with minimal disruption.

6.12 Concurrency Best Practices

Effective use of concurrency in Scala requires adherence to several best practices to achieve efficient and error-free applications. This section highlights key principles and techniques that are instrumental in writing high-quality concurrent programs.

Immutable Data Structures: The use of immutable data structures is crucial in concurrent programming. It eliminates the need for locking mechanisms, thereby avoiding typical synchronization issues such as deadlocks and race conditions. In Scala, List, Vector, and Map are examples of immutable collections that can be leveraged to maintain thread safety.

Avoid Blocking Calls: Blocking operations can severely degrade the performance of concurrent applications. By using non-blocking data structures and asynchronous programming constructs such as Future and Promise, we can ensure that threads remain responsive. The following example illustrates a non-blocking way to read from a file:

```
import scala.concurrent.Future
import scala.io.Source
import scala.concurrent.ExecutionContext.Implicits.global

def readFile(filePath: String): Future[String] = Future {
  Source.fromFile(filePath).getLines().mkString("\n")
}

val fileContent = readFile("example.txt")
```

This approach ensures that the I/O operation does not block the main thread, improving overall responsiveness and throughput.

Use Thread Pools Judiciously: Proper configuration of thread pools is essential for optimal resource utilization. Scala's ExecutionContext provides a thread pool mechanism to manage threads efficiently. It is advisable to avoid creating too many threads, as this can lead to context switching overhead and resource exhaustion. Configure the thread pool size based on the nature of tasks, balancing CPU-intensive and I/O-bound tasks efficiently:

```
import java.util.concurrent.Executors
import scala.concurrent.ExecutionContext

val cpuIntensiveEC = ExecutionContext.fromExecutor(Executors.newFixedThreadPool
    (4))
val ioBoundEC = ExecutionContext.fromExecutor(Executors.newCachedThreadPool())
```

Leverage Akka for Actor-Based Concurrency: The Akka toolkit provides robust support for the Actor model, facilitating efficient management of concurrency. Actors encapsulate state and behavior, communicating exclusively through message passing, which inherently avoids race conditions. To define an actor, extend the Actor trait and implement the receive method:

```
import akka.actor.{ Actor, ActorSystem, Props }

class MyActor extends Actor {
  def receive = {
    case "hello" => println("Hello, world!")
    case _ => println("Unknown message")
  }
}

val system = ActorSystem("MyActorSystem")
val myActor = system.actorOf(Props[MyActor], "myActor")

myActor ! "hello"
```

Akka's supervision strategy allows defining fault-tolerant systems where actors can gracefully recover from failures. Define a supervisor by extending the SupervisorStrategy trait, specifying the desired policy for handling exceptions.

Monitor and Tune Performance: Performance profiling and monitoring are vital for identifying bottlenecks in concurrent applications. Tools like VisualVM and YourKit provide insights into thread activities, memory consumption, and CPU usage. Regularly profile your application to fine-tune thread pool sizes, adjust concurrency levels, and optimize resource usage.

Practice Clean Code Principles: Maintain readability and maintainability by following clean code principles. Clearly document concurrent parts of the code, use meaningful variable names, and isolate concurrency logic from business logic. Encapsulation, modularity, and proper use of design patterns such as Futures, Promises, and Actors enhance codebase quality.

By adhering to these best practices, developers can harness the full potential of concurrency in Scala, leading to scalable, responsive, and robust applications.

Chapter 7

Error Handling and Exceptions

This chapter addresses error handling and exceptions in Scala. It includes traditional exception handling methods, the use of Try, Success, and Failure, and leveraging Option and Either for managing errors. The chapter also covers pattern matching for errors, resource management, custom exceptions, best practices, functional error handling approaches, and logging and monitoring errors to ensure robust and reliable code.

7.1   Introduction to Error Handling

Error handling is a critical aspect of robust software development. In Scala, as in many other languages, error handling aims to manage and mitigate potential runtime issues that could disrupt the normal flow of a program. Effective error handling improves program reliability and user experience, as well as facilitates easier debugging and maintenance.

Scala provides multiple mechanisms to handle errors and manage exceptions. These mechanisms can range from traditional try-catch blocks to more idiomatic functional approaches such as Try, Option, and Either. Understanding these approaches allows developers to write more resilient and predictable code.

Errors in Scala can be broadly categorized into three types:

183

- **Compile-time errors**: These errors are detected by the compiler and prevent the program from being compiled. Examples include syntax errors and type mismatches. Compile-time errors are not the primary focus in the context of runtime error handling.

- **Runtime errors**: These errors occur while the program is running, often due to unforeseen conditions such as invalid user input, file not found, network issues, etc.

- **Logical errors**: These errors are not typically caught by the compiler or runtime engine but result in incorrect program behavior due to flaws in the algorithm or code logic.

The fundamental unit of error handling in Scala is the *exception*. An exception is an event that disrupts the normal flow of the program's instructions. In Scala, all exceptions are represented by instances of Throwable or its subclasses. The primary subclasses of Throwable are Exception and Error. While Exception is used for conditions that a program might want to catch, Error is used for serious problems that a program typically cannot recover from, such as OutOfMemoryError.

```scala
def divide(x: Int, y: Int): Int = {
  try {
    x / y
  } catch {
    case e: ArithmeticException =>
      println("Error: Division by zero!")
      0
  }
}
```

In the example above, the try block measures code that might throw an exception. If an ArithmeticException (commonly arising from division by zero) occurs, the catch block handles the exception, prints an error message, and returns 0.

While the try-catch syntax provides a straightforward way to handle exceptions, it does have some limitations, particularly in functional programming paradigms. It introduces side effects and makes it harder to reason about program flow in a pure functional way. Additionally, every method potentially throwing an exception would need to be wrapped with try-catch, leading to verbose and less readable code.

Scala's functional programming features offer alternative mechanisms for handling errors more elegantly. The Try type provides a way to wrap computations that may result in an exception. If the computation succeeds, the result is wrapped in a Success; if it fails, the exception is wrapped in a Failure.

184

```scala
import scala.util.{Try, Success, Failure}

val result: Try[Int] = Try(10 / 0)

result match {
  case Success(value) => println(s"Result: $value")
  case Failure(exception) => println(s"Failed with exception: $exception")
}
```

In this code, the division by zero is safely encapsulated within a Try block. The result can then be pattern matched to appropriately handle success or failure cases, which provides a cleaner and more functional approach to error handling.

Another functional approach is using the Option type, which represents an optional value that can either be Some(value) or None. This is particularly useful when dealing with operations that might not return a value, such as looking up an element in a map.

```scala
val numbers = Map("one" -> 1, "two" -> 2)
val result: Option[Int] = numbers.get("three")

result match {
  case Some(value) => println(s"Found: $value")
  case None => println("Key not found")
}
```

The Option type reduces the need for null checks and potential null pointer exceptions, making the code safer and more readable.

For more complex scenarios involving errors, the Either type is beneficial as it can represent a value of one of two possible types—typically a success or an error. By convention, Either[Left, Right] is used where Left signifies an error, and Right indicates a success.

```scala
def divide(x: Int, y: Int): Either[String, Int] = {
  if (y == 0) Left("Division by zero")
  else Right(x / y)
}

val result: Either[String, Int] = divide(10, 0)

result match {
  case Right(value) => println(s"Result: $value")
  case Left(error) => println(s"Error: $error")
}
```

Either provides better context information by allowing a message or error object to be passed, making debugging easier.

Putting it all together, understanding and effectively utilizing Scala's diverse error-handling mechanisms significantly contribute to creating reliable, maintainable, and idiomatic Scala code. Each method—be it try-catch, Try, Option, or Either—serves different needs and use cases, giving developers a powerful toolkit for error management.

7.2   Exception Handling in Scala

Exception handling in Scala is pivotal for creating robust and reliable applications. In this section, we will explore the mechanisms available in Scala for handling exceptions, focusing on the traditional try-catch-finally blocks, Scala-specific enhancements, and best practices for error handling.

When a program encounters an unexpected condition, it may throw an exception. An exception is an object representing an error condition that disrupts the normal flow of the program. Scala provides a structured way to handle these exceptions using traditional 'try-catch-finally' blocks, which are conceptually similar to those in Java.

```scala
def divide(a: Int, b: Int): Int = {
  try {
    a / b
  } catch {
    case e: ArithmeticException => {
      println("Division by zero error!")
      0
    }
  } finally {
    println("Division operation attempted.")
  }
}
```

In this example, the divide function tries to divide a by b. If b is zero, an ArithmeticException is caught, a message is printed, and the function returns zero. The finally block executes regardless of whether an exception was thrown or not, indicating that the division operation was attempted.

Scala's exception handling can be enhanced through its robust pattern matching capabilities, allowing more expressive and concise error handling:

```scala
def divide(a: Int, b: Int): Int = {
  try {
    a / b
  } catch {
    case e: ArithmeticException => {
      println("Division by zero error!")
      0
    }
```

```scala
    case e: Exception => {
      println("Unknown error occurred: " + e.getMessage)
      -1
    }
  }
}
```

Here, pattern matching is used in the catch block to handle ArithmeticException separately from other exceptions. The Exception case ensures that any other unforeseen errors are also caught and handled appropriately.

Scala allows nested try-catch-finally blocks, although it is generally advisable to keep exception handling as simple as possible to avoid complex and hard-to-read code. The following example demonstrates a nested try-catch-finally scenario:

```scala
def complexOperation(a: Int, b: Int): Int = {
  try {
    try {
      val result = a / b
      println("Result: " + result)
      result
    } catch {
      case ae: ArithmeticException => {
        println("Inner catch: Division by zero.")
        0
      }
    }
  } catch {
    case e: Exception => {
      println("Outer catch: An error occurred.")
      -1
    }
  } finally {
    println("Operation complete.")
  }
}
```

Here, the inner try-catch block specifically handles ArithmeticException, while the outer try-catch block handles any other exceptions that may occur. The finally block executes after the nested blocks are completed, regardless of whether an exception was thrown.

Another aspect of exception handling in Scala is the use of throw. Exceptions can be thrown manually using the throw keyword:

```scala
def validateAge(age: Int): Unit = {
  if (age < 0) {
    throw new IllegalArgumentException("Age cannot be negative.")
  } else {
    println("Valid age: " + age)
  }
}
```

In the validateAge function, if the passed age is negative, an IllegalArgumentException is thrown, which the caller of this function is expected to handle. Exception objects are created using the standard new keyword followed by the exception class name and its message.

To handle resources such as files, database connections, or network sockets, Scala provides the try-with-resources mechanism using the Using trait from the scala.util.Using package, which ensures that resources are closed properly after use:

```scala
import scala.util.Using
import scala.io.Source

def readFile(filename: String): Unit = {
  Using(Source.fromFile(filename)) { source =>
    source.getLines().foreach(println)
  } match {
    case scala.util.Success(_) => println("File read successfully.")
    case scala.util.Failure(exception) => println("Error reading file: " + exception.
        getMessage)
  }
}
```

The Using block ensures that the Source is closed properly after reading the file. The match statement on the Using result helps to handle success and failure outcomes effectively.

It is important for developers to balance between handling exceptions gracefully and avoiding excessive use of try-catch blocks, which can lead to unwieldy code. Scala facilitates a variety of error handling constructs including pattern matching, Try, Option, and Either, which will be discussed in subsequent sections. Through effective use of these constructs, developers can manage errors in a clean and functional manner, ensuring the robustness of their Scala applications.

7.3   Try, Success, and Failure

The Try type in Scala is a powerful tool for handling exceptions in a more functional and declarative way. It encapsulates methods that might result in a successful computation (represented by Success) or an exception (represented by Failure), abstracting away traditional try-catch blocks and enhancing code readability and maintainability.

The Try type is an abstract sealed class, and it has two subclasses: Success and Failure. The primary goal of Try is to provide a way to manage exceptions that might arise from operations, such as input/output (I/O) actions, that could potentially fail.

To work with Try, you need to import the necessary Scala package:

```
import scala.util.{Try, Success, Failure}
```

Creating Try Instances

Try instances are created by wrapping code that may throw exceptions within a Try constructor.

```
val result = Try {
  // code that may throw an exception
  10 / 0
}
```

The result of the above expression will be a Failure because dividing by zero throws an ArithmeticException. If the operation had been successful, result would contain a Success.

Handling Try, Success, and Failure

Handling Try results effectively requires understanding its two possible outcomes: Success and Failure. To inspect or act upon the result, pattern matching is often used.

```
result match {
  case Success(value) => println(s"Success: $value")
  case Failure(exception) => println(s"Error: ${exception.getMessage}")
}
```

This pattern matching construct distinguishes between a successful computation and a failure, gracefully handling both scenarios.

Chaining Operations with Try

Chaining operations on Try instances allows for composing multiple computations that may fail. Methods like map, flatMap, recover, and recoverWith are instrumental in achieving this.

map and flatMap can be used to transform or chain additional computations on a successful result:

```
val result = Try {
  42
}.map(x => x + 1)

val chainedResult = result.flatMap(x => Try(x * 2))
```

In the above code, if the initial Try is a Success, map and flatMap will perform the transformations. If it is a Failure, the error will propagate through without applying the functions.

189

Error Recovery

To handle errors in a Try context, recover and recoverWith methods can be used. These methods allow for defining alternative computations or returning a default value in case of failure.

```
val result = Try {
  10 / 0
}.recover {
  case e: ArithmeticException => 42
}

val complexRecovery = result.recoverWith {
  case e: ArithmeticException => Try(42 / 2)
}
```

In the first example, recover catches the ArithmeticException and returns a default value. In the second example, recoverWith allows for another Try to be executed in case of failure.

Combining Multiple Try Instances

Combining multiple Try instances can be performed using for-comprehensions. This approach allows for elegant handling of sequential operations where each step might fail:

```
val combinedResult = for {
  a <- Try(10)
  b <- Try(20 / a)
} yield a + b
```

If any Try in the sequence fails, the entire result will be a Failure, propagating the error through.

Practical Use Cases

Reading from a File:

```
import scala.io.Source

def readFile(filename: String): Try[String] = Try {
  val source = Source.fromFile(filename)
  val content = try source.mkString finally source.close()
  content
}
```

The readFile method wraps file reading logic within a Try to capture potential exceptions. Pattern matching can be applied to handle the returned Try instance appropriately.

```
val content = readFile("test.txt")
content match {
  case Success(text) => println(text)
  case Failure(e) => println(s"Failed to read the file: ${e.getMessage}")
}
```

Failed to read the file: /test.txt (No such file or directory)

Database Operations:

```
def queryDatabase(query: String): Try[List[Map[String, Any]]] = Try {
  // Assume we have a database connection object db
  val resultSet = db.executeQuery(query)
  val results = resultSet.map { row =>
    Map(
      "id" -> row.getInt("id"),
      "name" -> row.getString("name")
    )
  }
  results.toList
}
```

Database operations can similarly be encapsulated within a Try to manage potential SQL exceptions gracefully.

Using Try, Success, and Failure in Scala offers a structured and functional approach to exception handling, replacing imperative try-catch blocks with cleaner and more readable code.

7.4 Using Option for Error Handling

In functional programming, the Option type is a powerful tool for handling the presence and absence of values without resorting to null references or throwing exceptions. This section delves into using Option for error handling in Scala, providing a comprehensive explanation of its structure, usage patterns, and best practices.

Option is a container type that represents a value that might be present (defined) or absent (undefined). It can either be an Option[T], where T is the type of the value, and it can take one of two forms:

- Some(value) - signifies that a value is present.

- None - indicates that no value is present.

The following Scala code examples demonstrate how to use Option:

```
val someValue: Option[Int] = Some(5)
val noneValue: Option[Int] = None
```

A common use case for Option is safely accessing elements in collections. For instance, accessing an element by index in a List can return

191

an Option.

```
val list = List(1, 2, 3)
val firstElement: Option[Int] = list.headOption
val fifthElement: Option[Int] = list.lift(4)
```

In the example above, list.headOption retrieves the first element of the list, wrapped in an Option. If the list is empty, it returns None. Similarly, list.lift(4) attempts to access the fifth element but will return None since the list contains only three elements.

Option promotes safe, functional access to values through pattern matching and higher-order functions like map, flatMap, and getOrElse. Below are usage scenarios illustrating these approaches:

```
val maybeValue: Option[Int] = Some(10)

// Using pattern matching
maybeValue match {
  case Some(value) => println(s"Value is $value")
  case None => println("No value found")
}

// Using map
val incrementedValue: Option[Int] = maybeValue.map(_ + 1)

// Using flatMap
val doubledValue: Option[Int] = maybeValue.flatMap(v => Some(v * 2))

// Using getOrElse
val valueOrDefault: Int = maybeValue.getOrElse(0)
```

Pattern matching provides explicit control over the presence and absence cases, ensuring both cases are handled. The map function transforms the contained value if it exists, while flatMap allows chaining operations that also return Option. The getOrElse method retrieves the value if present, or it returns a provided default.

When dealing with functions that may fail, returning an Option is preferable to throwing exceptions, as it naturally integrates with the functional paradigm. Consider the following function that attempts to parse an integer from a string:

```
def parseInt(str: String): Option[Int] = {
  try {
    Some(str.toInt)
  } catch {
    case _: NumberFormatException => None
  }
}
```

In this example, parseInt returns Some(value) if the string is successfully parsed as an integer, and None if a NumberFormatException occurs.

This allows clients of the function to handle parsing errors without dealing with exceptions.

When dealing with multiple Option values, for-comprehensions provide a concise, readable syntax for combining operations that could return None. The following example demonstrates how you can chain multiple optional computations:

```
val first: Option[Int] = Some(2)
val second: Option[Int] = Some(3)

val result: Option[Int] = for {
  a <- first
  b <- second
} yield a + b
```

Here, the for-comprehension extracts values from first and second if both are Some, and computes their sum. If any of these values is None, the result is None.

Proper use of Option leads to more resilient code by avoiding null pointer exceptions and using a type-safe manner to represent optional values. It aligns with the functional programming paradigm, encouraging more predictable and maintainable error handling patterns.

7.5 Either and Its Uses

Scala provides the Either type as a powerful tool for error handling that can encapsulate a value of one of two possible types. It is particularly useful for functions that can return either a success value or an error, making it a critical component in functional error handling.

The Either type is defined as follows:

```
sealed abstract class Either[+A, +B]
case class Left[+A, +B](value: A) extends Either[A, B]
case class Right[+A, +B](value: B) extends Either[A, B]
```

In this definition, Left typically represents a failure or an error, while Right represents a successful result. This convention is widely used, but it is crucial to understand that Either itself does not enforce any semantic meaning—developers must consistently apply this convention in their code.

To illustrate the usage of Either, consider a simple example of dividing two numbers where division by zero results in an error.

```
def divide(a: Int, b: Int): Either[String, Int] = {
```

```
  if (b == 0) Left("Division by zero error")
  else Right(a / b)
}
```

In this example, the divide function returns Either[String, Int]. If the divisor b is zero, the function returns Left with an error message. Otherwise, it returns Right with the result of the division.

Consuming the result of an Either is typically done through pattern matching. For instance:

```
val result = divide(10, 0)
result match {
  case Left(error) => println(s"Failed: $error")
  case Right(value) => println(s"Result: $value")
}
```

Failed: Division by zero error

Using pattern matching, we can handle both the success and failure cases accordingly.

Another useful method in the Either class is the fold method, which allows handling both Left and Right values in a more succinct manner:

```
result.fold(
  error => println(s"Failed: $error"),
  value => println(s"Result: $value")
)
```

This method takes two functions: one for handling Left and another for handling Right. The corresponding function is executed based on whether the Either is a Left or Right.

Chaining Operations with Either

Either also supports chaining operations through for-comprehensions. This is particularly useful when a sequence of operations may fail, and each step depends on the previous one. To illustrate this, consider a function that combines several operations that may each fail:

```
def divide(a: Int, b: Int): Either[String, Int] = {
  if (b == 0) Left("Division by zero error")
  else Right(a / b)
}

def reciprocal(x: Int): Either[String, Double] = {
  if (x == 0) Left("Reciprocal of zero error")
  else Right(1.0 / x)
}
```

194

```
def program(a: Int, b: Int): Either[String, Double] = {
  for {
    quotient <- divide(a, b)
    result <- reciprocal(quotient)
  } yield result
}
```

In this example, the program function performs a division and then computes the reciprocal of the result. Both operations may fail, but the for-comprehension allows for concise error handling and propagation. The result of the for-comprehension is an Either containing the final result or an error message:

```
val computation = program(10, 2)
computation match {
  case Left(error) => println(s"Operation failed: $error")
  case Right(result) => println(s"Operation succeeded: $result")
}
```

Operation succeeded: 0.5

Transforming Either

Methods such as map and flatMap are provided to transform the Right value while leaving the Left value unchanged. This functional approach to error handling aligns with the principles of immutability and chainable transformations that Scala promotes.

map applies a function to the Right value:

```
val right = Right(5)
val result = right.map(_ * 2)
// result: Either[Nothing, Int] = Right(10)
```

flatMap is useful for chaining operations that return Either:

```
val result = Right(5).flatMap(x => Right(x * 2))
// result: Either[Nothing, Int] = Right(10)
```

leftMap allows transforming the Left value:

```
val left = Left("Error")
val result = left.left.map(_.toUpperCase)
// result: Either[String, Nothing] = Left("ERROR")
```

Swap method switches the context from Right to Left and vice versa:

```
val right = Right(10)
val swapped = right.swap
// swapped: Either[Int, Nothing] = Left(10)
```

195

The use of these methods ensures clean, readable, and maintainable code by handling success and failure cases in a type-safe and declarative manner.

7.6 Pattern Matching for Error Handling

Pattern matching is a powerful feature in Scala that can be leveraged for concise and expressive error handling. It allows developers to check a value against a pattern and execute code based on the match. This section explores how pattern matching can be used to handle errors effectively within different contexts.

Consider the following basic example where a division by zero might occur:

```
def divide(a: Int, b: Int): Either[String, Int] = {
  if (b == 0) Left("Division by zero")
  else Right(a / b)
}
```

In the divide function, we return an Either[String, Int], with Left representing an error (in this case, "Division by zero") and Right representing a successful division result. Below is an example of using pattern matching to handle the result of this division function:

```
val result = divide(10, 0)
result match {
  case Left(error) => println(s"Error: $error")
  case Right(value) => println(s"Result: $value")
}
```

When divide(10, 0) is executed, the output will be:

```
Error: Division by zero
```

This demonstrates how pattern matching can be used to check for errors and handle them accordingly. The flexibility and readability of pattern matching make it a crucial technique for error handling in Scala.

Pattern matching is not limited to Either but can also be used with Try, Success, and Failure. Here is an example:

```
import scala.util.{Try, Success, Failure}

def divideWithTry(a: Int, b: Int): Try[Int] = Try(a / b)

val result = divideWithTry(10, 0)
result match {
  case Success(value) => println(s"Result: $value")
  case Failure(exception) => println(s"Error: ${exception.getMessage}")
```

```
}
```

The output from $\text{divideWithTry}(10, 0)$ will be:

```
Error: / by zero
```

Using pattern matching with Try abstracts away the need for explicit error handling logic seen with Either, leveraging Scala's built-in structures to manage exceptions.

Pattern matching can also be integrated with the Option type. Consider the following example:

```
def findElement(xs: List[Int], element: Int): Option[Int] = {
  xs.find(_ == element)
}

val result = findElement(List(1, 2, 3), 4)
result match {
  case Some(value) => println(s"Element found: $value")
  case None => println("Element not found")
}
```

The output when searching for the number 4 in the list $\text{List}(1, 2, 3)$ will be:

```
Element not found
```

Pattern matching with Option simplifies the structural handling of missing values. The Some and None cases clearly express when an element is found or not, improving code readability.

Pattern matching is also powerful for handling custom exceptions. Here is an example using a custom exception:

```
case class CustomException(message: String) extends Exception(message)

def riskyOperation(x: Int): Either[CustomException, Int] = {
  if (x < 0) Left(CustomException("Negative value error"))
  else Right(x * 2)
}

val result = riskyOperation(-1)
result match {
  case Left(ex) => println(s"Handled Custom Exception: ${ex.message}")
  case Right(value) => println(s"Operation Successful: $value")
}
```

The output for $\text{riskyOperation}(-1)$ will be:

```
Handled Custom Exception: Negative value error
```

By defining a CustomException and using pattern matching, the handling of specific error conditions becomes clear and structured.

197

Utilizing pattern matching for error handling in Scala allows developers to create more maintainable and readable code. The ability to directly decompose and act upon different error conditions through pattern matching is invaluable, making it an essential technique in a Scala programmer's toolkit.

7.7 Resource Management and Using Clause

Managing resources efficiently is pivotal in ensuring robust and clean code in Scala, particularly when dealing with file I/O, database connections, and network communications. Improper management of these resources can lead to memory leaks, resource contention, and other critical issues.

In this section, we focus on the using clause, introduced to simplify and enhance resource management in Scala. This technique ensures that resources are correctly acquired and released, providing a cleaner and more concise approach compared to traditional try-finally blocks.

Scala provides the Using object in the scala.util package, designed to manage resources using the AutoCloseable interface. By employing the Using object, you can ensure that resources are closed automatically, even if an exception occurs during their use.

```
import scala.util.{Try, Using}
import java.io._

val result: Try[String] = Using(new BufferedReader(new FileReader("example.txt"))) {
    reader =>
  reader.readLine()
}
```

In this example, Using is utilized to manage a BufferedReader object. The resource is opened and provided to the block of code where it is used. After the block is executed, whether it succeeds or an exception is thrown, the BufferedReader is automatically closed.

Nested Resource Management

In complex applications, it is common to manage multiple resources simultaneously. You can nest Using blocks to handle multiple resources. Here is an example demonstrating nested Using blocks for reading from one file and writing to another.

```
val result: Try[Unit] = Using(new BufferedReader(new FileReader("input.txt"))) {
    reader =>
  Using(new BufferedWriter(new FileWriter("output.txt"))) { writer =>
    var line = reader.readLine()
    while (line != null) {
      writer.write(line)
      writer.newLine()
      line = reader.readLine()
    }
  }
}
```

In this snippet, both BufferedReader and BufferedWriter are managed within their respective Using blocks. Each resource is safely closed once its corresponding block of code has been executed.

Resource Management with Custom Resources

In addition to standard library resources, you can manage custom resources by ensuring they implement the AutoCloseable interface. Here is an example of a custom resource:

```
class CustomResource extends AutoCloseable {
  def operate(): Unit = println("Operating on custom resource")
  def close(): Unit = println("Custom resource closed")
}

val result: Try[Unit] = Using(new CustomResource) { resource =>
  resource.operate()
}
```

In this case, CustomResource implements the AutoCloseable interface with a close method. The Using construct ensures that operate is called safely, and close is invoked automatically after execution.

Handling Multiple Exceptions

One of the advantages of the Using clause is the ability to handle multiple exceptions more gracefully. Here's an advanced example showcasing this capability:

```
val result: Try[Unit] = Using(new BufferedReader(new FileReader("input.txt"))) {
    reader =>
  Using(new BufferedWriter(new FileWriter("output.txt"))) { writer =>
    try {
      var line = reader.readLine()
      while (line != null) {
        writer.write(line)
        writer.newLine()
        line = reader.readLine()
      }
    } catch {
      case e: IOException => println(s"Error during I/O operations: ${e.getMessage}")
    }
  }
}
```

Here, a try-catch block is used within the Using blocks to catch and handle any IOException that may occur during read/write operations. The Using construct ensures that both the reader and writer resources are always closed properly, even if an exception is thrown.

Best Practices for Resource Management

To mitigate the risk of resource leaks and enhance the reliability of your Scala applications, adhere to the following best practices:

- Prefer the Using clause over manual resource management methods.

- Ensure all custom resources implement the AutoCloseable interface.

- Handle exceptions within Using blocks to ensure resources are released correctly.

- Test resource-handling code thoroughly to verify automatic closure and detection of potential leaks.

Applying these practices not only simplifies your code but also ensures resources are managed efficiently, thus avoiding common pitfalls associated with manual resource handling.

7.8 Custom Exceptions

In Scala, as in many other programming languages, it is often necessary to define custom exceptions to handle specific error conditions more gracefully and meaningfully. Custom exceptions allow developers to create exception types tailored to their application's particular needs, providing clearer insights into what went wrong and how to handle it. This section explores the process of defining and using custom exceptions in Scala, emphasizing best practices to ensure code clarity and maintainability.

To create a custom exception in Scala, you typically extend one of the existing exception classes. The most common parent class for custom exceptions is Exception, but depending on the context, extending other classes like RuntimeException or IOException might be more appropriate.

Consider the following example, where a custom exception InvalidOp-erationException is defined to signal an invalid operation attempt in some hypothetical application.

```
class InvalidOperationException(message: String) extends Exception(message)
```

Here, InvalidOperationException inherits from Exception, and its con-structor takes a String message argument that describes the error. This custom exception can now be thrown using the throw keyword and caught using a try-catch block.

To see it in action, consider the following code snippet, which throws the custom exception if an operation is deemed invalid:

```
object OperationHandler {
  def performOperation(op: String): Unit = {
    if(op == "invalid") {
      throw new InvalidOperationException("Invalid operation requested")
    } else {
      println(s"Performing operation: $op")
    }
  }
}

try {
  OperationHandler.performOperation("invalid")
} catch {
  case e: InvalidOperationException => println(s"Caught custom exception: ${e.
      getMessage}")
}
```

In this example, when an invalid operation is requested, the custom exception is thrown and subsequently caught in the catch block, where the error message is printed.

It is crucial to ensure that exception messages are informative and pre-cise. This practice aids in diagnosing the error's source more effectively during debugging and error handling. Additionally, custom exceptions can be augmented with more context-specific information by adding extra parameters to the constructor. For example:

```
class InvalidOperationException(message: String, errorCode: Int) extends Exception(
      message) {
  def getErrorCode: Int = errorCode
}

object OperationHandler {
  def performOperation(op: String): Unit = {
    if(op == "invalid") {
      throw new InvalidOperationException("Invalid operation requested", 1001)
    } else {
      println(s"Performing operation: $op")
    }
  }
}
```

```
try {
  OperationHandler.performOperation("invalid")
} catch {
  case e: InvalidOperationException =>
    println(s"Caught custom exception: ${e.getMessage}, Error Code: ${e.getErrorCode
      }")
}
```

In this more sophisticated example, the InvalidOperationException includes an additional integer parameter, errorCode, which can store a specific error code related to the exception. This makes error handling more robust, as additional context about the error is available.

Creating an exception hierarchy with multiple levels of custom exceptions improves maintainability and scalability in complex applications. Consider an application dealing with various user-related errors:

```
abstract class UserException(message: String) extends Exception(message)

class UserNotFoundException(userId: String) extends UserException(s"User with ID
    $userId not found")

class InvalidUserCredentialsException(username: String) extends UserException(s"
    Invalid credentials for user $username")
```

Here, UserException serves as a base class for user-related exceptions, while UserNotFoundException and InvalidUserCredentialsException provide specific error conditions.

Now, we can handle these custom exceptions in a more general way:

```
object UserService {
  def findUser(userId: String): Unit = {
    throw new UserNotFoundException(userId)
  }

  def authenticateUser(username: String, password: String): Unit = {
    throw new InvalidUserCredentialsException(username)
  }
}

try {
  UserService.findUser("12345")
} catch {
  case e: UserNotFoundException => println(s"Caught specific custom exception: ${e.
      getMessage}")
  case e: InvalidUserCredentialsException => println(s"Caught another custom
      exception: ${e.getMessage}")
  case e: UserException => println(s"Caught general user exception: ${e.getMessage}")
}
```

This structured hierarchy makes it possible to catch both specific and general user-related exceptions effectively. The ability to distinguish between different error conditions allows more precise and meaningful error handling.

When defining custom exceptions, it is also beneficial to follow established conventions. Here are a few best practices:

- Naming conventions: Custom exception names should end with Exception to clearly indicate their purpose.

- Avoid extending Throwable: Always extend Exception or its subclasses to avoid issues with error handling mechanisms.

- Provide constructor parameters that add meaningful context to the exception.

- Document each custom exception class: Clearly describe the error conditions that the exception represents.

By following these conventions, you ensure that your custom exceptions are well-defined, maintainable, and aligned with standard practices, significantly enhancing the robustness and readability of your Scala codebase.

7.9   Best Practices for Error Handling

Error handling is a critical aspect of software development, aiming to manage unexpected situations and maintain program robustness. Proper error handling enhances code readability, maintainability, and overall reliability. This section outlines best practices for error handling in Scala, facilitating the creation of resilient applications.

1. Prioritize Functional Error Handling

Functional programming in Scala promotes immutability and first-class functions. Prioritize using functional constructs like Option, Either, and Try for error handling instead of traditional exception handling. These constructs encapsulate successful and failed computations, making error scenarios explicit and manageable within function compositions.

```
def divide(a: Double, b: Double): Try[Double] = {
    if (b == 0) Failure(new ArithmeticException("Division by zero"))
    else Success(a / b)
}

val result: Try[Double] = divide(4, 2)
result match {
    case Success(value) => println(s"Result: $value")
```

```
    case Failure(exception) => println(s"Error: ${exception.getMessage}")
}
```

2. Leverage Pattern Matching

Pattern matching simplifies the handling of different error types. Utilize pattern matching to process the results of computations that may fail. This method enhances readability by clearly delineating success and failure paths.

```
val result: Either[String, Int] = Right(42)

result match {
    case Right(value) => println(s"Success: $value")
    case Left(error) => println(s"Error: $error")
}
```

3. Fail Fast and Provide Context

Detecting errors as early as possible and providing sufficient context aids in quick diagnosis. Ensure errors are caught at the point they occur, and additional information is included to facilitate debugging.

```
def parseInt(s: String): Either[String, Int] = {
    try {
        Right(s.toInt)
    } catch {
        case ex: NumberFormatException => Left(s"Failed to parse '$s' as Int: ${ex.
            getMessage}")
    }
}
```

4. Avoid Catching Generic Exceptions

Catching generic exceptions like Throwable may obscure specific issues and make debugging difficult. Catch specific exceptions to handle known error conditions appropriately and allow unknown exceptions to propagate, potentially revealing unanticipated errors.

```
try {
    // Some code that may throw exceptions
} catch {
    case ex: IOException => handleIOException(ex)
    case ex: SQLException => handleSQLException(ex)
    // Avoid: case ex: Throwable => handleAllExceptions(ex)
}
```

5. Limit the Use of Side Effects

Functional programming discourages side effects, promoting pure functions. Limit side effects within error handling to maintain function purity. Utilizing constructs such as Try, Option, and Either implicitly manages side effects by encapsulating them.

6. Use Finally to Clean Up Resources

When dealing with resource management, ensure resources like file handles or network connections are properly closed using finally. Scala's try-with-resources pattern can help manage resources effectively.

```
import scala.util.{Try, Using}

val source = Using(scala.io.Source.fromFile("example.txt")) { source =>
    // Perform operations on the file
    source.getLines().mkString("\n")
}

source match {
    case Success(content) => println(content)
    case Failure(exception) => println(s"Failed to read file: ${exception.getMessage}")
}
```

7. Document and Communicate Errors Clearly

Maintaining clear and informative error messages helps users and developers understand issues. Document potential error conditions and ensure error messages provide actionable information.

```
def connect(url: String): Either[String, Connection] = {
    try {
        // Attempt connection
        Right(new Connection(url))
    } catch {
        case ex: ConnectionException => Left(s"Failed to connect to $url: ${ex.getMessage}")
    }
}
```

8. Centralize Error Handling Logic

Consolidate error handling logic into reusable methods or objects to avoid redundancy and ensure consistency across the application. This centralization can simplify error management and align with the DRY (Don't Repeat Yourself) principle.

```
object ErrorHandler {
    def handleException(ex: Exception): String = {
        ex match {
            case _: NullPointerException => "Null value encountered."
            case _: IllegalArgumentException => "Invalid argument provided."
            case _ => "An unexpected error occurred."
        }
    }
}
```

9. Utilize Logging for Error Tracking

Implement logging to record errors and application states, aiding in di-

205

agnosis and monitoring. Ensure logs contain sufficient detail to trace issues without overwhelming the log files with verbosity.

```
import org.slf4j.LoggerFactory

val logger = LoggerFactory.getLogger(getClass)

def process(data: String): Either[String, Int] = {
  try {
    // Some processing that may throw exceptions
    Right(data.toInt)
  } catch {
    case ex: NumberFormatException =>
      logger.error(s"Failed to process data: ${data}", ex)
      Left(s"Error processing data: ${ex.getMessage}")
  }
}
```

Implementing these best practices will enhance the reliability, maintainability, and readability of Scala applications. Proper error handling ensures applications can gracefully manage unexpected conditions and provide meaningful feedback to users and developers.

7.10 Functional Error Handling

Functional programming promotes pure functions, immutability, and declarative code, providing a robust foundation for managing errors without relying on traditional exceptions. In Scala, functional error handling embraces these principles by utilizing monadic constructs such as Option, Either, and Try, along with higher-order functions. This allows developers to write concise, expressive, and less error-prone code.

Option is widely used to represent the presence or absence of a value, avoiding the pitfalls of null references. The type Option[A] can be either Some[A] for a value or None to indicate the absence of a value. Here's an example of how to use Option:

```
def parseInteger(input: String): Option[Int] = {
  try {
    Some(input.toInt)
  } catch {
    case _: NumberFormatException => None
  }
}
```

In this function, the parseInteger method returns Some integer if parsing succeeds or None if it fails. This approach prevents runtime exceptions and provides a clear contract.

Try is another construct that is more expressive than Option when dealing with computations that may fail. Try can represent a computation that either returns a value (Success) or results in an error (Failure). Here's how Try can be used:

```scala
import scala.util.{Try, Success, Failure}

def divide(dividend: Int, divisor: Int): Try[Int] = {
  Try(dividend / divisor)
}

val result = divide(10, 0)
result match {
  case Success(value) => println(s"Result: $value")
  case Failure(exception) => println(s"Failed: ${exception.getMessage}")
}
```

In this example, the divide function wraps the division operation in a Try. If the division is successful, Success is returned; if it results in an error (such as division by zero), Failure is returned.

Either is a type that can represent a value of one of two possible types, conventionally named Left and Right. By convention, Left is used for failure and Right for success. Here's an example:

```scala
def safeDivide(dividend: Int, divisor: Int): Either[String, Int] = {
  if (divisor == 0)
    Left("Division by zero error.")
  else
    Right(dividend / divisor)
}

val result = safeDivide(10, 0)
result match {
  case Left(error) => println(s"Error: $error")
  case Right(value) => println(s"Result: $value")
}
```

In this example, safeDivide returns a Left with an error message in case of a failure, or a Right with the result of the division if successful.

One of the significant advantages of using these constructs is their ability to be composed using combinator methods like map, flatMap, filter, and for-comprehensions. Here is an example using Try with for-comprehension:

```scala
def safeAdd(a: Int, b: Int): Try[Int] = Try(a + b)
def safeSubtract(a: Int, b: Int): Try[Int] = Try(a - b)
def safeMultiply(a: Int, b: Int): Try[Int] = Try(a * b)

val result = for {
  sum <- safeAdd(10, 5)
  diff <- safeSubtract(sum, 3)
  product <- safeMultiply(diff, 2)
} yield product
```

```
result match {
  case Success(value) => println(s"Computation result: $value")
  case Failure(exception) => println(s"Computation failed: ${exception.getMessage}")
}
```

In this example, safeAdd, safeSubtract, and safeMultiply are composed sequentially using a for-comprehension. This ensures that the computation is halted immediately if any step fails, and the error is propagated effectively.

Functional error handling in Scala is further enhanced by libraries such as cats, which introduces type classes like MonadError to handle error-prone computations within monadic contexts. Here is a brief look into using the cats library for error handling:

```
import cats.MonadError
import cats.instances.either._

type ErrorOr[A] = Either[String, A]

def example[F[_]](implicit M: MonadError[F, String]): F[Int] = {
  M.pure(42)
}

val result: ErrorOr[Int] = example[ErrorOr]
result match {
  case Left(error) => println(s"Error: $error")
  case Right(value) => println(s"Value: $value")
}
```

In this example, example showcases how to use a type class MonadError to abstract over error handling. This approach enables writing generic functions that are agnostic to the specific error handling mechanism used.

Functional error handling not only aligns with the principles of functional programming but also leads to more predictable, testable, and maintainable code. By utilizing constructs like Option, Try, Either, and leveraging advanced libraries, developers can write code that gracefully handles errors without confusing control flow or hidden side effects.

7.11 Logging and Monitoring Errors

Logging and monitoring errors are crucial aspects of maintaining robust and reliable applications. In Scala, these practices help developers track the occurrence and frequency of errors, diagnose issues, and monitor the overall health of their systems. This section will discuss various strategies and tools for implementing effective logging and monitoring.

Logging in Scala:

Logging in Scala can be achieved by using libraries such as Logback and SLF4J. These libraries offer both asynchronous and synchronous logging capabilities, support for various logging levels, and integration with different logging frameworks.

To implement logging in Scala, add the necessary dependencies to your build.sbt file:

```
libraryDependencies += "ch.qos.logback" % "logback-classic" % "1.2.3"
libraryDependencies += "org.slf4j" % "slf4j-api" % "1.7.25"
```

Next, create a logger instance within your Scala code as follows:

```
import org.slf4j.LoggerFactory

object MyLogger {
  val logger = LoggerFactory.getLogger(this.getClass)
}
```

With the logger instance ready, you can log messages at various levels:

```
MyLogger.logger.debug("This is a debug message")
MyLogger.logger.info("This is an info message")
MyLogger.logger.warn("This is a warning message")
MyLogger.logger.error("This is an error message")
```

By configuring Logback through a logback.xml file, users can specify details on log formatting, log file locations, and the logging granularity.

```
<configuration>
  <appender name="FILE" class="ch.qos.logback.core.FileAppender">
    <file>my_log_file.log</file>
    <encoder>
      <pattern>%d{yyyy-MM-dd HH:mm:ss} - %msg%n</pattern>
    </encoder>
  </appender>

  <root level="debug">
    <appender-ref ref="FILE" />
  </root>
</configuration>
```

Monitoring Errors:

Monitoring errors involves tracking application metrics, alerts, and log aggregation. Tools such as Prometheus, Grafana, and ELK Stack (Elasticsearch, Logstash, and Kibana) are commonly used for this purpose.

To start with Grafana and Prometheus, include necessary dependencies in your build.sbt file:

```
libraryDependencies += "io.prometheus" % "simpleclient" % "0.8.1"
libraryDependencies += "io.prometheus" % "simpleclient_httpserver" % "0.8.1"
libraryDependencies += "io.prometheus" % "simpleclient_hotspot" % "0.8.1"
```

Initialize the Prometheus metrics in your code:

```
import io.prometheus.client.exporter.HTTPServer
import io.prometheus.client.hotspot.DefaultExports

object MyMetrics {
  def init(): Unit = {
    DefaultExports.initialize()
    new HTTPServer(9091)
  }
}
```

This code creates an HTTP server at port 9091, where Prometheus can scrape the metrics.

For more sophisticated log management, the ELK Stack offers a comprehensive solution with Elasticsearch for storing logs, Logstash for processing logs, and Kibana for visualizing logs. Configuration can be complex and requires setting up each component to collect, process, and visualize logs effectively.

Example configuration for Logstash can include filters for parsing logs from various sources:

```
input {
  file {
    path => "/path/to/log/file.log"
    start_position => "beginning"
  }
}

filter {
  grok {
    match => { "message" => "%{TIMESTAMP_ISO8601:timestamp} - %{
        LOGLEVEL:level} - %{GREEDYDATA:message}" }
  }
}

output {
  elasticsearch {
    hosts => ["localhost:9200"]
    index => "my_logs"
  }
}
```

Finally, Kibana configurations allow for the visualization and analyses of logs:

```
Setup Kibana dashboards, saved searches, and visualizations via the Kibana web UI.
```

> Use Elasticsearch indices created by Logstash to create charts, graphs, and alerts.

By combining strong logging practices with effective monitoring tools, developers can ensure their Scala applications are both reliable and maintainable.

Chapter 8

Scala for Data Processing

This chapter focuses on using Scala for data processing tasks. It covers file input and output, working with CSV and JSON data, and data parsing and transformation. The chapter introduces Apache Spark for distributed data processing, including working with RDDs, DataFrames, and performing SQL queries. It also discusses stream processing with Spark Streaming and data visualization using Scala libraries.

8.1 Introduction to Data Processing in Scala

Scala provides a robust environment for data processing, catering to both functional and object-oriented paradigms. The language facilitates seamless integration with Java libraries, while offering powerful features like pattern matching, immutability, and higher-order functions. The syntax is expressive yet concise, making it particularly suitable for handling complex data operations efficiently.

File Operations: One of the fundamental tasks in data processing involves file input and output operations. Scala's scala.io.Source and java.io.PrintWriter classes provide an intuitive manner for reading from and writing to files.

```
import scala.io.Source

val filename = "data.txt"
val lines = Source.fromFile(filename).getLines().toList
lines.foreach(println)
```

213

```
import java.io.{File, PrintWriter}

val data = List("line1", "line2", "line3")
val file = new File("output.txt")
val writer = new PrintWriter(file)

data.foreach(writer.println)
writer.close()
```

Working with CSV and JSON: Data often comes in CSV or JSON formats. Scala's standard library, combined with external libraries such as scala-csv and json4s, enables efficient reading, parsing, and processing of these formats.

Reading a CSV file using the scala-csv library:

```
import com.github.tototoshi.csv._

val reader = CSVReader.open(new File("data.csv"))
val allData = reader.all()
reader.close()
```

Parsing a JSON file using json4s library:

```
import org.json4s._
import org.json4s.jackson.JsonMethods._

val json = parse(Source.fromFile("data.json").mkString)
val extracted = (json \ "key").extract[String]
```

Data Transformation: Efficient data processing requires robust methods for transforming data. Scala provides comprehensive support through its collection library, which includes methods such as map, filter, reduce, and many more.

Example of transforming a list of integers:

```
val nums = List(1, 2, 3, 4, 5)
val squared = nums.map(x => x * x)
val sum = squared.reduce((a, b) => a + b)
```

Integration with Apache Spark: Scala is the primary language for Apache Spark, a distributed data processing framework. With Spark, we can handle large-scale data processing tasks using Resilient Distributed Datasets (RDDs), DataFrames, and Datasets.

Creating an RDD and performing a simple transformation:

```
import org.apache.spark.{SparkConf, SparkContext}

val conf = new SparkConf().setAppName("Simple Application").setMaster("local")
val sc = new SparkContext(conf)
val data = sc.parallelize(Seq(1, 2, 3, 4, 5))
```

```
val squaredRDD = data.map(x => x * x)
val result = squaredRDD.collect()

result.foreach(println)
```

Stream Processing: Real-time data processing is achieved through Spark Streaming. Data streams are created, manipulated, and processed in fault-tolerant ways using Spark's high-level APIs.

Example of streaming text data from a TCP source:

```
import org.apache.spark.SparkConf
import org.apache.spark.streaming.{Seconds, StreamingContext}

val conf = new SparkConf().setMaster("local[2]").setAppName("NetworkWordCount")
val ssc = new StreamingContext(conf, Seconds(10))

val lines = ssc.socketTextStream("localhost", 9999)
val words = lines.flatMap(_.split(" "))
val wordCounts = words.map(x => (x, 1)).reduceByKey(_ + _)

wordCounts.print()
ssc.start()
ssc.awaitTermination()
```

Data Visualization: Visualizing processed data enhances comprehension and insight extraction. Scala's integration with visualization libraries such as Breeze and Vegas simplifies creating interactive and informative visual representations.

Creating a simple plot using Breeze:

```
import breeze.plot._

val fig = Figure()
val plt = fig.subplot(0)
val x = linspace(0.0, 1.0)
plt += plot(x, x :^ 2.0)
plt.xlabel = "x"
plt.ylabel = "y"
fig.saveas("plot.png")
```

Scala's powerful and versatile ecosystem, along with its ability to interoperate with Java, makes it an ideal choice for data processing tasks from experimental analysis to production systems involving large-scale data.

8.2 Reading and Writing Files

In data processing, reading from and writing to files is a fundamental task. Scala provides various tools to facilitate file I/O operations efficiently. This section will delve into the methods for reading from and writing to files, with an emphasis on practical examples and use cases.

Reading Files

Scala's scala.io.Source object is a versatile and straightforward way to read files. The following example demonstrates how to read the contents of a file line-by-line:

```
import scala.io.Source

val filename = "example.txt"
val fileContent = Source.fromFile(filename).getLines().toList

fileContent.foreach(println)
```

In this example, Source.fromFile(filename) creates a source to read from the specified file. The getLines() method retrieves an iterator over the lines of the file, which is then converted to a List using toList. Finally, foreach(println) prints each line to the console.

For reading the entire content of a file into a single string, use the mkString method:

```
val fileContent = Source.fromFile(filename).mkString
println(fileContent)
```

To ensure resources are properly managed and avoid resource leaks, it's prudent to close the source after reading. Here's how you can accomplish this:

```
val source = Source.fromFile(filename)
try {
  val fileContent = source.mkString
  println(fileContent)
} finally {
  source.close()
}
```

Writing Files

For writing to files, Scala leverages the java.io.PrintWriter class. Below is a basic example of writing to a file:

```
import java.io.PrintWriter

val pw = new PrintWriter("output.txt")
pw.write("Hello, Scala!\nThis is an example of writing to a file.")
pw.close()
```

In this snippet, the PrintWriter class is used to write text to output.txt. The write method writes a string to the file. After writing, the close method ensures the file is properly saved and closed.

When dealing with multiple lines, println within PrintWriter can be utilized:

```
val lines = List("Line 1", "Line 2", "Line 3")

val pw = new PrintWriter("output_lines.txt")
lines.foreach(pw.println)
pw.close()
```

Here, a list of lines is written to output_lines.txt, with each line appended in its own line in the file.

Working with File Paths

Scala supports working with file paths through java.nio.file. This is beneficial for platform-independent file handling. The following example demonstrates creating a file and writing to it using Paths and Files:

```
import java.nio.file.{Paths, Files}
import java.nio.charset.StandardCharsets

val path = Paths.get("output_nio.txt")
val content = "This content is written using NIO."

Files.write(path, content.getBytes(StandardCharsets.UTF_8))
```

In this example, Paths.get("output_nio.txt") creates a Path object. The Files.write method writes the byte array of the content to the specified path. The charset StandardCharsets.UTF_8 ensures proper encoding.

Appending to Files

To append data to an existing file, use a FileWriter with the append flag set to true. Here's an illustration:

```
import java.io.{FileWriter, BufferedWriter}

val fw = new FileWriter("append_example.txt", true)
val bw = new BufferedWriter(fw)

bw.write("This line will be appended.\n")
bw.close()
```

In this code, new FileWriter("append_example.txt", true) creates a FileWriter in append mode. The BufferedWriter then writes the new content to the file without overwriting the existing data.

Advanced Error Handling

Handling errors during file I/O operations is crucial to ensure robustness. Scala provides exceptions that can be caught and appropriately handled:

```
import java.io.{FileNotFoundException, IOException}

try {
  val source = Source.fromFile("non_existent_file.txt")
  try {
    source.getLines().foreach(println)
  } finally {
    source.close()
  }
} catch {
  case e: FileNotFoundException => println(s"File not found: ${e.getMessage}")
  case e: IOException => println(s"I/O error occurred: ${e.getMessage}")
}
```

In this example, a try-catch block is employed to catch FileNotFoundException and IOException. The error messages are printed, ensuring that the program handles file-related errors gracefully.

This section has explored the facets of reading and writing files in Scala, providing foundational knowledge required for data processing tasks. The detailed examples illustrate how to manage file operations efficiently, ensuring that the reader is equipped with practical skills for real-world applications.

8.3   Working with CSV and JSON Data

Handling CSV and JSON data is often critical in data processing tasks. This section explores how to read, manipulate, and write CSV and JSON data using Scala, ensuring data integrity and efficiency.

Reading CSV data in Scala can be performed using various libraries such as Apache Commons CSV, univocity-parsers, and Spark's CSV module. We will utilize the Spark's CSV module since it integrates seamlessly with Apache Spark, enhancing distributed data processing capabilities.

```
import org.apache.spark.sql.SparkSession

val spark = SparkSession.builder()
  .appName("CSV Reader")
  .config("spark.master", "local")
  .getOrCreate()

val csvPath = "path/to/your/csvfile.csv"
val csvDF = spark.read
  .option("header", "true")
  .option("inferSchema", "true")
  .csv(csvPath)
```

```
csvDF.show()
```

In the code above, SparkSession is created to initiate the Spark application. The read method of SparkSession provides various options for reading a CSV file, where header option indicates whether the CSV file contains a header row, and inferSchema automatically infers the schema of the CSV file.

To write the data back to a CSV file, it is crucial to manage options such as header inclusion and delimiter configuration.

```
csvDF.write
    .option("header", "true")
    .option("delimiter", ",")
    .csv("path/to/output/csvfile.csv")
```

Writing JSON data in Scala follows a similar approach, utilizing the Spark's JSON module. Reading JSON files is straightforward:

```
val jsonPath = "path/to/your/jsonfile.json"
val jsonDF = spark.read
    .option("multiline", "true")
    .json(jsonPath)

jsonDF.show()
```

Here, the multiline option specifies if the JSON file contains data entries across multiple lines. Writing back to JSON involves the write method:

```
jsonDF.write
    .option("compression", "gzip")
    .json("path/to/output/jsonfile.json")
```

The compression option handles data compression, beneficial for reducing storage space.

Data manipulation often necessitates transforming CSV and JSON data structures. Utilizing DataFrame operations can facilitate such transformations effectively. For CSV data, consider filtering rows based on certain criteria:

```
val filteredDF = csvDF.filter("age > 30")
filteredDF.show()
```

For JSON data, you might select a subset of fields:

```
val selectedDF = jsonDF.select("name", "age")
selectedDF.show()
```

Combining data from multiple CSV or JSON files can be performed via union operations.

```
val csvDF2 = spark.read
  .option("header", "true")
  .option("inferSchema", "true")
  .csv("path/to/another/csvfile.csv")

val combinedDF = csvDF.union(csvDF2)
combinedDF.show()
```

Similarly, JSON files can be combined in a straightforward manner:

```
val jsonDF2 = spark.read
  .json("path/to/another/jsonfile.json")

val combinedJSON = jsonDF.union(jsonDF2)
combinedJSON.show()
```

Handling nested JSON structures, often encountered in real-world data, requires special attention. Spark provides robust mechanisms to flatten these structures:

```
val flattenedDF = jsonDF.selectExpr("id", "details.name as name", "details.address as
    address")
flattenedDF.show()
```

Here, the selectExpr method allows the extraction and renaming of nested fields.

Performing large-scale distributed data processing with CSV and JSON files becomes efficient through Spark's transformative capabilities, leveraging DataFrames and Datasets.

8.4   Parsing and Transforming Data

Parsing and transforming data are essential tasks in data processing pipelines. In Scala, these tasks involve reading raw data, converting it into more useful formats, and transforming it as required for further analysis or processing. This section will demonstrate how to parse various data formats including CSV and JSON, and how to perform data transformations using Scala's robust functional programming features.

We will first explore parsing CSV data and transforming the resulting data structures, followed by examples of parsing JSON data and manipulating the parsed objects.

CSV (Comma-Separated Values) is a common data format for tabular data exchange. Each line in a CSV file represents a data record, with fields separated by commas. Parsing CSV data in Scala can be efficiently accomplished using libraries such as PureCSV or opencsv. Below is an example using PureCSV.

```scala
import purecsv.safe._
import scala.util.{Try, Success, Failure}
import java.io.File

case class Person(name: String, age: Int, email: String)

val file = new File("data/people.csv")

val parsedData: Try[List[Person]] = CSVReader[Person].readCSVFromFile(file)

parsedData match {
  case Success(data) => data.foreach(println)
  case Failure(ex) => println(s"Failed to parse CSV data: ${ex.getMessage}")
}
```

In the above code, we define a case class Person that corresponds to the structure of the CSV file. We use CSVReader to read and parse the CSV data into a list of Person objects. Handling the parsing result using the Try monad allows for elegant error handling.

Next, let's consider transforming the parsed CSV data. Suppose we want to filter out all persons below the age of 18 and transform the dataset to include only the names and emails of the remaining persons.

```scala
parsedData match {
  case Success(data) =>
    val adults: List[Person] = data.filter(_.age >= 18)
    val transformedData: List[(String, String)] = adults.map(person => (person.name,
        person.email))
    transformedData.foreach {
      case (name, email) => println(s"Name: $name, Email: $email")
    }
  case Failure(ex) => println(s"Failed to parse CSV data: ${ex.getMessage}")
}
```

Here, we first filter the data for adults using the filter method. We then transform the list of Person objects into a list of tuples containing only the name and email fields.

Next, we will parse JSON data. JSON (JavaScript Object Notation) is widely used for data interchange because of its readability and ease of use. Scala provides powerful libraries such as play-json and circe for working with JSON. Below is an example using circe.

```scala
import io.circe._, io.circe.parser._, io.circe.generic.auto._

case class Book(title: String, author: String, publishedYear: Int)

val jsonString = """
  |[
  | {"title": "1984", "author": "George Orwell", "publishedYear": 1949},
```

221

```
| {"title": "To Kill a Mockingbird", "author": "Harper Lee", "publishedYear": 1960}
|]
|""".stripMargin

val parsedJson: Either[Error, List[Book]] = decode[List[Book]](jsonString)

parsedJson match {
  case Right(books) => books.foreach(println)
  case Left(error) => println(s"Failed to parse JSON data: ${error.getMessage}")
}
```

In this example, we use circe to parse a JSON string representing a list of books into a list of Book case class instances. The decode function provides an Either type for result handling, ensuring errors are managed effectively.

Similarly to the CSV example, we can perform transformations on the parsed JSON data. Let's filter books published after 1950 and transform the resulting list to include only the titles.

```
parsedJson match {
  case Right(books) =>
    val recentBooks: List[Book] = books.filter(_.publishedYear > 1950)
    val titles: List[String] = recentBooks.map(_.title)
    titles.foreach(println)
  case Left(error) => println(s"Failed to parse JSON data: ${error.getMessage}")
}
```

In this case, we filter the list of books using the filter method and then transform it to a list of strings containing only the book titles.

An often-encountered task in data processing is transforming data structures. Scala's collection library offers numerous methods to manipulate data, such as map, flatMap, filter, groupBy, and fold. These methods can be chained together to perform complex transformations concisely and efficiently.

Here is an example demonstrating some of these operations. Suppose we have a list of people and we want to transform it into a map of ages to lists of names.

```
val people: List[Person] = List(
  Person("Alice", 30, "alice@example.com"),
  Person("Bob", 25, "bob@example.com"),
  Person("Charlie", 30, "charlie@example.com")
)

val ageToNames: Map[Int, List[String]] = people.groupBy(_.age).view.mapValues(_.
    map(_.name)).toMap

ageToNames.foreach {
  case (age, names) => println(s"Age: $age, Names: ${names.mkString(", ")}")
}
```

In this example, we use groupBy to group people by age, then transform the grouped values to lists of names using mapValues. Finally, toMap is called to convert the transformed view back into a standard Map.

Understanding and effectively utilizing Scala's parsing and transformation capabilities is pivotal for any data processing workflow. These functionalities allow for the creation of clean, efficient, and readable data pipelines that can handle a variety of data formats and transformation requirements.

8.5 Using Scala Collections for Data Manipulation

Scala collections provide a rich set of tools to handle and manipulate data efficiently. Understanding and effectively using these collections is crucial for performing data processing tasks. Scala offers various types of collections such as lists, arrays, sets, maps, and sequences which are designed to handle diverse data processing needs.

Collections in Scala are categorized into mutable and immutable collections. Immutable collections do not change their state after they are created, whereas mutable collections can be updated. The preference for immutability in functional programming paradigms ensures safer and more predictable code.

Lists

Lists in Scala are immutable collections that maintain the order of the elements. A list is a linked-list structure with efficient access to the head element but potentially less efficient access to its tail.

Creating a list in Scala:

```
val fruits = List("apple", "banana", "orange")
```

Accessing elements:

```
val firstFruit = fruits.head
val remainingFruits = fruits.tail
```

Common operations on lists include map, filter, and fold:

```
val upperCaseFruits = fruits.map(_.toUpperCase)
val shortNamedFruits = fruits.filter(_.length <= 5)
val allFruits = fruits.fold("")((acc, fruit) => acc + ", " + fruit).drop(2)
```

Arrays

Arrays are mutable collections with a fixed size and indexed access. They are suitable for situations where constant-time access to elements is required.

Creating an array:

```
val numbers = Array(1, 2, 3, 4, 5)
```

Accessing and modifying elements:

```
val firstNumber = numbers(0)
numbers(2) = 10
```

Applying operations:

```
val doubledNumbers = numbers.map(_ * 2)
val evenNumbers = numbers.filter(_ % 2 == 0)
```

Sets

Sets are collections that maintain unique elements. Scala provides both mutable and immutable sets.

Creating a set:

```
val fruitSet = Set("apple", "banana", "orange", "apple")
```

Sets automatically ensure uniqueness:

```
fruitSet: Set("apple", "banana", "orange")
```

Set operations include intersection, union, and difference:

```
val set1 = Set(1, 2, 3)
val set2 = Set(3, 4, 5)

val intersection = set1 & set2
val union = set1 | set2
val difference = set1 &~ set2
```

Maps

Maps are collections of key-value pairs, offering efficient lookups by key. Scala supports both immutable and mutable maps.

Creating a map:

```
val fruitPrices = Map("apple" -> 1.0, "banana" -> 0.5, "orange" -> 1.2)
```

Accessing and updating values:

```
val applePrice = fruitPrices("apple")
val updatedFruitPrices = fruitPrices + ("banana" -> 0.55)
```

Transforming maps:

```
val discountedPrices = fruitPrices.map { case (fruit, price) -> (fruit, price * 0.9) }
```

Sequences

Sequences are collections that provide a well-defined order of elements. They include lists, arrays, vectors, and ranges.

Creating and manipulating sequences:

```
val sequence = Seq(1, 2, 3, 4, 5)
val incrementedSequence = sequence.map(_ + 1)
val filteredSequence = sequence.filter(_ % 2 == 1)
```

Scala collections provide powerful abstractions and utilities to perform complex data manipulations concisely and efficiently. Employing these functional transformations allows developers to write clean, modular, and expressive code.

8.6 Introduction to Spark with Scala

Apache Spark is a powerful open-source distributed computing system that provides an interface for programming entire clusters with implicit data parallelism and fault tolerance. Spark extends the MapReduce model to efficiently support more types of computations, including interactive queries and stream processing.

Scala is one of the primary languages for interacting with Apache Spark, thanks to its concise syntax and strong type system. Using Scala with Spark offers several advantages, including better performance and quicker code execution due to its static type system and functional programming capabilities.

To utilize Spark with Scala effectively, it is essential to understand both the architecture of Spark and the basic constructs used within the Scala programming language. This section delves into the integral aspects of Spark, including its components, architecture, and the fundamental programming constructs necessary for data processing.

Spark Components

Spark consists of several key components:

- Spark Core

- Spark SQL

- Spark Streaming

- MLlib (Machine Learning Library)

- GraphX

Spark Core is the foundation of Spark. It provides basic functionalities such as task scheduling, memory management, fault recovery, and interaction with storage systems. The other components extend the capabilities of Spark Core for specialized tasks.

Spark Architecture

Spark adopts a master-slave architecture:

- Driver Program: The process where the main() function of the application runs. This program translates user code into a set of tasks that are executed by distributed worker nodes.

- Cluster Manager: Manages the cluster resources. Common Cluster Managers include Spark Standalone, Apache Mesos, and Hadoop YARN.

- Workers: These execute tasks assigned to them by the driver. They process data and return results to the driver.

The Driver Program creates a SparkContext, which is the entry point to Spark functionality. Within the workers, data is processed across multiple nodes, ensuring parallel execution and speed.

```
import org.apache.spark.{SparkConf, SparkContext}

val conf = new SparkConf().setAppName("Spark Example").setMaster("local")
val sc = new SparkContext(conf)
```

In the above example, SparkConf is used to configure the application, setting the application name to "Spark Example" and the master URL to local, which means Spark will run locally on a single node.

Resilient Distributed Datasets (RDDs)

RDDs are the primary abstraction in Spark. They represent an immutable, distributed collection of objects that can be processed in parallel. RDDs can be created in two ways:

- Parallelizing a collection in the driver program

- Referencing a dataset in an external storage system

```
val data = Array(1, 2, 3, 4, 5)
val distData = sc.parallelize(data)
```

In this example, an array of integers is converted into an RDD using the parallelize method.

```
val textFile = sc.textFile("path/to/file.txt")
```

Here, textFile is an RDD created by loading a text file from a given path.

Transformations and Actions are the two types of operations that can be performed on RDDs.

- Transformations: These are operations that create a new RDD from an existing one. For example, map, filter, and flatMap.

- Actions: These are operations that return a value to the driver after running a computation on the RDD. For example, collect, count, and first.

```
val lines = sc.textFile("path/to/file.txt")
val lineLengths = lines.map(s => s.length)
val totalLength = lineLengths.reduce((a, b) => a + b)
println(s"Total length of all lines: $totalLength")
```

In this example:

- lines is an RDD created from reading a text file.

227

- lineLengths is a transformed RDD where each line in lines is mapped to its length.

- totalLength is calculated by using the reduce action to sum all elements in lineLengths.

DataFrame API

A DataFrame is a distributed collection of data organized into named columns, conceptually equivalent to a table in a relational database. DataFrames provide a higher-level abstraction than RDDs and come with optimizations such as catalyst query optimization and Tungsten execution engine.

```
import org.apache.spark.sql.{SparkSession, DataFrame}

val spark = SparkSession.builder
    .appName("DataFrame Example")
    .master("local")
    .getOrCreate()

val df: DataFrame = spark.read.json("path/to/people.json")
df.show()
```

In this example, a SparkSession is initialized and used to create a DataFrame by reading a JSON file. The show() method displays the content of the DataFrame.

Transformations and Actions on DataFrames

Similar to RDDs, DataFrames support transformations and actions. However, operations on DataFrames are performed using domain-specific language (DSL) functions rather than lambda functions.

```
df.filter("age > 21").show()
df.groupBy("age").count().show()
```

In this example, filter is a transformation that filters rows based on the condition age > 21, and groupBy followed by count() groups the data by age and counts the number of occurrences.

Understanding the basics of Spark's architecture, its components, and how to perform operations with RDDs and DataFrames provides a strong foundation for utilizing Spark with Scala for distributed data processing tasks. The next sections will delve deeper into advanced functionalities and optimizations.

8.7 RDDs: Resilient Distributed Datasets

Resilient Distributed Datasets (RDDs) are a fundamental abstraction in Apache Spark, enabling distributed data processing in a fault-tolerant manner. RDDs are immutable distributed collections of objects that can be processed in parallel, supporting two types of operations: transformations and actions. This section delves into the creation, manipulation, and utilization of RDDs, focusing on their critical role in efficient, scalable data processing through Scala.

Creating RDDs: RDDs can be created in multiple ways, including:

- Parallelizing an existing collection in the driver program.

- Loading from an external dataset, such as a file in the Hadoop Distributed File System (HDFS).

To parallelize a collection, use the parallelize method. Consider the following example, which creates an RDD from an array:

```
val data = Array(1, 2, 3, 4, 5)
val distData = sc.parallelize(data)
```

Loading data from an external dataset such as a text file involves the textFile method. Here's an example of loading a file from HDFS:

```
val distFile = sc.textFile("hdfs://path/to/file.txt")
```

RDD Operations: RDDs support two types of operations:

- Transformations: Operations that create a new RDD from an existing one.

- Actions: Operations that return a value to the driver after running a computation on the dataset.

Transformations are lazy and are not computed immediately; they are executed only when an action is called. Common transformations include map, filter, flatMap, groupByKey, and reduceByKey. Actions include operations like collect, count, take, and reduce.

Consider the following example using map and filter transformations:

```
val distFile = sc.textFile("hdfs://path/to/file.txt")
val words = distFile.flatMap(line => line.split(" "))
val wordPairs = words.map(word => (word, 1))
val wordCounts = wordPairs.reduceByKey(_ + _)
wordCounts.collect
```

In this example, flatMap splits each line into words, map transforms each word into a pair, and reduceByKey aggregates the pairs. The collect action triggers the computation and returns the results.

Persistence: RDDs can be cached or persisted for efficient re-use. Spark provides the cache and persist methods. The cache method is shorthand for setting the storage level to MEMORY_ONLY, whereas persist allows fine control over the storage levels. Here is an example:

```
val wordCounts = wordPairs.reduceByKey(_ + _)
wordCounts.cache()
wordCounts.count()
```

Fault Tolerance: RDDs achieve fault tolerance through lineage. Each RDD maintains a graph of transformations (called the lineage graph) that can be recomputed in case of partition loss. This approach allows RDDs to recover lost data without requiring checkpointing.

Dependency Types: Dependencies between RDDs can be narrow or wide. Narrow dependencies, such as those resulting from map or filter, allow each partition of the parent RDD to be used by at most one partition of the child RDD. In contrast, wide dependencies, such as those from groupByKey, cause multiple child partitions to depend on one parent partition.

Example: Word Count: To put these concepts into practice, consider a full example of the word count program using RDDs in Scala.

```
import org.apache.spark.{SparkConf, SparkContext}
val conf = new SparkConf().setAppName("WordCount").setMaster("local")
val sc = new SparkContext(conf)
val distFile = sc.textFile("hdfs://path/to/file.txt")
val words = distFile.flatMap(line => line.split(" "))
val wordPairs = words.map(word => (word, 1))
val wordCounts = wordPairs.reduceByKey(_ + _)
wordCounts.collect().foreach(println)
```

This example begins with Spark context initialization, followed by the text file loading, transformation through flatMap and map, aggregation with reduceByKey, and finally, collecting and printing the results.

8.8   DataFrames and Datasets

DataFrames and Datasets are fundamental abstractions in Apache Spark that allow for efficient and expressive data processing. Both structures build on the Resilient Distributed Dataset (RDD) abstraction and are optimized for large-scale data processing tasks.

DataFrames are distributed collections of data organized into named columns, conceptually equivalent to a table in a relational database or a data frame in R or Python's pandas library. They offer a higher-level, more expressive API for data manipulation compared to RDDs.

Datasets, introduced more recently, are strongly-typed, distributed collections of data. They integrate the functionality of RDDs with Spark SQL's optimized execution engine, providing both compile-time type safety and the ability to use SQL-like query expressions.

```scala
import org.apache.spark.sql.{SparkSession, DataFrame, Dataset}

// Initialize Spark Session
val spark = SparkSession.builder()
  .appName("DataFrames and Datasets")
  .config("spark.master", "local")
  .getOrCreate()

// Creating a DataFrame from a JSON file
val df: DataFrame = spark.read.json("path/to/jsonfile.json")

// Defining a case class for the dataset
case class Person(name: String, age: Int)

// Creating a DataFrame and then converting it to a Dataset
import spark.implicits._
val ds: Dataset[Person] = df.as[Person]
```

The transformation to a Dataset from a DataFrame requires a case class or a row definition that matches the schema of the data. This transformation brings the benefits of compile-time type checking, which helps catch errors early in the development cycle.

DataFrames support a wide range of operations for data manipulation:

- select(expr: String, exprs: String*): DataFrame: Selects columns based on expressions.

- filter(condition: Column): DataFrame: Filters rows using the provided condition.

- groupBy(col1: String, cols: String*): GroupedData: Groups rows by specified columns.

- agg(exprs: (String, String)*): DataFrame: Performs aggregate functions on the grouped data.

```scala
import org.apache.spark.sql.functions._

// Select specific columns
val selectedColumnsDF = df.select("name", "age")
```

231

```
// Filter rows
val filteredDF = df.filter(col("age") > 21)

// Group by and aggregate
val aggregatedDF = df.groupBy("status").agg(avg("salary"), max("age"))
```

Datasets provide similar functionalities but with the added advantages of type safety and functional programming paradigms, like map, flatMap, filter, etc.

```
import org.apache.spark.sql.Encoders

val personEncoder = Encoders.product[Person]

// Select specific columns
val selectedColumnsDS = ds.map(person => (person.name, person.age))(Encoders.
    tuple(Encoders.STRING, Encoders.INT))

// Filter rows
val filteredDS = ds.filter(_.age > 21)

// Group by and aggregate
val aggregatedDS = ds.groupBy("status").agg(avg("salary"), max("age"))
```

Algorithm 3: Filtering and Aggregating Data with Datasets

Input: DataFrame or Dataset of people
Output: Filtered and aggregated DataFrame or Dataset

1 **Function** filterByAge(*(data: Dataset[Person], ageThreshold: Int): Dataset[Person]*):

2   data.filter(person => person.age > ageThreshold)

3 **Function** calculateAggregates(*(data: Dataset[Person]): DataFrame*):

4   data.groupBy("age").agg(
     avg("salary").as("average_salary"),
     max("salary").as("max_salary"))

5 val filteredData = filterByAge(*(ds, 21)*)

6 val result = calculateAggregates(*(filteredData)*)

DataFrames offer the benefit of Catalyst optimizer, which efficiently plans the query execution. When working with datasets with a known schema, it can be beneficial to use Datasets for their type safety and the benefit of functional programming operations.

```
df.createOrReplaceTempView("people")

// Performing SQL query
val sqlDF = spark.sql("SELECT name, age FROM people WHERE age > 21")
```

232

Dataset operations achieve robust type safety while leveraging the efficient execution engine provided by the Spark SQL optimizer. This combination facilitates both error prevention at compile time and performance improvements during execution.

Utilizing DataFrames and Datasets comprehensively enhances the ability to manage and manipulate large-scale data structures in a type-safe and optimized manner, thereby leveraging the full capabilities of the Spark SQL engine.

8.9   Performing SQL Queries with Spark SQL

Spark SQL is a component on top of Apache Spark that allows for querying data using SQL and the DataFrame API. It integrates relational processing with Spark's functional programming API, providing a powerful synergy of SQL and general-purpose data processing. This section delves into how to perform SQL queries with Spark SQL, including creating DataFrames, running SQL queries, and registering and querying temporary views.

To begin, ensure that you have the necessary libraries imported and a Spark session initialized. Here's a basic setup:

```
import org.apache.spark.sql.SparkSession

val spark = SparkSession.builder
    .appName("Spark SQL Example")
    .config("spark.master", "local")
    .getOrCreate()
```

To work with SQL, the data must first be loaded into a DataFrame. As an example, consider a JSON file containing data about users:

```
val df = spark.read.json("path/to/your/users.json")
```

Once the data is loaded into a DataFrame, you can perform SQL-like operations. For instance, to show the content of the DataFrame:

```
df.show()
```

The output will be:

233

```
+----+-------+
| age|  name|
+----+-------+
| null|Michael|
|  30|  Andy |
|  19| Justin|
+----+-------+
```

Spark SQL allows the DataFrame to be registered as a temporary view, enabling SQL queries to be executed directly. Register the DataFrame as a view:

```
df.createOrReplaceTempView("users")
```

With the temporary view 'users' created, SQL queries can be run. To select specific columns:

```
val sqlDF = spark.sql("SELECT name FROM users WHERE age BETWEEN 13 AND
     19")
sqlDF.show()
```

The output will be:

```
+-------+
|   name|
+-------+
| Justin|
+-------+
```

Beyond simple queries, Spark SQL supports complex operations including joins, aggregations, and subqueries. Assume another JSON file containing user preferences:

```
val prefsDF = spark.read.json("path/to/your/userprefs.json")
prefsDF.createOrReplaceTempView("userprefs")
```

Example of a join operation combining 'users' and 'userprefs':

```
val joinedDF = spark.sql(
    """
    SELECT u.name, p.pref
    FROM users u
    JOIN userprefs p
    ON u.name = p.name
    """
)
joinedDF.show()
```

The output will look like:

```
+-------+------+
|   name|  pref|
+-------+------+
| Justin| music|
|  Andy | sports|
+-------+------+
```

Spark SQL also supports aggregations. For example, to calculate the average age of users:

```
val avgAgeDF = spark.sql("SELECT AVG(age) as avg_age FROM users")
avgAgeDF.show()
```

The output will be:

```
+-----------------+
|         avg_age|
+-----------------+
|            24.5|
+-----------------+
```

Additionally, Spark SQL can be extended with User-Defined Functions (UDFs). Create and register a simple UDF that adds a greeting to each name:

```
import org.apache.spark.sql.functions.udf

val addGreeting = udf((name: String) => s"Hello, $name!")
spark.udf.register("addGreeting", addGreeting)

val greetingDF = spark.sql("SELECT addGreeting(name) as greeted_name FROM
    users")
greetingDF.show()
```

The output will be:

```
+--------------+
| greeted_name|
+--------------+
| Hello, null!|
|  Hello, Andy!|
| Hello, Justin!|
+--------------+
```

By this point, you should have a clear understanding of how to leverage Spark SQL to perform a variety of SQL queries on your data. Whether handling simple read operations, executing complex joins, performing aggregations, or enhancing functionalities with UDFs, Spark SQL provides a robust framework that integrates SQL querying capabilities seamlessly within the Scala programming environment.

8.10 Stream Processing with Spark Streaming

Stream processing involves the real-time processing and analysis of data as it is ingested. Apache Spark Streaming is an extension of the core Spark API that enables high-throughput, scalable, fault-tolerant stream processing of live data streams. In this section, we will delve into the core concepts and functionalities of Spark Streaming, including DStreams, transformations, actions, and window operations. We will also cover how to integrate Spark Streaming with various data sources and sinks.

Discretized Streams (DStreams)

The fundamental abstraction in Spark Streaming is a discretized stream, or DStream. A DStream represents a continuous stream of data, divided into small batches. DStreams can be created from various input sources, such as Kafka, Flume, or directly from the socket.

```scala
import org.apache.spark.streaming._
import org.apache.spark.streaming.StreamingContext._
import org.apache.spark.SparkConf

val conf = new SparkConf().setMaster("local[*]").setAppName("NetworkWordCount")
val ssc = new StreamingContext(conf, Seconds(1))

val lines = ssc.socketTextStream("localhost", 9999)
val words = lines.flatMap(_.split(" "))

val wordCounts = words.map(x => (x, 1)).reduceByKey(_ + _)
wordCounts.print()

ssc.start()
ssc.awaitTermination()
```

In this example, a DStream is created from a socket stream on localhost, listening to port 9999. The data received is divided into 1-second batches.

Transformations on DStreams

DStreams support many transformations that are similar to RDD transformations. Some commonly used transformations include map, flatMap, filter, reduceByKey, and updateStateByKey. These operations allow you to manipulate the data within each batch of the stream.

```scala
val filteredLines = lines.filter(line => line.contains("ERROR"))
val errorWords = filteredLines.flatMap(_.split(" "))
val errorWordCounts = errorWords.map(word => (word, 1)).reduceByKey(_ + _)

errorWordCounts.print()
```

Here, we filter lines containing the word "ERROR" and then count the

236

occurrences of each word.

Window Operations

Spark Streaming also supports window-based computations, which allow transformations over a sliding window of data. These are useful when you want to perform operations on a larger time span of the data stream.

```
val windowedWordCounts = words.map(x => (x, 1))
                              .reduceByKeyAndWindow((a: Int, b: Int) => a + b,
                              Seconds(30), Seconds(10))

windowedWordCounts.print()
```

In this example, we use a window duration of 30 seconds and a sliding interval of 10 seconds to compute the word counts for the window of data.

Stateful Operations

Spark Streaming allows the maintenance of state across batches of data using stateful transformations like updateStateByKey. This facilitates advanced use-cases like sessionization and tracking running totals.

```
def updateFunction(newValues: Seq[Int], runningCount: Option[Int]): Option[Int] = {
  val newCount = runningCount.getOrElse(0) + newValues.sum
  Some(newCount)
}

val runningCounts = words.map(word => (word, 1))
                         .updateStateByKey(updateFunction)

runningCounts.print()
```

The updateStateByKey function keeps a running count of every word received in the stream using a user-defined update function.

Integration with Data Sources and Sinks

Spark Streaming can integrate with various data sources such as Kafka, Flume, and Kinesis. Similarly, it can output processed data to various sinks like HDFS, databases, or dashboards.

```
import org.apache.spark.streaming.kafka010._
```

```
import org.apache.kafka.common.serialization.StringDeserializer

val kafkaParams = Map[String, Object](
  "bootstrap.servers" -> "localhost:9092",
  "key.deserializer" -> classOf[StringDeserializer],
  "value.deserializer" -> classOf[StringDeserializer],
  "group.id" -> "consumer-group"
)

val topics = Array("test-topic")
val stream = KafkaUtils.createDirectStream[String, String](ssc,
  LocationStrategies.PreferConsistent,
  ConsumerStrategies.Subscribe[String, String](topics, kafkaParams))

val messages = stream.map(record => (record.key, record.value))
```

This example demonstrates how to set up a direct connection to a Kafka stream. The Kafka messages are then processed as a DStream.

Fault Tolerance

Spark Streaming provides fault tolerance using checkpointing. Checkpointing is a process of saving the state of the computation for recovery in case of a failure.

```
ssc.checkpoint("/path/to/checkpoint-directory")

val runningCounts = words.map(word => (word, 1))
                    .updateStateByKey(updateFunction)

runningCounts.print()
```

Checkpointing enables Spark Streaming to recover from failures by using the saved state.

Streaming processing with Spark Streaming allows efficient and scalable real-time data processing. The use of DStreams, window operations, stateful transformations, and integration with various data sources and sinks make Spark Streaming a robust framework for stream processing tasks.

8.11   Data Visualization with Scala Libraries

Scala offers a diverse ecosystem for data visualization, providing powerful libraries that integrate seamlessly with its functional programming paradigm. Data visualization is crucial for interpreting large datasets, revealing underlying patterns, trends, and outliers. In this section, we will examine two prominent Scala libraries for data visualization: Breeze and Vegas. These libraries provide the functionality needed to create a variety of visual representations like scatter plots, line charts, bar charts, and more.

Breeze is primarily known for its numerical processing capabilities but also includes a plotting library. Vegas abstracts the complexities of visualization by providing a high-level interface to Vega-Lite, a concise JSON grammar for creating and sharing interactive visualizations.

Breeze is a powerful library for numerical computing. It supports plotting through an integrated module called Breeze-viz. To utilize Breeze for plotting, include the library in the build definition file. Add the following lines to your build.sbt file:

```
libraryDependencies += "org.scalanlp" %% "breeze" % "1.1"
libraryDependencies += "org.scalanlp" %% "breeze-viz" % "1.1"
```

To render plots using Breeze-viz, the application must run in a graphical environment. Below is an example of plotting a simple sine function using Breeze:

```
// Import necessary packages
import breeze.linalg._
import breeze.plot._

// Define the x values
val x = linspace(0.0, 1.0, 100)

// Define the y values as the sine of x
val y = x.map(xi => math.sin(2 * math.Pi * xi))

// Create a figure
val fig = Figure()

// Add a subplot
val p = fig.subplot(0)

// Plot y versus x
p += plot(x, y)

// Set the labels for the axes
p.xlabel = "x axis"
p.ylabel = "y axis"

// Display the plot
fig.refresh()
```

This example demonstrates Breeze's intuitive syntax for linear algebra and plotting. The linspace function generates a vector of 100 evenly spaced values between 0.0 and 1.0. The plot function creates a line plot of the sine values against the x values.

Moving on to another powerful tool, Vegas is a high-level library for producing plots. It leverages the Vega-Lite visualization grammar, which allows for the generation of complex visualizations through concise specifications. To include Vegas in your project, add the following dependency:

```
libraryDependencies += "org.vegas-viz" %% "vegas" % "0.3.11"
```

The following example illustrates how to create a scatter plot using Vegas:

```
// Import necessary packages
import vegas._
import vegas.render.WindowRenderer._

// Define the data for the plot
val data = Seq(
  Map("x" -> 1, "y" -> 2),
  Map("x" -> 2, "y" -> 3),
  Map("x" -> 3, "y" -> 5),
  Map("x" -> 4, "y" -> 7)
)

// Create the scatter plot
val plot = Vegas("Scatter Plot").
  withData(data).
  encodeX("x", Quantitative).
  encodeY("y", Quantitative).
  mark(Point)

// Render the plot
plot.show
```

In this script, the data is represented as a sequence of maps, with keys corresponding to columns x and y. The withData method binds this data to the plot. The encodeX and encodeY methods specify the axes' data types, and the mark method defines the plot type: Point, for a scatter plot.

For interactive and more customized visualizations, we can extend these basics. Adding layers, tooltips, and adjusting scales are some of the advanced functionalities that Vegas supports.

Consider an example of a layered visualization using a combination of line and point marks:

```
val layeredPlot = Vegas.layered("Line and Point Layers").
  withData(data).
  encodeX("x", Quantitative).
  encodeY("y", Quantitative).

  layer(
    Layer().mark(Line).
      encodeX("x", Quantitative).
      encodeY("y", Quantitative),
```

240

```
   Layer().mark(Point).
     encodeX("x", Quantitative).
     encodeY("y", Quantitative)
 )
layeredPlot.show
```

This layered plot uses the same dataset but represents it with both line and point marks, showing the flexibility of Vegas in combining different mark types within a single visualization.

Both Breeze and Vegas offer distinct advantages for different types of users and use cases. Breeze is particularly suitable for users who are already familiar with its numerical capabilities and prefer an integrated environment. Vegas, on the other hand, provides a more versatile and higher-level approach to visualization, especially for users who need to create complex and interactive visualizations without delving into lower-level details.

When choosing a library for visualization in Scala, consider the specific requirements of the project, the type of visualizations needed, and the ease of integration with existing codebases. Both libraries discussed here are highly capable and serve as robust tools in the Scala data scientist's toolkit.

Chapter 9

Working with External Libraries

This chapter explores how to effectively work with external libraries in Scala. It includes managing dependencies with sbt, and introduces popular libraries for various tasks, such as JSON processing with json4s, Circe, and Play JSON, database connectivity with Slick and Doobie, and HTTP clients like Akka HTTP and sttp. Additionally, it covers unit testing with ScalaTest, building REST APIs with Akka HTTP, integrating with Apache Kafka, and managing library versioning and compatibility.

9.1 Introduction to External Libraries in Scala

In Scala, the use of external libraries is a fundamental aspect of modern software development. Libraries extend the functionality of the language, allowing developers to leverage pre-built solutions for common tasks, thereby improving efficiency and reducing the likelihood of errors. This section provides an in-depth examination of the role of external libraries in Scala, how they integrate into projects, and best practices for their utilization.

Scala supports a rich ecosystem of external libraries that cater to a range of functionalities including data processing, web development,

243

database interaction, and more. The primary tool for managing these libraries is sbt (Simple Build Tool), which simplifies dependency management and project configuration. It is essential for developers to understand how to effectively declare, manage, and update library dependencies to maintain a robust and scalable codebase.

To include an external library in a Scala project, you must first declare the dependency in the build.sbt file. This file is crucial as it defines the project settings, dependencies, and more. Here is an example of a build.sbt file that includes dependencies for various popular libraries:

```
name := "ExampleProject"

version := "0.1"

scalaVersion := "2.13.6"

libraryDependencies ++= Seq(
  "org.json4s" %% "json4s-native" % "3.6.7",
  "com.typesafe.akka" %% "akka-http" % "10.2.4",
  "com.typesafe.slick" %% "slick" % "3.3.3",
  "org.scalatest" %% "scalatest" % "3.2.9" % Test
)
```

The libraryDependencies setting is used to declare the libraries required by the project. Each dependency is defined by its groupId, artifactId, and version. The "%" symbol separates these components, while the "%%" symbol is a shorthand to include the Scala version in the dependency coordinates.

To manage dependencies effectively, one should be aware of transitive dependencies, which are dependencies of the libraries you are using. Transitive dependencies can sometimes introduce version conflicts known as *dependency hell*. sbt provides mechanisms to exclude or override transitive dependencies to resolve such conflicts.

```
libraryDependencies += "org.apache.commons" % "commons-lang3" % "3.12.0" exclude
    ("commons-logging", "commons-logging")
```

In the above example, the commons-lang3 dependency is included, but its transitive dependency commons-logging is excluded to avoid potential conflicts.

External libraries in Scala are versioned, and managing these versions is vital for maintaining the compatibility and stability of the project. It is advisable to use specific versions rather than dynamic version ranges to prevent unexpected behavior due to untested versions. To further ensure consistency across different environments and builds, one can use sbt plugins like sbt-dependency-check to audit dependencies for known vulnerabilities.

Another aspect of working with libraries is understanding their licensing. Open-source libraries come with various licenses such as MIT, Apache License 2.0, GPL, etc. Ensure compliance with these licenses to avoid legal issues. Tools like sbt-license-report can be used to generate reports of the licenses of all project dependencies.

Example of using an external library

Suppose you want to use the json4s library for JSON processing in a Scala project. First, add the dependency to the build.sbt file as shown in the earlier example. Then, you can write Scala code to parse a JSON string:

```scala
import org.json4s._
import org.json4s.native.JsonMethods._

object JsonExample {
  implicit val formats: DefaultFormats = DefaultFormats // Brings in default date
      formats etc.

  case class Person(name: String, age: Int)

  def main(args: Array[String]): Unit = {
    val jsonString = """{"name": "John", "age": 30}"""
    val json = parse(jsonString)
    val person = json.extract[Person]

    println(s"Name: ${person.name}, Age: ${person.age}")
  }
}
```

Upon execution, the output will be:

Name: John, Age: 30

This example demonstrates the integration of an external library (json4s) into a Scala project for JSON parsing. External libraries, when used properly, can drastically reduce development time and increase the capabilities of a Scala project.

In this section, we have discussed key considerations and steps for using external libraries in Scala projects. It is essential to manage dependencies with care, ensuring compatibility and compliance with licenses to build effective and maintainable Scala applications.

245

9.2   Dependency Management with sbt

Scala Build Tool (sbt) is the primary build tool for Scala projects. It not only automates tasks like compiling, testing, and packaging your code, but it also manages project dependencies efficiently. Dependency management in sbt leverages Apache Ivy under the hood, allowing developers to specify external libraries their projects require by listing dependencies in a standard format.

Dependencies in sbt are declared within the build.sbt file located at the root of your project directory. The build.sbt file employs a straightforward syntax, making it accessible even to those new to Scala.

Consider the following example of a simple build.sbt file:

```
name := "MyScalaProject"

version := "0.1.0"

scalaVersion := "2.13.8"

libraryDependencies += "org.scala-lang" % "scala-library" % scalaVersion.value
```

In this file, name, version, and scalaVersion are basic settings that define the project's name, its version, and the Scala version to use, respectively. The libraryDependencies setting is where we declare external dependencies. Dependencies are specified using a triple of groupId, artifactId, and version.

"org.scala-lang" % "scala-library" % scalaVersion.value breaks down as follows:

- "org.scala-lang" is the groupId indicating the organization or group that produces the library.

- "scala-library" is the artifactId, denoting the specific library or module.

- scalaVersion.value dynamically references the version of Scala being used in this project.

Multiple dependencies can be added in a Seq, as shown below:

```
libraryDependencies ++= Seq(
  "org.typelevel" %% "cats-core" % "2.6.1",
  "org.scalatest" %% "scalatest" % "3.2.9" % Test
)
```

Here, the libraryDependencies setting uses the $++=$ operator to concatenate the existing dependencies with a Seq of new dependencies.
Notice the %% operator instead of %. The double percent operator
%% automatically appends the current Scala version to the artifactId. For example, "org.typelevel" %% "cats-core" % "2.6.1" becomes
"org.typelevel" % "cats-core_2.13" % "2.6.1" when scalaVersion :=
"2.13.8" is set. This is used for Scala libraries that are cross-published
for multiple Scala versions.

The % Test qualifier at the end of the ScalaTest dependency indicates
that this particular library is only required for the test configuration,
rather than the main project runtime.

Dependency configurations are more flexible through sbt. Developers
can manage transitive dependencies, conflict resolution, and exclusion
rules to maintain a clean and manageable dependency tree. For instance, to exclude a transitive dependency that would otherwise be
included, you can use the exclude method:

```
libraryDependencies += "org.apache.spark" %% "spark-core" % "3.1.2" exclude("org.
    slf4j", "slf4j-log4j12")
```

This line adds Apache Spark Core version 3.1.2 while excluding the
slf4j-log4j12 dependency from the org.slf4j group. This is particularly
useful when you encounter version conflicts between transitive dependencies of different libraries.

Another essential feature is resolvers. By default, sbt uses Maven Central and Ivy repositories to fetch dependencies. However, you might
want to add custom or internal repositories. This is achieved with the
resolvers setting:

```
resolvers += "Sonatype OSS Snapshots" at "https://oss.sonatype.org/content/
    repositories/snapshots"
```

This declaration adds the Sonatype OSS Snapshots repository, enabling your project to fetch libraries published to that repository.

To summarize, sbt automates dependency management through a
combination of straightforward syntax and powerful features. By specifying dependencies, exclusion rules, configurations, and resolvers in
the build.sbt file, you ensure that all necessary libraries are included,
conflicts are resolved, and your build process remains smooth and efficient.

9.3   Popular Scala Libraries and Their Uses

Scala, with its powerful standard library and ecosystem, provides a diverse set of external libraries that extend its capabilities, allowing developers to efficiently solve a wide range of problems. This section introduces some of the most popular Scala libraries and delves into their common uses, demonstrating how they can streamline development processes.

1. json4s

json4s is a library that simplifies working with JSON in Scala. Its integration with both Scala's object model and functional programming paradigms makes it an excellent choice for JSON processing.

```
import org.json4s._
import org.json4s.native.JsonMethods._

case class Person(name: String, age: Int)

// Serialization
val person = Person("Alice", 25)
val jsonString = write(person)

// Deserialization
val json = parse(jsonString)
val extractedPerson = json.extract[Person]
```

The above code demonstrates how to serialize a Scala case class to JSON and deserialize JSON back to a case class using json4s. This library simplifies these operations, ensuring minimal boilerplate code.

2. Circe

Circe is another popular library for JSON processing, especially fitting for users who appreciate a purely functional approach. It integrates seamlessly with the Cats library for functional programming.

```
import io.circe._
import io.circe.generic.auto._
import io.circe.parser._
import io.circe.syntax._

case class Person(name: String, age: Int)

// Serialization
val person = Person("Bob", 30)
val jsonString = person.asJson.noSpaces

// Deserialization
val decodedPerson = decode[Person](jsonString)
```

Circe's use of automatic derivation through annotations and its functional programming style make it an appealing choice for projects that prioritize functional paradigms.

3. Play JSON

Known for its relation to the Play Framework, Play JSON is another robust option for JSON processing. It integrates well with other Play Framework components but can be used independently.

```
import play.api.libs.json._

case class Person(name: String, age: Int)

implicit val personFormat = Json.format[Person]

// Serialization
val person = Person("Charlie", 35)
val jsonString = Json.toJson(person).toString()

// Deserialization
val json = Json.parse(jsonString)
val personResult = json.as[Person]
```

Play JSON's strong typing and straightforward APIs make it a practical choice, especially for developers already using the Play Framework.

4. Akka HTTP

Akka HTTP, part of the Akka toolkit, allows developers to build scalable REST APIs using actor-based concurrency models.

```
import akka.actor.ActorSystem
import akka.http.scaladsl.Http
import akka.http.scaladsl.model._
import akka.http.scaladsl.server.Directives._
import akka.stream.ActorMaterializer

implicit val system = ActorSystem()
implicit val materializer = ActorMaterializer()
implicit val executionContext = system.dispatcher

val route =
  path("hello") {
    get {
      complete(HttpEntity(ContentTypes.`text/html(UTF-8)`, "<h1>Hello World!</h1
          >"))
    }
  }

Http().bindAndHandle(route, "localhost", 8080)
```

Akka HTTP's ability to handle a vast number of connections concurrently, along with its integration with other Akka components, makes it ideal for developing high-performance web services.

5. Slick

249

Slick is the library for functional-relational mapping in Scala, enabling database operations using composable functional constructs.

```
import slick.jdbc.H2Profile.api._

case class User(id: Int, name: String)

class Users(tag: Tag) extends Table[User](tag, "USERS") {
  def id = column[Int]("ID", O.PrimaryKey)
  def name = column[String]("NAME")
  def * = (id, name) <> (User.tupled, User.unapply)
}

val db = Database.forConfig("h2mem1")
val users = TableQuery[Users]

// Database operations
val setup = DBIO.seq(
  users.schema.create,
  users += User(1, "Dave")
)

val resultFuture = db.run(setup)
```

Slick's typesafe querying capabilities and its ability to leverage Scala abstractions for complex database schemas and queries distinguish it from traditional ORM libraries.

6. Doobie

Doobie is a functional JDBC layer for Scala, designed for compositional and functional database programming. It works excellently with Cats and other functional libraries.

```
import doobie._
import doobie.implicits._
import cats.effect.IO

val xa = Transactor.fromDriverManager[IO](
  "org.h2.Driver", // PostgreSQL driver class
  "jdbc:h2:mem:test;DB_CLOSE_DELAY=-1", // connect URL
  "user", // username
  "pass" // password
)

case class Country(code: String, name: String, pop: Int)

val program = sql"SELECT code, name, population FROM COUNTRY".query[Country
    ].to[List]

val result = program.transact(xa).unsafeRunSync()
```

By promoting immutability and purity, Doobie enhances the maintainability and scalability of database-related code in large-scale systems.

7. ScalaTest

250

ScalaTest is a popular testing library that supports a range of styles, from behavior-driven development (BDD) to property-based testing.

```
import org.scalatest.flatspec.AnyFlatSpec

class ExampleSpec extends AnyFlatSpec {
  "An empty Set" should "have size 0" in {
    assert(Set.empty.size == 0)
  }
}
```

ScalaTest's flexibility in describing tests and the breadth of testing paradigms it supports make it a versatile tool for validating Scala applications.

Exploring these widely-used Scala libraries and understanding their specific use cases empowers developers to make informed choices, thus optimizing both productivity and code quality in Scala development.

9.4   Using Apache Commons Libraries

Apache Commons is a collection of reusable Java components that can be utilized in Scala projects to enhance functionality and streamline development processes. These libraries provide a wide range of utilities, from mathematical operations to file handling and data manipulation. Scala, being interoperable with Java, allows seamless integration of Apache Commons libraries, thus leveraging their robustness and efficiency.

To begin using Apache Commons libraries in a Scala project managed by sbt (Simple Build Tool), include the relevant dependencies in the build.sbt file. For instance, to use commons-lang3 for string utilities and commons-io for file operations, add the following lines:

```
libraryDependencies ++= Seq(
  "org.apache.commons" % "commons-lang3" % "3.12.0",
  "commons-io" % "commons-io" % "2.11.0"
)
```

The above configuration specifies the required versions, ensuring the selected libraries are downloaded and included in the project. Once the dependencies are included, functionalities from these libraries can be accessed directly in Scala code.

For illustration, consider commons-lang3, which provides extensive utilities for manipulating core Java objects such as String, Number, and

251

Array. **Below is a Scala example leveraging** StringUtils **from** commons-lang3 **to demonstrate various string operations:**

```scala
import org.apache.commons.lang3.StringUtils

object StringOpsExample {
  def main(args: Array[String]): Unit = {
    val originalString: String = " Apache Commons Lang "

    val trimmedString: String = StringUtils.trim(originalString)
    println(s"Trimmed: '$trimmedString'")

    val capitalizedString: String = StringUtils.capitalize(trimmedString)
    println(s"Capitalized: '$capitalizedString'")

    val reversedString: String = StringUtils.reverse(capitalizedString)
    println(s"Reversed: '$reversedString'")

    val isNumeric: Boolean = StringUtils.isNumeric(capitalizedString)
    println(s"Is Numeric: '$isNumeric'")
  }
}
```

Executing the above program yields the following output:

```
Trimmed: 'Apache Commons Lang'
Capitalized: 'Apache commons lang'
Reversed: 'gnal sremmoc ehpA'
Is Numeric: 'false'
```

StringUtils **provides methods like** trim() **to remove surrounding whitespace,** capitalize() **to convert the first character of the string to uppercase,** reverse() **to reverse the string, and** isNumeric() **to check if the string contains only numeric characters. Utilizing these ready-made methods significantly reduces boilerplate code and enhances readability.**

Another crucial library, commons-io, **simplifies file operations. Below is an example showcasing reading from and writing to a file using** FileUtils **from** commons-io:

```scala
import org.apache.commons.io.FileUtils
import java.io.File
import java.nio.charset.StandardCharsets

object FileOpsExample {
  def main(args: Array[String]): Unit = {
    val filePath: String = "example.txt"
    val file: File = new File(filePath)

    // Writing to a file
    FileUtils.writeStringToFile(file, "Hello, Apache Commons IO!", StandardCharsets.
        UTF_8)
    println(s"Written to file: $filePath")

    // Reading from a file
    val fileContents: String = FileUtils.readFileToString(file, StandardCharsets.UTF_8)
    println(s"Read from file: $fileContents")
```

```
  }
}
```

Running this code results in:

```
Written to file: example.txt
Read from file: Hello, Apache Commons IO!
```

This example demonstrates writeStringToFile() and readFileToString() methods to handle file write and read operations using UTF-8 encoding. These methods abstract the complexities of file I/O operations, providing a simpler and more intuitive interface.

Beyond commons-lang3 and commons-io, Apache Commons libraries cover diverse functionalities, including:

- commons-math3: Provides mathematical and statistical components, such as distributions, regression models, and optimization algorithms.

- commons-collections4: Enhances the Java Collections Framework with additional data structures and algorithms.

- commons-codec: Provides implementations of common encoders and decoders, such as Base64 and Hexadecimal.

- commons-dbcp2: Database connection pooling library, reducing resource usage and improving performance for database-driven applications.

Integrating Apache Commons libraries into Scala projects offers extensive pre-built utilities, optimizing development efficiency and maintaining code quality. This integration exemplifies the versatility and strengths of using Java libraries within the Scala ecosystem.

9.5 Working with JSON: json4s, Circe, and Play JSON

In many Scala applications, managing JSON data efficiently is critical, given its widespread use in RESTful APIs, configuration files, and data interchange. The Scala ecosystem offers several robust libraries for JSON processing. This section dives into three popular libraries: json4s, Circe, and Play JSON, illustrating their usage and advantages.

json4s is a library that supports seamless integration with Scala's existing data types while maintaining ease of use. It leverages the power of native JValue representations. Here's a basic example of serializing and deserializing JSON using json4s:

```
import org.json4s._
import org.json4s.native.JsonMethods._
import org.json4s.native.Serialization.{ read, write }
import org.json4s.native.Serialization

// Define a case class for our data
case class Person(name: String, age: Int)

// Setup required implicit formats
implicit val formats = Serialization.formats(NoTypeHints)

// Serialize an instance of Person to JSON
val person = Person("John Doe", 30)
val json: String = write(person)

// Deserialize the JSON back to Person
val personFromJson: Person = read[Person](json)

println(json)
println(personFromJson)
```

```
Output:
{"name":"John Doe","age":30}
Person(John Doe,30)
```

In this example, we first import necessary components from json4s. We then define a Person case class and establish the implicit formats for serialization and deserialization. Utilizing write and read, we can easily convert between a Person object and its JSON representation.

Moving to **Circe**, it emphasizes compile-time safety and highly functional programming paradigms. Circe utilizes Encoder and Decoder type classes to handle JSON transformations:

```
// Import circe libraries
import io.circe._, io.circe.parser._, io.circe.generic.auto._, io.circe.syntax._

// Define a case class for our data
case class Person(name: String, age: Int)

// Encode an instance of Person to JSON
val person = Person("Jane Doe", 25)
val json: Json = person.asJson

// Decode the JSON back to Person
val personFromJson: Either[Error, Person] = decode[Person](json.noSpaces)

println(json)
println(personFromJson)
```

254

```
Output:
{
  "name" : "Jane Doe",
  "age" : 25
}
Right(Person(Jane Doe,25))
```

With Circe, JSON encoding and decoding involve derivation of Encoder and Decoder. Here, the method asJson serializes the Person object to JSON, while the function decode performs the reverse. The use of Either facilitates error handling in the parsing process.

Lastly, **Play JSON**, a component of the Play framework, is versatile and straightforward. It enables concise JSON transformations through a feature-rich API:

```
// Import Play JSON library
import play.api.libs.json.

// Define a case class and its companion object
case class Person(name: String, age: Int)

object Person {
  implicit val personFormat: OFormat[Person] = Json.format[Person]
}

// Serialize an instance of Person to JSON
val person = Person("Bob Smith", 40)
val json: JsValue = Json.toJson(person)

// Deserialize the JSON back to Person
val personFromJson: JsResult[Person] = Json.fromJson[Person](json)

json.validate[Person] match {
  case JsSuccess(person, _) => println(s"Deserialized: $person")
  case JsError(errors) => println(s"Errors: $errors")
}

println(json)
```

```
Output:
{
  "name" : "Bob Smith",
  "age" : 40
}
```

Deserialized: Person(Bob Smith,40)

In Play JSON, the Json.format method generates JSON formatting code automatically for any case class, provided we define an implicit OFormat. Serialization is achieved with Json.toJson, and deserialization is performed by Json.fromJson or json.validate for more comprehensive validation.

These examples showcase the fundamental functionalities of each library. Users can expand on these by leveraging advanced features like custom serializers, combinators for complex data types, and error

255

handling mechanisms tailored to specific applications.

9.6 Database Connectivity with Slick and Doobie

When building Scala applications that require persistent data, choosing the appropriate database connectivity library is crucial. This section delves into two powerful libraries: Slick and Doobie. Both libraries enable straightforward and effective interaction with relational databases, facilitating the writing and execution of database queries within Scala applications while leveraging the language's functional programming capabilities.

Slick, short for Scala Language-Integrated Connection Kit, provides a functional interface for data access. It abstracts SQL queries, translating Scala code into SQL, allowing compile-time verification and optimizations.

Doobie, on the other hand, is a pure functional JDBC layer for Scala, focusing on composability and type safety. It enables the creation of robust database interactions using only idiomatic Scala code, ensuring that interactions are type-checked at compile-time.

Setting Up Dependencies

To use Slick and Doobie in a Scala project managed with sbt, you must include the necessary dependencies in your build.sbt file. Below is an example of dependencies required for Slick and Doobie:

```
libraryDependencies ++= Seq(
  "com.typesafe.slick" %% "slick" % "3.3.3",
  "org.postgresql" % "postgresql" % "42.2.12",
  "com.zaxxer" % "HikariCP" % "3.4.1",
  "org.tpolecat" %% "doobie-core" % "0.9.0",
  "org.tpolecat" %% "doobie-hikari" % "0.9.0",
  "org.tpolecat" %% "doobie-postgres" % "0.9.0",
  "org.tpolecat" %% "doobie-specs2" % "0.9.0" % "test"
)
```

Using Slick

To start with Slick, initialize a database connection using the Database object. Below is an example:

```
import slick.jdbc.PostgresProfile.api._

// Database configuration
val db = Database.forConfig("mydb")
```

256

```
// Example configuration in application.conf
/*
mydb = {
  url = "jdbc:postgresql://localhost:5432/mydb"
  driver = "org.postgresql.Driver"
  connectionPool = "HikariCP"
  keepAliveConnection = true
  user = "username"
  password = "password"
}
*/

// Simple table definition
class Users(tag: Tag) extends Table[(Int, String)](tag, "users") {
  def id = column[Int]("id", O.PrimaryKey, O.AutoInc)
  def name = column[String]("name")

  def * = (id, name)
}

// Table query
val users = TableQuery[Users]

// Action to select all users
val allUsersQuery = users.result

// Execute action
val allUsers: Future[Seq[(Int, String)]] = db.run(allUsersQuery)
```

This example demonstrates a basic table schema definition for a Users
table, a table query, and executing a query to retrieve all users from the
database.

Using Doobie

Doobie requires the establishment of a Transactor for managing
database connections. Below is an example of setting up a Transactor
and performing a query:

```
import doobie._
import doobie.implicits._
import cats.effect.{IO, ContextShift}
import scala.concurrent.ExecutionContext

// Transactor definition
implicit val cs: ContextShift[IO] = IO.contextShift(ExecutionContext.global)

val xa = Transactor.fromDriverManager[IO](
  "org.postgresql.Driver",
  "jdbc:postgresql://localhost:5432/mydb",
  "username",
  "password"
)

// Example query to fetch all users
val allUsersQuery = sql"SELECT id, name FROM users".query[(Int, String)]

// Execute the query
```

```
val allUsers: IO[List[(Int, String)]] = allUsersQuery.to[List].transact(xa)

val usersList: List[(Int, String)] = allUsers.unsafeRunSync()
```

This Doobie example showcases initializing a Transactor using a Post-greSQL database, defining a SQL query to fetch user data, and executing this query to obtain results.

Comparison and Best Practices

Both Slick and Doobie offer robust capabilities for database connectivity in Scala, each with distinct advantages:

- **Slick**: Offers a highly abstract and type-safe API for constructing database queries. It is suitable for developers who prefer a more DSL-like approach to SQL within Scala code. Slick enables compile-time query verification and leverages Scala's powerful type system to prevent runtime errors.

- **Doobie**: Provides a lower-level, more compositional approach to database interactions. Ideal for developers favoring explicit SQL and functional programming patterns. Doobie ensures that interactions are type-checked at compile-time and allows for extensive customization.

Best Practices:

- Use **connection pooling** to manage database connections efficiently. HikariCP is a popular choice that integrates well with both Slick and Doobie.

- **Leverage type safety**: Both libraries provide mechanisms to ensure type-safe queries, reducing runtime errors.

- **Transactional control** is crucial for ensuring data integrity. Use the provided mechanisms in Slick and Doobie to handle transactions.

- **Optimize queries** and monitor performance to ensure that the database interactions are efficient and scalable.

By understanding and utilizing the strengths of both Slick and Doobie, Scala developers can build robust, efficient, and highly maintainable database applications, ensuring optimal performance and type-safe database interactions.

9.7 HTTP Clients: Akka HTTP and sttp

When building applications that communicate with web services, it is essential to choose a robust HTTP client that simplifies handling HTTP requests and responses. Scala provides several powerful libraries for this purpose, with Akka HTTP and sttp being amongst the most popular due to their comprehensive feature sets and ease of use.

Akka HTTP is built upon the Akka Actor framework and delivers asynchronous, event-driven IO to handle HTTP requests, making it suitable for building high-performance applications. It provides a convenient dsl for routing, and leveraging Akka Streams, it efficiently manages HTTP connections with backpressure support.

sttp (Scala HTTP Client) is a more lightweight HTTP client library that offers both synchronous and asynchronous APIs, suited for both simple and advanced HTTP request scenarios. It's highly modular and integrates well with other libraries, providing flexibility to developers to choose the desired backend (such as Akka, Cats Effect, Future, or Monix) and pluggable features like retries, request logging, and more.

Here, we delve into the practical utilization of these two libraries, contrasting their APIs, capabilities, and use cases.

Akka HTTP: To include Akka HTTP in your project, add the following dependencies to your sbt build file:

```
libraryDependencies ++= Seq(
  "com.typesafe.akka" %% "akka-http" % "10.2.6",
  "com.typesafe.akka" %% "akka-stream" % "2.6.16"
)
```

Creating a basic HTTP client with Akka HTTP involves creating an ActorSystem, Materializer, and using the Http() extension to perform requests. Here is a simple example of performing an HTTP GET request:

```
import akka.actor.ActorSystem
import akka.http.scaladsl.Http
import akka.http.scaladsl.model._
import akka.stream.Materializer

import scala.concurrent.{ExecutionContextExecutor, Future}
import scala.util.{Failure, Success}

implicit val system: ActorSystem = ActorSystem()
implicit val materializer: Materializer = Materializer(system)
implicit val executionContext: ExecutionContextExecutor = system.dispatcher

val responseFuture: Future[HttpResponse] = Http().singleRequest(HttpRequest(uri = "
    https://api.example.com/data"))
```

259

```
responseFuture.onComplete {
  case Success(res) =>
    println(s"Response: ${res.status}")
  case Failure(exception) =>
    println(s"Failed to fetch data: $exception")
}
```

This code snippet demonstrates the fundamental process for making a request and handling the response asynchronously. Akka HTTP's powerful routing dsl is handy for building RESTful services, integrating smoothly with Akka Streams for reactive streams processing.

sttp: Add the following dependency to your sbt build file to include sttp:

```
libraryDependencies ++= Seq(
  "com.softwaremill.sttp.client3" %% "core" % "3.3.16"
)
```

For sttp, you can create both synchronous and asynchronous clients. By default, it uses Future for asynchronous computations, but other backends can be used as needed. Here is an example of an HTTP GET request using sttp with Future backend:

```
import sttp.client3._
import scala.concurrent.Future
import scala.concurrent.ExecutionContext.Implicits.global

val backend: SttpBackend[Future, Any] = AsyncHttpClientFutureBackend()

val request = basicRequest.get(uri"https://api.example.com/data")
val response: Future[Response[Either[String, String]]] = request.send(backend)

response.onComplete {
  case scala.util.Success(value) => println(s"Response: ${value.body}")
  case scala.util.Failure(exception) => println(s"Failure: $exception")
}
```

This example illustrates how concise the code is using sttp. The basicRequest object facilitates constructing the request, while the send method executes it. The response handling remains asynchronous and integrates seamlessly with the standard Scala Future.

Choosing between Akka HTTP and sttp typically depends on the specific needs of the application. Akka HTTP is often preferred for its integration with Akka Streams and the actor model, making it suitable for building reactive stream-based applications and services. On the other hand, sttp is appreciated for its simplicity, modularity, and flexibility, making it a compelling choice when ease of integration and flexibility in backend selection are priorities. Both libraries offer strong typing and immutable data structures, ensuring the reliability and maintainability of your Scala applications.

9.8 Unit Testing with ScalaTest and Specs2

Unit testing is a critical aspect of software development, ensuring that individual components of your codebase are functioning as expected. In Scala, two of the most popular frameworks for unit testing are ScalaTest and Specs2. This section delves into the functionalities and usage of both frameworks, enabling you to write robust tests for your Scala applications.

ScalaTest is a versatile and comprehensive testing library that supports different styles of testing such as behavior-driven development (BDD), and fixtures-based testing. Specs2 is another powerful library that focuses on providing a clear and concise syntax for testing and adopts a more declarative style. Both frameworks integrate seamlessly with sbt and provide rich features for assertions, mocking, and property-based testing.

Setting Up ScalaTest with sbt

To use ScalaTest in your Scala project, you need to add the appropriate dependency to your build.sbt file:

```
libraryDependencies += "org.scalatest" %% "scalatest" % "3.2.10" % Test
```

This command specifies that ScalaTest version 3.2.10 should be included as a test dependency.

Basic ScalaTest Example

Below is a simple example of a ScalaTest specification that tests a basic addition function:

```
import org.scalatest.funsuite.AnyFunSuite

class AdditionTest extends AnyFunSuite {
  test("addition of two positive numbers") {
    val sum = 2 + 3
    assert(sum === 5)
  }

  test("addition of two negative numbers") {
    val sum = -2 + -3
    assert(sum === -5)
  }
}
```

In this code, we used the AnyFunSuite trait, which is designed for writing simple tests. The test method is used for defining individual test cases, and the assert function ensures that the expected condition holds true.

261

Using Fixtures in ScalaTest

Fixtures allow you to set up common objects or conditions that are used by multiple tests. ScalaTest provides various ways to manage fixtures. An example is shown below using the FeatureSpec trait to illustrate the use of fixtures:

```scala
import org.scalatest.featurespec.AnyFeatureSpec
import org.scalatest.BeforeAndAfter

class SampleSpec extends AnyFeatureSpec with BeforeAndAfter {

  var database: Database = _

  before {
    database = new Database()
    database.connect()
  }

  after {
    database.disconnect()
  }

  Feature("Database operations") {
    Scenario("data insertion") {
      val data = "sample data"
      val result = database.insert(data)
      assert(result)
    }

    Scenario("data retrieval") {
      val data = database.retrieve("id123")
      assert(data === "expected data")
    }
  }
}
```

Here, the before and after hooks ensure that the database connection setup and teardown occur before and after each test case.

Property-based Testing in ScalaTest

ScalaTest also supports property-based testing, which allows you to define properties that should hold for a range of input values. This is implemented through the ScalaCheckDrivenPropertyChecks trait. For example:

```scala
import org.scalatest.propspec.AnyPropSpec
import org.scalatestplus.scalacheck.ScalaCheckDrivenPropertyChecks

class PropertiesTest extends AnyPropSpec with ScalaCheckDrivenPropertyChecks {

  property("addition is commutative") {
    forAll { (a: Int, b: Int) =>
      assert(a + b == b + a)
    }
  }
}
```

In the above example, the forAll method tests the commutativity property of addition over a wide range of integer inputs.

Setting Up Specs2 with sbt

To incorporate Specs2 into your project, add the following dependency to your build.sbt file:

```
libraryDependencies += "org.specs2" %% "specs2-core" % "4.10.6" % Test
```

Basic Specs2 Example

The following example demonstrates a simple Specs2 specification:

```
import org.specs2.mutable.Specification

class AdditionSpecs2Test extends Specification {
  "Addition" should {
    "add two positive numbers correctly" in {
      val sum = 2 + 3
      sum must beEqualTo(5)
    }

    "add two negative numbers correctly" in {
      val sum = -2 + -3
      sum must beEqualTo(-5)
    }
  }
}
```

Here, we used the mutable.Specification trait, which allows mutable variables and a more flexible testing style. The must matcher is used for assertions.

Using Traits and Contexts in Specs2

Specs2 provides traits and contexts to share setup code among tests. Here's an example using the BeforeAfterEach trait:

```
import org.specs2.mutable.Specification
import org.specs2.specification.BeforeAfterEach

class DatabaseSpec extends Specification with BeforeAfterEach {

  var database: Database = _

  def before = {
    database = new Database()
    database.connect()
  }

  def after = {
    database.disconnect()
  }

  "Database" should {
    "insert data correctly" in {
      val data = "sample data"
```

263

```
    val result = database.insert(data)
    result must beTrue
  }

  "retrieve data correctly" in {
    val data = database.retrieve("id123")
    data must beEqualTo("expected data")
  }
 }
}
```

The BeforeAfterEach trait ensures setup and teardown are applied to each test case.

Property-based Testing in Specs2

Specs2 also supports property-based testing through integration with ScalaCheck. Below is an example:

```
import org.specs2.ScalaCheck
import org.specs2.mutable.Specification

class PropertiesSpec extends Specification with ScalaCheck {
  "addition" should {
    "be commutative" ! prop { (a: Int, b: Int) =>
      a + b must beEqualTo(b + a)
    }
  }
}
```

The prop method is used to define properties with randomly generated inputs.

Both ScalaTest and Specs2 are powerful tools for unit testing in Scala, each offering unique advantages. ScalaTest is known for its flexibility and extensive ecosystem, while Specs2 is appreciated for its readable syntax and integration with behavior-driven development. With these tools, you can ensure your codebase remains robust and reliable.

9.9 Building REST APIs with Akka HTTP

Akka HTTP is a powerful toolkit for building RESTful APIs in Scala. It is built on top of Akka actors and provides both client-side and server-side HTTP functionalities. Akka HTTP is highly asynchronous and non-blocking, which makes it well-suited for building scalable web services. In this section, we will cover the essential concepts of building REST APIs using Akka HTTP, including setting up the project, defining routes, handling requests, and structuring the application.

Project Setup

To start using Akka HTTP, add the following dependencies to your build.sbt file:

```
libraryDependencies += "com.typesafe.akka" %% "akka-http" % "10.2.7"
libraryDependencies += "com.typesafe.akka" %% "akka-stream" % "2.6.17"
libraryDependencies += "com.typesafe.akka" %% "akka-http-spray-json" % "10.2.7"
```

These dependencies pull in Akka HTTP, Akka Streams, and JSON support using spray-json.

Defining Routes

Routes in Akka HTTP are defined by combining multiple Directive instances.

Here is an example of a simple route:

```
import akka.http.scaladsl.server.Directives.
import akka.http.scaladsl.server.Route

val route: Route = path("hello") {
  get {
    complete("Hello, World!")
  }
}
```

This route responds with "Hello, World!" when a GET request is made to the '/hello' path.

Starting the Server

To start an Akka HTTP server, use the Http().newServerAt method:

```
import akka.actor.ActorSystem
import akka.http.scaladsl.Http
import akka.stream.ActorMaterializer

import scala.io.StdIn

object WebServer {
  def main(args: Array[String]): Unit = {
    implicit val system: ActorSystem = ActorSystem("my-system")
    implicit val materializer: ActorMaterializer = ActorMaterializer()
    implicit val executionContext = system.dispatcher

    val bindingFuture = Http().newServerAt("localhost", 8080).bind(route)

    println("Server online at http://localhost:8080/\nPress RETURN to stop...")
    StdIn.readLine()
    bindingFuture
      .flatMap(_.unbind())
      .onComplete(_ => system.terminate())
  }
}
```

265

This example creates a server bound to localhost on port 8080, using the previously defined route.

Handling JSON Requests and Responses

For handling JSON, it is common to use spray-json. First, define case classes for the data model:

```
case class Person(name: String, age: Int)
```

Next, create an implicit formatter using DefaultJsonProtocol:

```
import spray.json.DefaultJsonProtocol._
import akka.http.scaladsl.marshallers.sprayjson.SprayJsonSupport._

implicit val personFormat = jsonFormat2(Person)
```

Now, you can create routes that consume and produce JSON:

```
val jsonRoute: Route = path("person") {
  post {
    entity(as[Person]) { person =>
      complete(person.copy(name = person.name.toUpperCase))
    }
  }
}
```

This route accepts a POST request containing a JSON representation of a Person and returns a new Person with the name converted to uppercase.

Structuring the Application

For larger applications, it is beneficial to structure the code into separate components. Encapsulate route definitions within different classes or objects and then combine them. For example:

```
trait PersonRoutes {
  val personRoutes: Route =
    pathPrefix("api" / "person") {
      pathEnd {
        post {
          entity(as[Person]) { person =>
            complete(person.copy(name = person.name.toUpperCase))
          }
        }
      }
    }
}

object WebServer extends PersonRoutes {
  def main(args: Array[String]): Unit = {
    implicit val system: ActorSystem = ActorSystem("my-system")
    implicit val materializer: ActorMaterializer = ActorMaterializer()
    implicit val executionContext = system.dispatcher
```

```
val bindingFuture = Http().newServerAt("localhost", 8080).bind(personRoutes)

println("Server online at http://localhost:8080/\nPress RETURN to stop...")
StdIn.readLine()
bindingFuture
  .flatMap(_.unbind())
  .onComplete(_ => system.terminate())
  }
}
```

This approach promotes modularity and maintainability by separating concerns and organizing code logically.

Seamlessly integrating Akka HTTP into your Scala applications allows you to build efficient and scalable REST APIs, leveraging its powerful asynchronous processing model and extensive toolkit.

9.10   Integrating with Apache Kafka

Apache Kafka is a distributed event streaming platform capable of handling trillions of events a day. Integrating Scala applications with Kafka allows for robust stream processing capabilities, making it suitable for various use cases such as real-time analytics, machine learning pipelines, and event-driven architectures.

Scala developers can leverage popular libraries such as Kafka Streams, Akka Streams, and Alpakka Kafka for seamless integration. This section provides detailed steps and examples to accomplish this.

Adding Kafka Dependencies

To begin integrating Apache Kafka, ensure that the necessary dependencies are included in the build.sbt file. For Kafka Streams, Akka Streams, and Alpakka Kafka, add:

```
libraryDependencies ++= Seq(
  "org.apache.kafka" %% "kafka-streams-scala" % "2.8.0",
  "com.typesafe.akka" %% "akka-stream" % "2.6.14",
  "com.typesafe.akka" %% "akka-stream-kafka" % "2.1.0",
  "org.apache.kafka" % "kafka-clients" % "2.8.0"
)
```

Kafka Producer Example

A Kafka producer is responsible for publishing records to Kafka topics. Below is an example using Kafka's producer API in Scala:

```
import java.util.Properties
import org.apache.kafka.clients.producer.{KafkaProducer, ProducerRecord}
```

```
object SimpleKafkaProducer {
  def main(args: Array[String]): Unit = {
    val props = new Properties()
    props.put("bootstrap.servers", "localhost:9092")
    props.put("key.serializer", "org.apache.kafka.common.serialization.StringSerializer")
    props.put("value.serializer", "org.apache.kafka.common.serialization.StringSerializer"
        )

    val producer = new KafkaProducer[String, String](props)
    val topic = "example-topic"

    for (i <- 1 to 10) {
      val record = new ProducerRecord[String, String](topic, s"key-$i", s"value-$i")
      producer.send(record)
    }

    producer.close()
  }
}
```

In this example, a KafkaProducer instance is created with the necessary configuration and publishes ten records to the topic named
example-topic.

Kafka Consumer Example

A Kafka consumer subscribes to topics and processes records from
them. Below is an example using Kafka's consumer API in Scala:

```
import java.time.Duration
import java.util.Properties
import org.apache.kafka.clients.consumer.{KafkaConsumer, ConsumerRecords}

object SimpleKafkaConsumer {
  def main(args: Array[String]): Unit = {
    val props = new Properties()
    props.put("bootstrap.servers", "localhost:9092")
    props.put("group.id", "example-group")
    props.put("key.deserializer", "org.apache.kafka.common.serialization.
        StringDeserializer")
    props.put("value.deserializer", "org.apache.kafka.common.serialization.
        StringDeserializer")

    val consumer = new KafkaConsumer[String, String](props)
    consumer.subscribe(java.util.Arrays.asList("example-topic"))

    while (true) {
      val records: ConsumerRecords[String, String] = consumer.poll(Duration.ofMillis
          (100))
      records.forEach(record => println(s"Consumed record with key ${record.key()}
          and value ${record.value()}"))
    }
  }
}
```

In this example, a KafkaConsumer instance subscribes to the example-
topic and continuously polls for new records, printing their keys and
values.

Stream Processing with Kafka Streams

Kafka Streams is a powerful library for building streaming applications with Apache Kafka. Below is an example showcasing a simple stream processing application in Scala:

```
import org.apache.kafka.streams.{KafkaStreams, StreamsBuilder, StreamsConfig}
import org.apache.kafka.streams.scala._
import org.apache.kafka.streams.scala.ImplicitConversions._
import org.apache.kafka.streams.scala.Serdes._
import java.util.Properties

object SimpleKafkaStreams {
  def main(args: Array[String]): Unit = {
    val props = new Properties()
    props.put(StreamsConfig.APPLICATION_ID_CONFIG, "example-streams")
    props.put(StreamsConfig.BOOTSTRAP_SERVERS_CONFIG, "localhost:9092")
    props.put(StreamsConfig.DEFAULT_KEY_SERDE_CLASS_CONFIG, Serdes.
        stringSerde.getClass)
    props.put(StreamsConfig.DEFAULT_VALUE_SERDE_CLASS_CONFIG, Serdes.
        stringSerde.getClass)

    val builder = new StreamsBuilder()
    val inputTopic = "input-topic"
    val outputTopic = "output-topic"

    val stream = builder.stream[String, String](inputTopic)
    stream.mapValues(value => value.toUpperCase)
        .to(outputTopic)

    val streams = new KafkaStreams(builder.build(), props)
    streams.start()

    sys.ShutdownHookThread {
      streams.close(Duration.ofSeconds(10))
    }
  }
}
```

Here, the application reads messages from input-topic, converts the message values to uppercase, and writes them to output-topic.

Integration with Akka Streams and Alpakka Kafka

Alpakka Kafka integrates Kafka with Akka Streams, enabling reactive stream processing. Below is an example demonstrating how to integrate with Alpakka Kafka to consume messages:

```
import akka.actor.ActorSystem
import akka.kafka.{ConsumerSettings, Subscriptions}
import akka.kafka.scaladsl.{Consumer, Producer}
import akka.kafka.scaladsl.Consumer.DrainingControl
import akka.stream.ActorMaterializer
import akka.stream.scaladsl.Sink
import org.apache.kafka.common.serialization.{ByteArrayDeserializer,
    StringDeserializer}

object AlpakkaKafkaConsumerExample {
  def main(args: Array[String]): Unit = {
```

269

```
  implicit val system: ActorSystem = ActorSystem("AlpakkaKafkaConsumer")
  implicit val materializer: ActorMaterializer = ActorMaterializer()

  val consumerSettings = ConsumerSettings(system, new StringDeserializer, new
       StringDeserializer)
    .withBootstrapServers("localhost:9092")
    .withGroupId("example-group")
    .withProperty("auto.offset.reset", "earliest")

  Consumer
    .plainSource(consumerSettings, Subscriptions.topics("example-topic"))
    .map { msg => println(s"Consumed message: ${msg.value}") }
    .runWith(Sink.ignore)
  }
}
```

This example demonstrates an Akka Streams-based consumer that reads messages from example-topic and prints them.

Integrating with Apache Kafka using these libraries ensures reliable and efficient stream processing in Scala applications.

9.11   Library Versioning and Compatibility

Effective management of library versions and ensuring compatibility in Scala projects is crucial for maintaining stability and functionality. In this section, we delve into versioning strategies, the role of Semantic Versioning (SemVer), and methods for mitigating potential conflicts. We also discuss tools and practices specific to the Scala build tool (sbt) that help in managing dependencies and ensuring compatibility.

Versioning Strategies

Versioning is essential for tracking changes, updates, and bug fixes in libraries. The most widely adopted versioning strategy in the software development community is Semantic Versioning (SemVer). SemVer uses a three-part version number format: MAJOR.MINOR.PATCH.

- MAJOR version increases when there are incompatible API changes.

- MINOR version increases when new, backwards-compatible features are added.

- PATCH version increases when backwards-compatible bug fixes are made.

Compliance with SemVer helps to convey the nature of changes made in each release, which is particularly useful for developers integrating or contributing to libraries.

Managing Dependencies with sbt

When working with external libraries in Scala using sbt, dependencies are defined in the build.sbt file. Each dependency includes a group ID, artifact ID, and version. For instance, a typical dependency definition might look like:

```
libraryDependencies += "org.scalaz" %% "scalaz-core" % "7.3.3"
```

In this example, "org.scalaz" is the group ID, "scalaz-core" is the artifact ID, and "7.3.3" is the version. By maintaining accurate version specifications, it is possible to control the specific versions of libraries used, thereby ensuring consistency across different environments.

Conflict Resolution

Dependency conflicts often arise when multiple libraries depend on different versions of the same transitive dependency. sbt provides mechanisms to handle these conflicts through version overrides and eviction warnings.

Version Overrides

sbt allows specifying overrides for dependency versions directly in the build.sbt file. This can be achieved using the dependencyOverrides setting, which enforces specific versions of dependencies:

```
dependencyOverrides += "com.example" % "example-lib" % "1.4.5"
```

This directive ensures that example-lib version 1.4.5 is used throughout the project, no matter what version other dependencies may specify.

Eviction Warnings

Eviction warnings provide a mechanism to detect and alert users of potential conflicts. sbt can be configured to generate warnings if multiple versions of a dependency are being pulled in, allowing developers to address them proactively:

```
evictionWarningOptions in update := EvictionWarningOptions.full
```

Setting the EvictionWarningOptions to full ensures that sbt outputs detailed warnings about dependency evictions during the resolution process.

Cross-Building for Scala Versions

Scala's ecosystem includes multiple major versions such as Scala 2.11, 2.12, 2.13, and the upcoming Scala 3.x. Libraries need to be cross-built to support multiple versions, which can be done using the sbt-cross-project plugin.

To declare support for multiple Scala versions, define the Scala version and cross-version settings in the build.sbt:

```
crossScalaVersions := Seq("2.12.13", "2.13.5")
```

This setting informs sbt to compile the project against both Scala 2.12.13 and Scala 2.13.5. The % and %% symbols in dependency definitions aid compatibility by selecting the appropriate version suffix based on the Scala version in use.

Ensuring Binary Compatibility

Binary compatibility means that a compiled library should work across different versions of a language runtime, provided they adhere to certain compatibility guarantees. Scala guarantees binary compatibility within the same major version series (like 2.12.x) but not between major versions (such as 2.12.x and 2.13.x).

Maintaining binary compatibility can be complex and requires adherence to specific practices, such as avoiding changes to public API signatures that break compatibility. Tools like MiMa (Migration Manager for Scala) can aid in detecting binary incompatibilities. To integrate MiMa with sbt, add the following plugin in project/plugins.sbt:

```
addSbtPlugin("com.typesafe" % "sbt-mima-plugin" % "0.8.0")
```

MiMa checks can be configured in build.sbt to verify that changes remain compatible:

272

```
mimaPreviousArtifacts := Set(organization.value %% name.value % "2.0.0")
```

By setting mimaPreviousArtifacts, developers ensure that the project's current build is compatible with the specified previous version.

Responsible versioning and compatibility management are essential for the health of any Scala project, involving strategies for precise versioning, dependency conflict resolution, cross-building, and binary compatibility checks. Through meticulous application of these strategies, projects can achieve robust and reliable dependency management.

Chapter 10

Testing in Scala

This chapter delves into testing practices in Scala, covering setting up the testing environment, unit testing with ScalaTest, and behavior-driven development with Specs2. It also includes property-based testing with ScalaCheck, mocking and stubbing with Mockito, testing asynchronous code, using Akka TestKit for actor testing, integration testing, continuous integration practices, test-driven development (TDD), and performance testing and benchmarking.

10.1   Introduction to Testing in Scala

Software testing is a critical aspect of modern software development, providing a safeguard against defects and ensuring that code behaves as expected. In Scala, testing adopts various paradigms and tools, enabling developers to create reliable and maintainable systems. This section introduces fundamental concepts and key practices associated with testing in Scala.

Scala's testing ecosystem is rich and diversified, supporting multiple testing methodologies including unit testing, behavior-driven development (BDD), and property-based testing. Given Scala's interoperability with Java, Scala-based projects can leverage a wide array of testing frameworks and libraries.

Testing in Scala emphasizes both functional and object-oriented

275

paradigms, ensuring that code is evaluated under multiple perspectives. The functional paradigm encourages immutability and pure functions, simplifying the testing process by eliminating side effects. Conversely, the object-oriented paradigm, with its focus on state and behavior encapsulation, requires careful consideration of mock objects and dependency injection.

- Unit Testing: This involves testing individual units of code, typically functions or methods, in isolation from the rest of the application to verify that they perform as expected.

- Behavior-Driven Development (BDD): BDD extends the principles of test-driven development to describe how software should behave in narratives that are easily understood by non-developers.

- Property-Based Testing: This technique involves defining properties or invariants that should hold for a range of inputs, allowing for broader test coverage and discovering edge cases.

To create a conducive environment for testing in Scala, it is essential to structure projects effectively and integrate appropriate libraries and plugins. Popular build tools such as sbt (Scala Build Tool) facilitate the configuration of testing dependencies and the execution of tests seamlessly.

An example of a basic sbt configuration for including ScalaTest (a popular testing framework) can be defined as follows:

```
lazy val root = (project in file(".")).
  settings(
    name := "MyProject",
    version := "0.1",
    scalaVersion := "2.13.6",
    libraryDependencies ++= Seq(
      "org.scalatest" %% "scalatest" % "3.2.9" % Test
    )
  )
```

In the configuration above, the % Test suffix specifies that the ScalaTest dependency should be included in the test scope, preventing it from being part of the production build.

Testing frameworks for Scala provide rich APIs and DSLs tailored for writing expressive and concise test cases. ScalaTest, for instance, offers several styles such as FunSuite, FeatureSpec, and WordSpec, catering to different testing preferences.

276

A simple example of a FunSuite test in ScalaTest might look like this:

```
import org.scalatest.FunSuite

class ExampleSuite extends FunSuite {

  test("addition of positive numbers") {
    val sum = 2 + 3
    assert(sum === 5)
  }

  test("multiplication of negative numbers") {
    val product = -2 * -3
    assert(product === 6)
  }
}
```

The test keyword denotes individual test cases. Assertions such as assert, assertResult, and intercept ensure the correctness of the code under test.

Another important aspect is integrating with continuous integration (CI) systems, enabling automated testing and reporting. Tools like Jenkins, Travis CI, and GitHub Actions can be configured to run Scala test suites as part of the build pipeline, thereby ensuring that code changes are continuously verified.

To incorporate CI using GitHub Actions, for example, a workflow file might be set up as follows:

```
name: Scala CI

on: [push, pull_request]

jobs:
  build:

    runs-on: ubuntu-latest

    steps:
    - uses: actions/checkout@v2
    - name: Setup Scala
      uses: olafurpg/setup-scala@v11
      with:
        java-version: '11'
    - name: sbt test
      run: sbt test
```

This configuration specifies that the tests should run on each push or pull_request event, using an Ubuntu environment.

By employing the practices and tools discussed, developers can achieve a robust testing strategy in Scala. Mastery of these techniques leads to the development of high-quality, reliable software systems.

10.2   Setting Up Testing Environment

When setting up a testing environment for Scala, it is crucial to establish a robust foundation that facilitates seamless testing operations. This section will guide you through the necessary steps, including configuring your build tool, integrating vital testing libraries, and ensuring appropriate settings for an efficient testing workflow.

1. Configuring SBT (Simple Build Tool) Scala projects commonly use SBT as the build tool. SBT not only compiles and builds your Scala code but also manages dependencies, including testing libraries such as ScalaTest, Specs2, and ScalaCheck. Begin by creating or updating the build.sbt file to include the required dependencies.

```
name := "MyScalaProject"

version := "0.1.0"

scalaVersion := "2.13.6"

libraryDependencies ++= Seq(
  "org.scalatest" %% "scalatest" % "3.2.9" % Test,
  "org.specs2" %% "specs2-core" % "4.10.6" % Test,
  "org.scalacheck" %% "scalacheck" % "1.15.4" % Test,
  "org.mockito" %% "mockito-core" % "1.16.29" % Test,
  "com.typesafe.akka" %% "akka-testkit" % "2.6.14" % Test
)
```

The above libraryDependencies configuration includes ScalaTest for unit testing, Specs2 for behavior-driven development (BDD), ScalaCheck for property-based testing, Mockito for mocking and stubbing, and Akka TestKit for testing Akka actors. The '

2. Directory Structure

Organize your Scala project directory structure to differentiate between production code and test code. A typical Scala project directory layout looks like this:

```
MyScalaProject/
|-- build.sbt
|-- project/
|-- src/
    |-- main/
    |   |-- scala/
    |       |-- MainApp.scala
    |-- test/
        |-- scala/
            |-- MyTests.scala
```

- src/main/scala/ contains the main source code.

278

- src/test/scala/ houses the test code.

Having a clear separation between these directories helps maintain clean project organization and ensures that tests do not inadvertently interfere with production code.

3. Writing and Running Tests

To verify the configuration, let's write a simple unit test using ScalaTest. Create a file named ExampleSpec.scala in src/test/scala/ with the following content:

```
import org.scalatest.flatspec.AnyFlatSpec
import org.scalatest.matchers.should.Matchers

class ExampleSpec extends AnyFlatSpec with Matchers {

  "An empty list" should "have size 0" in {
    List.empty.size should be (0)
  }

  it should "throw NoSuchElementException when head is invoked" in {
    a [NoSuchElementException] should be thrownBy {
      List.empty.head
    }
  }
}
```

This simple test case checks that an empty list has a size of 0 and that invoking the head method on an empty list throws a NoSuchElementException. To run the test, execute the following SBT command in the terminal:

```
sbt test
```

Upon running this command, SBT compiles the code and runs the tests, displaying the results in the terminal:

```
[info] ExampleSpec:
[info] An empty list
[info] - should have size 0
[info] - should throw NoSuchElementException when head is invoked
[success] Total time: 2 s, completed ...
```

4. Continuous Testing and Integration

Setting up continuous testing is essential for maintaining code quality. Use SBT's test-quick command to run only the tests affected by recent changes:

```
sbt testQuick
```

For continuous integration (CI), integrate your SBT-based project with CI services such as Travis CI, Jenkins, or GitHub Actions. Create a

279

configuration file (e.g., .travis.yml for Travis CI) to automate the build
and testing process on every push to the repository:

```
language: scala

scala:
  - 2.13.6

script:
  - sbt clean compile test
```

This example configuration specifies Scala version 2.13.6, cleans the
project, compiles the source code, and runs the tests.

Following these steps ensures that your Scala project's testing environment is properly set up, allowing you to leverage powerful testing tools
and maintain high code quality. The next sections will delve deeper into
specific testing techniques and frameworks, building upon the foundation established here.

10.3   Writing Unit Tests with ScalaTest

When approaching unit testing within the Scala ecosystem, ScalaTest
serves as a widely adopted and robust testing framework. ScalaTest
facilitates various styles of testing, but for this part, we will focus on
testing using the FunSuite approach due to its simplicity and straightforward nature, especially for beginners.

To begin, ensure that ScalaTest is included as a dependency in your
project. In a typical SBT (Scala Build Tool) project, this can be done by
adding the following line to your build.sbt file:

```
libraryDependencies += "org.scalatest" %% "scalatest" % "3.2.10" % Test
```

After including the ScalaTest dependency, you can create a test file to
start writing unit tests. Consider a simple example where we intend to
test a basic arithmetic class named Calculator.

Here is the implementation of the Calculator class:

```
class Calculator {
  def add(a: Int, b: Int): Int = a + b
  def subtract(a: Int, b: Int): Int = a - b
  def multiply(a: Int, b: Int): Int = a * b
  def divide(a: Int, b: Int): Int = if (b == 0) throw new IllegalArgumentException("
      Division by zero") else a / b
}
```

In the above class, we have four methods: add, subtract, multiply, and divide. The goal is to write unit tests for each of these methods.

Create a new test file named CalculatorTest.scala. Within this file, we will use the FunSuite trait from ScalaTest.

```scala
import org.scalatest.FunSuite

class CalculatorTest extends FunSuite {
  val calculator = new Calculator

  test("addition of two positive numbers") {
    assert(calculator.add(3, 4) == 7)
  }

  test("subtraction of two positive numbers") {
    assert(calculator.subtract(10, 4) == 6)
  }

  test("multiplication of two positive numbers") {
    assert(calculator.multiply(3, 4) == 12)
  }

  test("division of two positive numbers") {
    assert(calculator.divide(8, 4) == 2)
  }

  test("division by zero should throw IllegalArgumentException") {
    assertThrows[IllegalArgumentException] {
      calculator.divide(8, 0)
    }
  }
}
```

Each test block declares a specific test case. The assert function verifies that the returned value matches the expected result, while assertThrows ensures that an IllegalArgumentException is thrown for an invalid operation like division by zero.

Run the tests using SBT with the following command in the terminal:

```
sbt test
```

If all tests pass, the output should be similar to:

```
[info] CalculatorTest:
[info] - addition of two positive numbers
[info] - subtraction of two positive numbers
[info] - multiplication of two positive numbers
[info] - division of two positive numbers
[info] - division by zero should throw IllegalArgumentException
[info] ScalaTest
[info] Run completed in 356 milliseconds.
[info] Total number of tests run: 5
[info] Suites: completed 1, aborted 0
[info] Tests: succeeded 5, failed 0, canceled 0, ignored 0, pending 0
[info] All tests passed.
```

Test names should be descriptive to improve readability and maintainability of the test suite. In complex systems, testing corner cases, edge cases, and erroneous inputs often results in high-quality, robust software.

10.4   Behavior-Driven   Development   with   Specs2

Behavior-Driven Development (BDD) is a software development approach that emphasizes collaboration among developers, QA, and non-technical or business participants in a software project. Specs2 is a library often used for BDD in Scala, offering concise, readable DSL for writing specifications and test cases.

Specs2 enables writing specifications in a way that closely resembles natural language. This allows for clear and understandable specification of behavior, making it easier to involve all stakeholders in the development process.

```
libraryDependencies += "org.specs2" %% "specs2-core" % "4.12.0" % Test
```

To begin creating Specs2 specifications, extend the Specification trait, which is a central component of the Specs2 DSL. Here is a basic example of how you might use Specs2 to test a Scala class:

```
// Class to be tested
class Calculator {
  def add(a: Int, b: Int): Int = a + b
}
```

```
// Specs2 Specification
import org.specs2.mutable.Specification

class CalculatorSpec extends Specification {
  "The Calculator" should {
    "return the correct sum when two numbers are added" in {
      val calculator = new Calculator
      calculator.add(2, 3) mustEqual 5
    }
  }
}
```

In this example, should and in are methods provided by Specs2 to create behavior-driven tests. The string inside the first should describes the behavior, while the in block contains the actual test case.

To run this specification, you can use the following sbt command:

```
sbt test
```

Specs2 also supports more complex specifications using different styles like acceptance and unit specification styles.

Here is an example of a more complex specification using the acceptance style:

```
import org.specs2.Specification

class ComplexCalculationSpec extends Specification {
  def is = s2"""
    The ComplexCalculator should
      return the correct product for multiplication $e1
      handle division correctly with non-zero divisor $e2
      throw an exception for division by zero $e3
  """

  def e1 = {
    val calculator = new ComplexCalculator
    calculator.multiply(3, 5) mustEqual 15
  }

  def e2 = {
    val calculator = new ComplexCalculator
    calculator.divide(10, 2) mustEqual 5
  }

  def e3 = {
    val calculator = new ComplexCalculator
    calculator.divide(10, 0) must throwA[ArithmeticException]
  }
}
```

In this specification, def is defines the structure of the specification. It lists every behavior that needs to be tested along with a corresponding method to implement each test. The methods e1, e2, and e3 are then implemented to perform the tests.

To get more elaborate with Specs2, you might include examples that have variable inputs using the Tables trait. Here is an example that tests the addition method using a table of values:

```
import org.specs2.mutable.Specification
import org.specs2.matcher.DataTables

class TableDrivenSpec extends Specification with DataTables {
  "add" should {
    "correctly add integers from a datatable" in {
      val calculator = new Calculator
      "a" | "b" | "result" |
       1 ! 2 ! 3 |
       2 ! 3 ! 5 |
       3 ! 4 ! 7 |
       4 ! 5 ! 9 | { (a, b, result) =>
        calculator.add(a, b) mustEqual result
      }
    }
```

```
  }
}
```

In this example, the Tables trait is used to create a table of input values and expected results. The ! and | operators fill out the table, and the test case iteratively checks each row to ensure the addition method returns the correct results.

Specs2 supports mocking through various mocking libraries like Mockito. The following example demonstrates how to mock dependencies in a class using Mockito with Specs2:

```
import org.specs2.mock.Mockito
import org.specs2.mutable.Specification

// Class to be tested
class DataService {
  def fetchData: String = "real data"
}

class DataFetcher(dataService: DataService) {
  def getData: String = s"Fetched: ${dataService.fetchData}"
}

// Specs2 Specification with Mockito
class DataFetcherSpec extends Specification with Mockito {
  "getData" should {
    "return data with fetched prefix" in {
      val mockDataService = mock[DataService]
      mockDataService.fetchData returns "mock data"
      val dataFetcher = new DataFetcher(mockDataService)
      dataFetcher.getData mustEqual "Fetched: mock data"
    }
  }
}
```

In this case, Mockito is used to create a mock instance of DataService, specifying the behavior of the fetchData method. This allows the test to verify the DataFetcher.getData method without relying on the actual implementation of DataService.

Asynchronous operations are common in Scala, and Specs2 handles testing these efficiently. For such cases, it integrates seamlessly with Futures. An example of testing asynchronous operations is as follows:

```
import org.specs2.mutable.Specification
import scala.concurrent._
import scala.concurrent.ExecutionContext.Implicits.global
import scala.concurrent.duration._

class AsyncSpec extends Specification {
  "Async operations" should {
    "return the correct result" in {
      val futureResult = Future {
        Thread.sleep(1000)
```

```
      "Asynchronous result"
    }
    Await.result(futureResult, 2.seconds) mustEqual "Asynchronous result"
    }
  }
}
```

In this asynchronous test, a Future is created to perform a long-running operation, and Await.result is used to wait for the result. Specs2 waits for the specified duration to complete the future and checks the correctness of the result.

Specs2 also integrates well with property-based testing libraries such as ScalaCheck, enabling the generation of test cases based on properties rather than specific examples, further enhancing the robustness and coverage of your test suite.

To install ScalaCheck with Specs2, include:

```
libraryDependencies += "org.specs2" %% "specs2-scalacheck" % "4.12.0" % Test
```

An example of property-based testing with ScalaCheck in Specs2 is shown below:

```
import org.specs2.ScalaCheck
import org.specs2.mutable.Specification
import org.scalacheck.Prop.forAll

class PropertySpec extends Specification with ScalaCheck {
  "addition" should {
    "be commutative" in {
      forAll { (a: Int, b: Int) =>
        a + b mustEqual b + a
      }
    }
  }
}
```

In property-based testing, forAll is used to specify that the property must hold for all values of a and b generated by the ScalaCheck library. This kind of testing ensures that the properties of the addition operation hold across a wide range of inputs, ensuring robustness.

Behavior-Driven Development with Specs2 not only enhances the readability and maintainability of the test code but also fosters better collaboration among team members by expressing test cases in a form that is close to the natural language and hence easier for non-developers to understand. It integrates seamlessly with existing Scala testing infrastructure and supports a wide range of testing styles and methodologies.

285

10.5   Property-Based   Testing   with ScalaCheck

Property-based testing is a testing technique where properties or invariants of the code are specified, and tests are generated to validate these properties across a wide range of inputs. ScalaCheck is a library designed for this kind of testing in the Scala programming language. Unlike traditional unit tests that focus on specific input-output pairs, property-based tests describe the general behavior of the program, allowing for broader validation.

ScalaCheck integrates seamlessly with ScalaTest, making it convenient to incorporate property-based tests into an existing unit testing suite. At its core, ScalaCheck relies on properties and generators. Properties describe behavior, and generators produce the inputs on which properties are validated.

Defining Properties:

Properties are defined using the Prop class. A property in ScalaCheck typically asserts that a condition should hold for all generated inputs. Consider the following simple example that checks the commutativity of integer addition:

```scala
import org.scalacheck.Properties
import org.scalacheck.Prop.forAll

object AdditionProperties extends Properties("Addition") {
  property("commutative") = forAll { (a: Int, b: Int) =>
    a + b == b + a
  }
}
```

The forAll construct creates a property that must hold for all values of a and b generated by the built-in integer generator.

Custom Generators:

ScalaCheck allows the creation of custom generators using the Gen class. These are useful when you need specific kinds of data structures or input ranges. Here is an example of a generator for even integers:

```scala
import org.scalacheck.Gen

val evenInts = Gen.choose(0, 100).suchThat(_ % 2 == 0)

val evenIntProp = forAll(evenInts) { n =>
  (n % 2) == 0
}
```

286

In this example, Gen.choose creates a generator for integers within the range of 0 to 100, and suchThat filters these values to only include even numbers. The property evenIntProp asserts that all generated numbers are indeed even.

Combining Properties:

Properties can be combined using logical connectors. This enables complex behavior to be described comprehensively. For instance:

```
val positiveInts = Gen.choose(1, 100)
val nonNegativeInts = Gen.choose(0, 100)

property("sum of positives is positive") = forAll(positiveInts, positiveInts) { (a: Int, b:
    Int) =>
  a + b > 0
}

property("sum is non-negative") = forAll(nonNegativeInts, nonNegativeInts) { (a: Int,
    b: Int) =>
  a + b >= 0
}
```

This example defines two properties: one that asserts the sum of two positive integers is positive, and another that ensures the sum of two non-negative integers is non-negative.

Testing with ScalaTest:

ScalaCheck properties can be integrated into a ScalaTest suite. This approach leverages the expressive test syntax of ScalaTest and the powerful property-based testing capabilities of ScalaCheck. Here's an illustration:

```
import org.scalatest.propspec.AnyPropSpec
import org.scalatestplus.scalacheck.ScalaCheckPropertyChecks
import org.scalacheck.Prop._

class AdditionSpec extends AnyPropSpec with ScalaCheckPropertyChecks {

  property("addition is commutative") {
    forAll { (a: Int, b: Int) =>
      assert(a + b == b + a)
    }
  }

  property("addition is associative") {
    forAll { (a: Int, b: Int, c: Int) =>
      assert((a + b) + c == a + (b + c))
    }
  }
}
```

Here, AnyPropSpec is used to create a property-based specification, and ScalaCheckPropertyChecks provides the forAll method to define properties within the ScalaTest framework.

Shrinking Failing Inputs:

When a property fails, ScalaCheck attempts to minimize the failing input. This process is known as *shrinking*. Consider a property that asserts the length of the concatenation of two lists equals the sum of their lengths:

```
property("list concatenation length") = forAll { (l1: List[Int], l2: List[Int]) =>
  (l1 ++ l2).length == l1.length + l2.length
}
```

If a failure occurs, ScalaCheck will shrink the lists to the smallest example that still fails. This helps in diagnosing and debugging issues more effectively.

Configuring Test Parameters:

ScalaCheck provides various options to configure the testing process, like the number of generated cases. These can be controlled using Test.Parameters. Here is how you can configure a test to run 500 cases:

```
import org.scalacheck.Test

property("configurable test") = forAll { (n: Int) =>
  n % 2 == 0
}

Test.check(Test.Parameters.default.withMinSuccessfulTests(500), property("
    configurable test"))
```

This snippet configures the test to run with a minimum of 500 successful cases.

Property-based testing with ScalaCheck offers an extensive suite of tools for validating program properties across a broad spectrum of inputs, significantly enhancing the robustness and reliability of your codebase. By combining custom generators, logical property combinations, and detailed configuration options, ScalaCheck enables precise and effective testing that extends beyond typical unit testing paradigms.

10.6   Mocking and Stubbing with Mockito

Mockito is a popular library for mocking objects in unit tests. Mocking is the practice of creating objects that simulate the behavior of real objects. This is particularly useful when the real object's behavior is complex, undesirable, or difficult to reproduce. Mockito allows for the creation of mocks easily and provides a fluent API for specifying their behavior.

Using Mockito in Scala requires adding the corresponding dependency. This can be achieved by including the following in the build.sbt file:

```
libraryDependencies ++= Seq(
  "org.mockito" %% "mockito-scala" % "1.16.37" % Test
)
```

With Mockito, you can define the behavior of a mock object using stubbing. Stubbing involves setting specific return values for method calls on mock objects. The when construct is used for this purpose, along with the thenReturn method to specify the return value.

Consider a scenario where you want to test a class OrderService that depends on OrderRepository. The OrderRepository itself might interact with a database, making it a candidate for mocking. Below is an example of how to achieve this:

```
import org.scalatest.flatspec.AnyFlatSpec
import org.mockito.scalatest.MockitoSugar
import org.mockito.Mockito._

class OrderServiceTest extends AnyFlatSpec with MockitoSugar {

  "OrderService" should "retrieve an order by ID" in {
    val mockOrderRepository = mock[OrderRepository]
    val orderService = new OrderService(mockOrderRepository)

    val sampleOrder = Order(1, "Sample Item", 100)

    when(mockOrderRepository.findOrder(1)).thenReturn(Some(sampleOrder))

    val result = orderService.getOrder(1)

    assert(result.contains(sampleOrder))
  }

}
```

In this example, OrderService uses OrderRepository to fetch orders. By mocking OrderRepository and specifying the behavior with when, we isolate the test for OrderService. This allows us to verify that orderService.getOrder(1) returns the expected sampleOrder.

Mockito also supports verifying the interactions with the mock objects. This is useful for ensuring that certain methods are called, and they are called with the correct parameters. The verify method helps achieve this:

```
"OrderService" should "call findOrder on OrderRepository" in {
  val mockOrderRepository = mock[OrderRepository]
  val orderService = new OrderService(mockOrderRepository)
```

```
orderService.getOrder(1)

verify(mockOrderRepository).findOrder(1)
}
```

The above code verifies that the method findOrder on OrderRepository was indeed called with argument 1 when orderService.getOrder(1) is invoked.

Stubbing methods with return values that are more complex than basic data types are also supported. For example, suppose OrderRepository has a method that returns a future, you could stub it like this:

```
import scala.concurrent.Future
import org.mockito.ArgumentMatchers.any

"OrderService" should "retrieve an order asynchronously" in {
  val mockOrderRepository = mock[OrderRepository]
  val orderService = new OrderService(mockOrderRepository)

  val sampleOrder = Order(1, "Sample Item", 100)

  when(mockOrderRepository.findOrderAsync(any[Int]))
    .thenReturn(Future.successful(Some(sampleOrder)))

  val result = orderService.getOrderAsync(1)

  result.map(order => assert(order.contains(sampleOrder)))
}
```

Additionally, Mockito supports argument matchers to provide more flexibility in specifying method call expectations. This is particularly useful when the exact argument is not known or irrelevant for the test.

It is also essential to handle exceptions. Mockito allows for stubbing methods to throw exceptions, which is crucial for testing error handling code paths. For example:

```
import org.mockito.Mockito.doThrow

"OrderService" should "handle exceptions from OrderRepository" in {
  val mockOrderRepository = mock[OrderRepository]
  val orderService = new OrderService(mockOrderRepository)

  doThrow(new RuntimeException("Database not available"))
    .when(mockOrderRepository).findOrder(1)

  assertThrows[RuntimeException] {
    orderService.getOrder(1)
  }
}
```

In this scenario, we expect a RuntimeException to be thrown when orderService.getOrder(1) is called, simulating a failure in OrderRepository.

The assertThrows method from ScalaTest ensures that this exception is properly detected.

By understanding and utilizing Mockito's capabilities, developers can effectively mock dependencies and test their Scala applications comprehensively.

10.7 Testing Asynchronous Code

Asynchronous programming plays a crucial role in modern software development, especially in applications that require non-blocking and concurrent operations. Testing asynchronous code in Scala involves ensuring that the code behaves correctly when executed asynchronously. Scala's rich ecosystem provides several tools and frameworks that facilitate the testing of asynchronous operations.

ScalaTest comes with built-in support for testing futures, promises, and other asynchronous constructs. This section will cover how to effectively write tests for asynchronous code using ScalaTest.

Futures are one of the primary constructs for managing asynchronous computations in Scala. A Future represents a value that may become available at some point or a computation that is yet to be completed. Testing Futures involves verifying that the eventual result of the Future meets the expected criteria.

Consider the following simple asynchronous function:

```scala
import scala.concurrent.Future
import scala.concurrent.ExecutionContext.Implicits.global

def asyncAdd(a: Int, b: Int): Future[Int] = Future {
  a + b
}
```

To test the asyncAdd function, ScalaTest provides several styles. Here is an example using ScalaTest's built-in Future support:

```scala
import org.scalatest.AsynchronousFunSuite

class AsyncAddTest extends AsynchronousFunSuite {

  test("asyncAdd should return correct result") {
    val futureResult = asyncAdd(3, 4)
    futureResult.map { result =>
      assert(result == 7)
    }
  }
}
```

291

```
}
```

The AsynchronousFunSuite trait from ScalaTest allows writing tests that return Future[Assertion]. This style is non-blocking and lets the test framework manage the asynchronous computation.

ScalaTest also provides the whenReady construct to simplify testing Futures. The whenReady function waits for a Future to complete and asserts its result.

```scala
import org.scalatest.concurrent.ScalaFutures
import org.scalatest.funsuite.AnyFunSuite
import scala.concurrent.Future

class AsyncAddTestWithWhenReady extends AnyFunSuite with ScalaFutures {

  test("asyncAdd should return correct result") {
    val futureResult = asyncAdd(3, 4)
    whenReady(futureResult) { result =>
      assert(result == 7)
    }
  }
}
```

The ScalaFutures trait enables the usage of whenReady for more readable and expressive tests. It allows developers to focus on the functional behavior without cluttering the test logic with Future handling details.

For testing more complex asynchronous workflows, ScalaTest's Async suite can be utilized. This suite integrates directly with Future-based APIs, orchestrating multiple asynchronous operations.

Consider a more involved example where multiple asynchronous operations need to be tested together:

```scala
def asyncComposeAdd(a: Int, b: Int, c: Int): Future[Int] = {
  for {
    sum1 <- asyncAdd(a, b)
    sum2 <- asyncAdd(sum1, c)
  } yield sum2
}
```

Testing this function involves verifying that all intermediate computations are conducted correctly.

```scala
import org.scalatest.AsynchronousFunSuite

class AsyncComposeAddTest extends AsynchronousFunSuite {

  test("asyncComposeAdd should correctly compose additions") {
    val futureResult = asyncComposeAdd(1, 2, 3)
    futureResult.map { result =>
```

```
    assert(result == 6)
    }
  }
}
```

Regarding the execution context, testing frameworks provide mechanisms to control the context under which asynchronous tests run. Using custom execution contexts can help isolate tests and manage test dependencies better.

Moreover, integration testing frameworks such as Akka TestKit provide additional tools tailored for actor-based asynchronous code. Ensuring the correct behavior of actors and their messaging patterns requires specialized tools provided by Akka TestKit.

Suppose you have the following actor to test:

```
import akka.actor.{ Actor, ActorSystem, Props }

class AdderActor extends Actor {
  def receive: Receive = {
    case (a: Int, b: Int) => sender() ! (a + b)
  }
}

object AdderActor {
  def props: Props = Props[AdderActor]
}
```

Using Akka TestKit, you can test the AdderActor:

```
import akka.actor.ActorSystem
import akka.testkit.{ TestKit, TestProbe }
import org.scalatest.BeforeAndAfterAll
import org.scalatest.wordspec.AnyWordSpecLike
import org.scalatest.matchers.should.Matchers

class AdderActorTest
  extends TestKit(ActorSystem("AdderActorTestSystem"))
    with AnyWordSpecLike
    with Matchers
    with BeforeAndAfterAll {

  override def afterAll: Unit = {
    TestKit.shutdownActorSystem(system)
  }

  "An AdderActor" must {
    "correctly add numbers and send back the result" in {
      val probe = TestProbe()
      val adderActor = system.actorOf(AdderActor.props)
      adderActor.tell((1, 2), probe.ref)
      probe.expectMsg(3)
    }
  }
}
```

Custom execution contexts, Akka TestKit, and tools like whenReady and ScalaFutures provide a robust toolkit for effectively testing asynchronous code. Employing these tools ensures that asynchronous operations in Scala code behave as expected and are resilient to concurrency issues.

10.8   Testing with Akka TestKit

Akka is a powerful toolkit for building concurrent, distributed, and resilient message-driven applications on the JVM. Testing Akka actors requires specialized tools to ensure proper functionality and performance. Akka TestKit provides the utilities necessary for testing Akka actors. This section explores the core components and practices for effective testing with Akka TestKit.

Akka TestKit is designed to simplify the process of writing unit tests for actor-based systems by providing a test actor system and useful assertions and probes. We begin by setting up the environment and introduce key concepts necessary for testing Akka actors.

Setting Up the Environment

First, ensure you have included the necessary dependencies in your build file. For sbt, add the following to your build.sbt file:

```
libraryDependencies += "com.typesafe.akka" %% "akka-testkit" % "2.6.17" % Test
```

Creating a Test Actor System

It is essential to create a dedicated test actor system for your tests. This ensures isolation from the main actor system and can be more easily tailored or disposed of as needed. Here's how you can initialize a test actor system using Akka TestKit in Scala:

```
import akka.actor.{Actor, Props}
import akka.testkit.{TestActorRef, TestKit, TestProbe}
import akka.util.Timeout
import org.scalatest.BeforeAndAfterAll
import org.scalatest.matchers.should.Matchers
import org.scalatest.wordspec.AnyWordSpecLike
import akka.actor.ActorSystem
import scala.concurrent.duration._

class ActorSpec extends TestKit(ActorSystem("TestSystem"))
  with AnyWordSpecLike
  with Matchers
  with BeforeAndAfterAll {

  override def afterAll(): Unit = {
```

```
    TestKit.shutdownActorSystem(system)
  }

  "An example actor" must {
    "respond with a message" in {
      // Test logic goes here
    }
  }
}
```

TestKit.shutdownActorSystem(system) ensures that the test actor system is properly shut down after all tests have completed, preventing resource leaks.

Writing Tests with TestProbes

TestProbe is a powerful utility provided by Akka TestKit. It acts both as an actor and a test utility, allowing you to intercept messages sent to actors and assert expected behaviors. Here's an example of how to use TestProbe to test an actor's message handling:

```
class MyActor extends Actor {
  def receive: Receive = {
    case "ping" => sender() ! "pong"
    case _ => sender() ! "unknown message"
  }
}

"An example actor" must {
  "respond with 'pong' when a 'ping' message is sent" in {
    val probe = TestProbe()
    val myActor = system.actorOf(Props[MyActor])

    myActor.tell("ping", probe.ref)
    probe.expectMsg("pong")
  }

  "respond with 'unknown message' for unrecognized messages" in {
    val probe = TestProbe()
    val myActor = system.actorOf(Props[MyActor])

    myActor.tell("hello", probe.ref)
    probe.expectMsg("unknown message")
  }
}
```

In the example above, TestProbe.expectMsg is used to assert that the messages received match the expected responses. This is critical for ensuring the correctness of actor logic.

Using TestActorRef for Synchronous Testing

TestActorRef provides direct access to an actor instance without the need for asynchronous message passing. This is useful for testing the internal state and behavior of an actor synchronously. Here's an example demonstrating the usage of TestActorRef:

```scala
class CounterActor extends Actor {
  var counter = 0
  def receive: Receive = {
    case "increment" => counter += 1
    case "get" => sender() ! counter
  }
}

"An example actor" must {
  "increment the counter" in {
    val counterActor = TestActorRef[CounterActor]

    counterActor ! "increment"
    counterActor.underlyingActor.counter should equal(1)
  }

  "return the current counter value" in {
    val counterActor = TestActorRef[CounterActor]

    counterActor ! "increment"
    counterActor ! "get"

    val result = Await.result(ask(counterActor, "get")(Timeout(5.seconds)).mapTo[Int],
        5.seconds)
    result should equal(1)
  }
}
```

TestActorRef allows you to interact with the actor directly and access its state. This can be particularly useful for complex logic or stateful actors, where inspecting the internal state directly simplifies the testing process.

Advanced Testing Techniques

For more advanced scenarios, such as testing actor supervision or failure handling, Akka TestKit offers additional utilities. The following example demonstrates testing an actor that supervises another actor and handles its failures:

```scala
class SupervisorActor extends Actor {
  val child = context.actorOf(Props[ChildActor], "child")
  override val supervisorStrategy = AllForOneStrategy(loggingEnabled = false) {
    case _: Exception => Restart
  }

  def receive: Receive = {
    case msg => child forward msg
  }
}

class ChildActor extends Actor {
  def receive: Receive = {
    case "fail" => throw new RuntimeException("Failure")
    case msg => sender() ! msg
  }
}
```

```
}
"An example actor" must {
  "restart the child actor upon failure" in {
    val supervisor = system.actorOf(Props[SupervisorActor])
    val probe = TestProbe()

    supervisor.tell("fail", probe.ref)
    probe.expectNoMessage(1.second)

    supervisor.tell("something else", probe.ref)
    probe.expectMsg("something else")
  }
}
```

In this example, the supervisor actor restarts its child upon receiving a failure. Using TestProbe and timing assertions (expectNoMessage), we can validate that the child actor is properly restarted and continues functioning as expected.

These examples illustrate the variety of tools and techniques available in Akka TestKit for robust and comprehensive actor testing. Understanding and effectively utilizing these tools will significantly enhance the reliability and maintainability of Akka-based systems.

10.9 Integration Testing

Integration testing in Scala focuses on testing the interactions between multiple components to verify they work together as expected. This ensures the cooperation between various parts of a system, such as modules, services, and external APIs. Integration testing is crucial for discovering issues related to data flow, interface adherence, and system-level functionality that unit testing cannot surface.

To perform effective integration testing, Scala developers leverage various libraries and frameworks. In this section, we explore the practical usage of these tools with step-by-step examples.

Integration tests often require the setup and teardown of external dependencies, such as databases or web services. Using libraries like ScalaTest and DockerTestKit, we can manage these dependencies efficiently.

```
import org.scalatest._
import com.whisk.docker._
import com.whisk.docker.impl.spotify._

class DatabaseIntegrationTest extends FlatSpec with Matchers with DockerTestKit {
```

```scala
val mysqlContainer = DockerContainer("mysql:5.7")
  .withPorts(3306 -> Some(3306))
  .withEnv("MYSQL_ROOT_PASSWORD=root", "MYSQL_DATABASE=testdb")
  .withReadyChecker(
    DockerReadyChecker
      .LogLineContains("ready for connections")
      .looped(20, 1.second)
  )

override val dockerContainers = mysqlContainer :: Nil

"Database" should "be ready and responsive" in {
  mysqlContainer.isRunning().futureValue shouldBe true
}

it should "perform a simple query" in {
  // Assuming a Database wrapper is already defined
  val db = new Database("jdbc:mysql://localhost:3306/testdb", "root", "root")
  val result = db.query("SELECT 1")
  result shouldBe 1
}
}
```

In the above example, a MySQL Docker container is defined using DockerContainer from the DockerTestKit library. The withReady-Checker method ensures the service is fully initialized before proceeding with the tests.

Integration tests often involve more than simple connectivity checks. They test complex interactions, requiring a comprehensive setup. Consider a scenario where an application communicates with both a database and an external REST API. By mocking the REST API and verifying the end-to-end process, we can ensure the different components interact seamlessly.

```scala
import org.scalatest._
import com.github.tomakehurst.wiremock.client.WireMock._
import com.github.tomakehurst.wiremock.WireMockServer
import com.github.tomakehurst.wiremock.core.WireMockConfiguration
import java.sql._

class FullIntegrationTest extends FlatSpec with Matchers {

  val wireMockServer = new WireMockServer(WireMockConfiguration.wireMockConfig
      ().port(8080))
  wireMockServer.start()
  configureFor("localhost", 8080)

  override def beforeAll(): Unit = {
    wireMockServer.stubFor(get(urlEqualTo("/endpoint"))
      .willReturn(aResponse()
        .withStatus(200)
        .withBody("""{"key":"value"}""")))
  }

  override def afterAll(): Unit = {
    wireMockServer.stop()
```

```
  }

  "Application" should "fetch data from API and save to database" in {
    val result = scala.io.Source.fromURL("http://localhost:8080/endpoint").mkString
    result shouldBe """{"key":"value"}"""

    val connection = DriverManager.getConnection("jdbc:mysql://localhost:3306/testdb
        ", "root", "root")
    val statement = connection.createStatement()
    statement.executeUpdate("INSERT INTO data (key, value) VALUES ('key', 'value')
        ")

    val resultSet = statement.executeQuery("SELECT value FROM data WHERE key
        = 'key'")
    resultSet.next()
    resultSet.getString("value") shouldEqual "value"
  }
}
```

In this example, a WireMock server is used to simulate the REST API. The test fetches data from the mocked API and performs a database insertion operation, followed by a retrieval to check the correct flow of data between the API and the database.

By leveraging $DockerTestKit$ for container management and $WireMock$ for API simulation, we can achieve robust integration tests that validate complex interactions within a system.

Integration testing also involves testing with real services, particularly in microservice architectures. This can be facilitated using test environments that mimic production as closely as possible. Continuous integration (CI) pipelines play a vital role in running these tests consistently.

Here is an example of setting up a CI configuration for running integration tests using GitHub Actions:

```
name: Scala CI

on:
  push:
    branches:
      - main
  pull_request:
    branches:
      - main

jobs:
  test:
    runs-on: ubuntu-latest

    services:
      mysql:
        image: mysql:5.7
        options: --health-cmd="mysqladmin ping" --health-interval=10s --health-timeout
            =5s --health-retries=3
```

```
  env:
    MYSQL_ROOT_PASSWORD: root
    MYSQL_DATABASE: testdb
  ports:
    - 3306:3306

steps:
  - name: Checkout code
    uses: actions/checkout@v2

  - name: Set up JDK 11
    uses: actions/setup-java@v2
    with:
      java-version: 11

  - name: Install sbt
    run: sudo curl -L -o /usr/local/bin/sbt https://example.com/path/to/sbt &&
         sudo chmod +x /usr/local/bin/sbt

  - name: Run tests
    run: sbt test
```

This GitHub Actions workflow defines a job that initializes a MySQL service container, sets up a JDK, installs sbt, and runs tests. The integration tests connect to the MySQL container, ensuring that the database-dependent tests are executed in an environment closely mimicking production.

Effective integration testing combines automated tests, containerized environments, and CI pipelines to verify that various components of a Scala application interact correctly and produce reliable outcomes. The discussed approaches provide a structured way to achieve this goal, enhancing the robustness and reliability of Scala applications.

10.10   Continuous Integration and Testing

Continuous Integration (CI) is a software development practice where developers regularly merge their code changes into a shared repository, which is then automatically verified by running tests. This practice aims to detect integration issues early, thereby improving the quality and reducing the time taken for delivery of software.

To set up a Continuous Integration pipeline for a Scala project, we can use tools like Jenkins, Travis CI, or CircleCI. These tools automate the process of building and testing code changes. Below, we will outline the key steps involved in configuring a CI pipeline for a Scala project.

- Set Up Version Control: Ensure that your project is under version control, using a tool such as Git. Push your code repository to a version control hosting service like GitHub, GitLab, or Bitbucket.

- Configure the CI Tool: Depending on the CI tool you choose, the configuration might vary. For example, with Travis CI, you need to create a .travis.yml file in the root directory of your repository. For Jenkins, you will configure jobs via its web interface or Jenkinsfile.

- Install Dependencies: Ensure that your CI configuration installs all required dependencies for building and testing the project. In Travis CI, you would specify these in your .travis.yml file, like so:

```
language: scala
jdk:
  - openjdk8

script:
  - sbt clean compile test
```

- Run Build and Tests: The CI tool will execute the specified build and test commands. For a Scala project, you typically use sbt (Scala Build Tool) for this purpose. In the example above, sbt clean compile test commands are used to clean the project, compile the source code, and run the tests.

- Monitor Build Status: Once the CI pipeline is set up, monitor the build status through the CI tool's web interface or via notifications (e.g., email, Slack). Address any build or test failures promptly to maintain a healthy codebase.

Consider the following example scenario using Jenkins and GitHub to set up a Continuous Integration pipeline:

First, ensure that Jenkins is installed and running. Install the Git plugin for Jenkins if it's not already installed. Then, create a new pipeline job in Jenkins:

1. In Jenkins, click on New Item, enter an item name (e.g., "Scala-CI-Pipeline"), select Pipeline, and click OK.

2. In the pipeline configuration, under the Pipeline section, set the Definition to Pipeline script from SCM. Choose Git for SCM and enter the repository URL.

3. Add a Jenkinsfile to your project repository. This file will contain the pipeline script:

```
pipeline {
```

```
agent any

tools {
    jdk 'openjdk-8'
    sbt 'sbt-1.3.13'
}

stages {
    stage('Checkout') {
        steps {
            git 'https://github.com/your-repository.git'
        }
    }
    stage('Build') {
        steps {
            sh 'sbt clean compile'
        }
    }
    stage('Test') {
        steps {
            sh 'sbt test'
        }
    }
}

post {
    always {
        junit '**/target/test-reports/*.xml'
        archiveArtifacts artifacts: '**/target/scala-*/test-reports/*.xml',
            allowEmptyArchive: true
    }
}
}
```

This Jenkinsfile defines a pipeline with three stages: Checkout, Build, and Test. The post section ensures that test results are recorded and any test reports are archived.

By integrating CI into your development workflow, you benefit from early detection of defects, consistent integration efforts, and rapid feedback on code quality. Regular and automated testing through CI improves collaboration and streamlines the development process, leading to more robust and maintainable software.

10.11 Test-Driven Development (TDD) Practices

Test-Driven Development (TDD) is an essential practice in modern software engineering, where developers write tests for their code prior to writing the implementation. The TDD cycle aims to enhance the quality and maintainability of codebases.

The TDD process can be understood through the following steps:

- Write a test for the new function or feature.

- Run the test and see it fail (since the feature is not yet implemented).

- Write the minimum amount of code required to make the test pass.

- Run the test to ensure it passes.

- Refactor the code while ensuring the tests continue to pass.

- Repeat the cycle for additional features and functions.

To illustrate TDD in Scala, we'll focus on creating a small feature using ScalaTest for unit testing.

First, we define an interface for a simple arithmetic calculator.

```scala
trait Calculator {
  def add(a: Int, b: Int): Int
  def subtract(a: Int, b: Int): Int
  def multiply(a: Int, b: Int): Int
  def divide(a: Int, b: Int): Option[Int]
}
```

Before implementing the methods, we will write test cases. Assume we are focusing on the 'add' function. Using ScalaTest, we define the tests as follows:

```scala
import org.scalatest.flatspec.AnyFlatSpec
import org.scalatest.matchers.should.Matchers

class CalculatorSpec extends AnyFlatSpec with Matchers {

  "Calculator" should "return the sum of two positive numbers" in {
    val calc = new BasicCalculator
    calc.add(1, 2) should be(3)
  }

  it should "return the sum of a positive and a negative number" in {
    val calc = new BasicCalculator
    calc.add(1, -1) should be(0)
```

```
        }

    it should "return the sum of two negative numbers" in {
        val calc = new BasicCalculator
        calc.add(-1, -2) should be(-3)
    }

}
```

Running the tests at this point will result in failures since the 'Basic-Calculator' class is not yet implemented. Now we define the simplest implementation that passes the tests:

```
class BasicCalculator extends Calculator {
    def add(a: Int, b: Int): Int = a + b
    def subtract(a: Int, b: Int): Int = ???
    def multiply(a: Int, b: Int): Int = ???
    def divide(a: Int, b: Int): Option[Int] = ???
}
```

We then run the tests:

```
Calculator
  - should return the sum of two positive numbers
  - should return the sum of a positive and a negative number
  - should return the sum of two negative numbers
```

With all tests passing for the 'add' method, we can proceed to implement and test other methods using the same TDD cycle.

Algorithm 4: TDD Cycle

    Data: Inputs: method name, test cases
    Result: Implemented method with passing tests
1 **while** *new method or feature* **do**
2   Write a failing test case;
3   Implement the minimum code to make the test pass;
4   Verify that the test passes;
5   Refactor the code if necessary, ensuring tests still pass;
6   Repeat for the next feature or method;
7 **end**

For the 'subtract' method, we add the following tests:

```
"Calculator" should "subtract two positive numbers" in {
    val calc = new BasicCalculator
```

```
    calc.subtract(5, 2) should be(3)
  }

  it should "subtract when the second number is larger" in {
    val calc = new BasicCalculator
    calc.subtract(2, 5) should be(-3)
  }
```

Implementing the 'subtract' method:

```
class BasicCalculator extends Calculator {
  def add(a: Int, b: Int): Int = a + b
  def subtract(a: Int, b: Int): Int = a - b
  def multiply(a: Int, b: Int): Int = ???
  def divide(a: Int, b: Int): Option[Int] = ???
}
```

This iterative process continues for each method or feature, ensuring robust and thoroughly tested code. In TDD, refactoring plays a crucial role in maintaining code quality and adhering to design principles without compromising functionality. The small increments of design and functionality achieved through the TDD methodology build a foundation of reliable code, resulting in improved software maintainability and easier debugging.

10.12 Performance Testing and Benchmarking

Performance testing and benchmarking are crucial aspects of software development that ensure your Scala applications run efficiently and scale effectively. This section will cover tools and methodologies for performance testing in Scala, with an emphasis on practical implementation and thorough analysis.

Performance testing involves evaluating the speed, responsiveness, and stability of a system under a particular workload. Benchmarking, on the other hand, compares the performance of various implementations to identify the most efficient one. Both these practices help in optimizing code, identifying bottlenecks, and ensuring that the application meets the required performance criteria.

Java Microbenchmark Harness (JMH)

JMH is a benchmarking tool specifically crafted for the Java and JVM ecosystem, which includes Scala. It is optimized to minimize the influence of the Common JVM pitfalls, such as Just-in-Time (JIT) compilation and warm-up phases, ensuring accurate performance measurements.

To use JMH in a Scala project, we use the sbt plugin. Add the following lines to your build.sbt file:

```
enablePlugins(JmhPlugin)

libraryDependencies += "org.openjdk.jmh" % "jmh-core" % "1.33"
libraryDependencies += "org.openjdk.jmh" % "jmh-generator-
    annprocess" % "1.33"
```

Create a benchmarking class to define the performance tests:

```
import org.openjdk.jmh.annotations._

@State(Scope.Thread)
class ExampleBenchmark {

  var list: List[Int] = _

  @Setup(Level.Trial)
  def setup(): Unit = {
    list = (1 to 1000000).toList
  }

  @Benchmark
  def sumList(): Int = {
    list.sum
  }

  @Benchmark
  def sumListPar(): Int = {
    list.par.sum
  }
}
```

This code defines a simple benchmark for two methods of summing a list: sequentially and using parallel collections. The sumList method

306

computes the sum in a single thread, while sumListPar employs parallelism.

To run the benchmarks, execute the following sbt command:

```
sbt jmh:runExampleBenchmark
```

The output will be displayed in the console, showing various statistics such as mean execution time, error, and confidence intervals:

```
Benchmark               Mode Cnt   Score    Error  Units
ExampleBenchmark.sumList    avgt   5   13.456 ±  0.045  ms/op
ExampleBenchmark.sumListPar avgt   5    8.234 ±  0.023  ms/op
```

Profiling Tools

Profiling tools offer insights into how a Scala application consumes system resources, such as CPU and memory. These tools help identify performance bottlenecks that purely benchmarking might miss.

VisualVM is a powerful profiler that supports the JVM. It provides a detailed view of your application's performance, including CPU and memory usage, thread activity, and garbage collection behavior.

To profile a Scala application, start VisualVM, locate the running JVM process, and attach to it. The tool provides real-time monitoring and recording of various performance metrics.

Gatling for Load Testing

For load testing web applications developed in Scala, Gatling is a prominent tool. It allows simulating numerous users accessing the application concurrently, thereby providing insights into how the application handles high traffic.

First, add Gatling dependencies to your build.sbt:

```
libraryDependencies += "io.gatling" % "gatling-core" % "3.6.1" % "
    test"
libraryDependencies += "io.gatling" % "gatling-http" % "3.6.1" % "
    test"
```

Define a load test scenario in a Scala class:

```
import io.gatling.core.Predef._
import io.gatling.http.Predef._
import scala.concurrent.duration._

class BasicSimulation extends Simulation {
```

```scala
val httpConf = http.baseUrl("http://localhost:8080")

val scn = scenario("Basic Simulation")
  .exec(http("request_1")
  .get("/"))
  .pause(5)

setUp(
  scn.inject(atOnceUsers(100))
).protocols(httpConf)
}
```

This code creates a simple scenario where 100 users simultaneously send GET requests to the URL http://localhost:8080/. The load test runs with the defined configuration, and Gatling generates detailed reports, including response times, error rates, and throughput.

Execute the Gatling simulation by running:

```
sbt test
```

The results will be available in the target/gatling directory, providing comprehensive metrics and graphs to analyze application performance under load.

ScalaTest's Duration Assertions

ScalaTest also offers tools for performance testing, enabling developers to assert that certain operations complete within a specified duration. This can ensure that performance regressions are detected during the standard test runs.

Here is an example using ScalaTest's eventually and within method:

```scala
import org.scalatest.concurrent.TimeLimits._
import org.scalatest.time.Span
import org.scalatest.time.Millis

class PerformanceSpec extends FunSuite {

  test("operation should complete within 500 millis") {
    failAfter(Span(500, Millis)) {
      // your code to test
    }
```

```
    }
}
```

By surrounding the operation with the failAfter method, you assert that it completes within the specified duration, catching any unexpected delays immediately.

Through a combination of benchmarking, profiling, load testing, and duration assertions, you can ensure that your Scala applications not only function correctly but also meet stringent performance requirements. These methodologies and tools facilitate identifying and resolving performance bottlenecks, thereby enhancing the application's overall efficiency and user satisfaction.